DOROTHY McMILLAN is a Senior Lecturer in English Literature at the University of Glasgow and a past President of the Association for Scottish Literary Studies. She has published widely on women's writing and co-edited *A History of Scottish Women's Writing* (EUP, 1997).

MICHEL BYRNE lectures in the Department of Celtic at the University of Glasgow. He is the editor of the definitive two-volume *Collected Poems and Songs of George Campbell Hay* (EUP, 2000).

Modern Scottish Women Poets

Edited and Introduced by
Dorothy McMillan and Michel Byrne

113

CANONGATE
Edinburgh · New York · Melbourne

First published as a Canongate Classic
in 2003 by Canongate Books Ltd,
14 High Street, Edinburgh EH1 1TE
This paperback edition published in 2005

Introduction © Dorothy McMillan, 2003
Selection © Dorothy McMillan and Michel Byrne, 2003
Translations from Gaelic © Michel Byrne, 2003 (except
as indicated)
Details of copyright permissions for poems
can be found on pp 310–12

10 9 8 7 6 5 4 3 2 1

The publishers gratefully acknowledge general subsidy from the
Scottish Arts Council towards the Canongate Classics series and
a specific grant towards the publication of this volume.

Typeset in Janson Text by
Palimpsest Book Production Limited,
Polmont, Stirlingshire

Printed and bound in Denmark by
Nørhaven Paperback A/S

British Library Cataloguing-in-Publication Data
A catalogue record for this book is available on
request from the British Library

ISBN 1 84195 526 4

CANONGATE CLASSICS
Series Editor: Roderick Watson
Editorial Board: Cairns Craig,
Dorothy McMillan

www.canongate.net

Contents

Contents

Contents

Acknowledgements

I want to thank the staff of the Scottish Poetry Library and particularly the librarian, Lizzie MacGregor, for assistance in finding details about the poets. The librarians of Level 5 of the Mitchell Library, Glasgow, have been most helpful in repeatedly supplying me with material from the Scottish Poetry Collection; this is a wonderful resource without which I could not have put the anthology together. Karen McCrossan of Canongate has been a most patient, efficient and supportive editor.

Dorothy McMillan

Taing mhòr do na bàird a thug comhairle dhomh air eadar-theangachadh nan dàn, agus do na daoine a leanas airson an cuideachaidh: John Boa, Raghnall MacIlleDhuibh, Fr Donald Mackay, Marion Morrison agus Joina NicDhòmhnaill.

Michel Byrne

Introduction

> Poetry was my first love in writing – is still my true
> love, even though I write few poems. But the writing
> of a poem is a pure delight, finished, complete, absolute,
> an experience.
>
> Marion Lochhead, 'Notebook'

I have taken Marion Lochhead's testimony to poetry as my
epigraph, as an assurance to the reader that although it
might seem tendentious to anthologise writing according
to gender and place, I have throughout been conscious of
the primacy of delight. Above all this anthology seeks to
celebrate the making of poetry, and the dedication to
making, of all the writers included in it.

Nevertheless, it would be disingenuous to pretend that
there is nothing problematic in the production of an
anthology of modern Scottish women's poetry. Arguments
about the propriety of such anthologies, depending, as they
do, on possibly dodgy classifications, and invoking, as they
must, debates about gender and place, have been well
rehearsed over the last thirty years, which have seen a
number of national anthologies and an even larger number
of anthologies of women's poetry, although Catherine
Kerrigan's pioneering *Scottish Women Poets* remains the only
anthology that covers both categories for Scotland.[1] And
there are also a number of collections of critical essays with

the same foci. Is this a proper or useful way to think about poetry? Do the notions of gender and nation or place liberate or constrain discussion? Are readers assisted or bullied by such groupings? The advantages of greater exposure for the writers generated by a variety of ways of conceiving their work must always be balanced against the dangers of ghettoisation and of the production of totalising figures for language, style, belief and concern that may well blur what is special in individual writers, or what these writers have in common with figures who could never be anthologised with them according to the principles of sex or nation.

Yet the persistence of such anthologies and essay collections suggests that interest in women's writing as a phenomenon different from writing by men remains at the forefront of academic concerns and continues to provoke the curiosity of the reading public. Equally, notions of nation and place refuse to go away, even when they are most fervently wished into oblivion. Of course, more collections of essays from academic publishers may seem to prove little more than that academics must write and hence find things to write about. But the involvement of the writers themselves in a number of such collections and anthologies somewhat validates the enterprises. Writers as well as academics contributed to *Sleeping with Monsters*, *Peripheral Visions*, *A History of Scottish Women's Writing*, *Gendering the Nation*, *Kicking Daffodils* and *Contemporary Women's Poetry*.[2]

WOMEN AND SCOTTISHNESS

The focus on women probably requires more justification than the focus on place. Place, as can easily be seen from the poetry in this collection, does seem to be, as Robert

Crawford suggests in *Identifying Poets*,[3] a pressing concern of modern poets – indeed, it can probably be shown to have exercised the imagination of most poets at all times. But the separation of women's writing from men's in anthologies has worried a number of poets of both sexes. Although I have begun by conceding the problem, I do not believe that this separation need be characterised as ghettoisation. In the 'Introduction' to *A History of Scottish Women's Writing* Douglas Gifford and I said that 'even if the only justification that can be offered for separatism is that it carves out more space to talk about women's writing, then that seems good enough to be going on with' (p.ix); but I now feel that this is over-apologetic. I think rather that we should be even more pragmatic: all the evidence suggests that the focus on women's writing over the last thirty-odd years has made a significant difference to the profile of women writers. That embarrassed 'Hadn't we better get a woman?' that was still a feature of some literary gatherings in the 1980s has, I think, completely disappeared, or at least it is a long time since I heard it. This does not, however, mean that it is time to stop; rather, this success should be built on.

Nor do I think that the shift in focus in gender studies to more varied and variable gender positions means that we have ceased to know what we mean when we talk about men and women, and it is the poetry of women that this volume is intended to celebrate, whether or not there is any consensus about the difference in kind of this poetry from poetry written by men.

What then of 'Scottishness'? If we extend the idea of the nation into the wider idea of place, and the situation – moral, emotional and linguistic – of the writer within place, we need perhaps look no further for justification of the Scottish side of this project. In *Identifying Poets* Robert

Crawford convincingly argues that 'the theme of home, crucial for the "identifying poet", is one of the great themes, perhaps the major theme of late twentieth-century poetry in the English-speaking world – using that last, problematic term only to fracture and problematize it by paying close attention to the world of poets who write in Scots' (p.15). Language and place are, of course, intimately bound together.

Not all the writers in the volume will be felt to be equally 'Scottish' but some relationship with Scotland and Scottishness, and the unique situation of the writer with respect to these ideas, will be found in most of the poems. My interpretation of Scottishness has been, however, as wide as possible. It agrees with Alasdair Gray's definition of anyone working and living in Scotland but it also includes those who have in the past lived or worked in Scotland and who have either thought about this at the time or subsequently. Thus, Carol Ann Duffy, who left when she was three but excitingly revisits the country in imagination and fact, is appropriated. It is to be assumed that she is gracious about the co-option since she accepted a commission for a poem to celebrate the opening of the Museum of Scotland on 30 November 1998. Kathleen Raine, who has an even more complicated emotional relationship with Scotland, is welcomed, as is Kate Clanchy, who spent her childhood and adolescence in Glasgow and Edinburgh. Kate Clanchy confirms Robert Crawford's sense of 'where's home?' as an important question for twentieth-century writers: '*Samarkand* is primarily about home – a sense of the right place in space and time.' And Marion Lomax, although less technically Scottish than Clanchy, nevertheless so engages with border crossings and with Lady Macbeth that I was anxious for her presence.

WOMEN AND TRADITION

If one then allows 'women' and 'Scottishness', what is to be done with them? What questions may we ask of the poetry? Do women/should women address a different subject matter from men? Do women/should women have a different language/languages from men? These are issues for all genres but they are peculiarly intense for poetry. If women have problems with a predominantly male tradition, are these problems always already in place, even when the social and political situation of women changes? Have some of the 'problems' that women have with poetry been created, sometimes retrospectively, by feminist criticism? In the course of a conference in Glasgow on Scottish women's writing in 1986 a number of these issues emerged: various academics – Glenda Norquay, Isobel Murray, myself – almost assumed that women had special problems with a male aesthetic, especially in poetry, given what still seemed the overwhelming masculinity of the Scottish poetic tradition. Liz Lochhead, who also spoke, felt that women poets must have a different relationship with the Muse. But Janet Caird, an older poet in the audience, although one who started writing poetry late in life, could not understand what people were going on about: 'You are a woman; you write poetry. What's the problem?' she asked. How, in the light of this, can there be a special female tradition?

It is always possible for the anthologist to load the dice here. For example, I think that there *are* special subject matters discernible among the women I have chosen and I think there are also special ways of writing about shared subject matter. About whether or not there is a different female poetic language, I am much less sure.[4] But the point, for the moment, is that I could easily have accentuated these special differences by my choice of poems. That is to say, I think I have already loaded the dice a little (any anthology is perhaps defined by dice-loading) but I could have been much more careful or wily in choosing poems that would illustrate or confirm a thesis.

An example may help here. A number of poems in the anthology invoke Ophelia: Bessie MacArthur's 'For a Modern Ophelia', Tracey Herd's 'Ophelia's Confession', Sheena Blackhall's 'Ophelia'. Of course, this is not an accident but I have in the end included none of the poems from Agnes Allan Macdiarmid's *Ophelia's Songs* (1935) and have not included the title poem from Elizabeth Burns's *Ophelia, and Other Poems*. In truth, the obsession with Ophelia disturbingly suggests a greater complicity with victimhood than I would wish to highlight. The process of revising female figures from legend or earlier writing is certainly a feature of modern women's verse and prose but we should probably worry if women persistently choose models of untransformable victimhood. Ophelia's suicide is not really recoverable for empowerment. I also have an odd feeling that I might have given a different notion of female figuring had I admitted every skein of wild geese that I encountered or every invocation of spindrift: these figures might leadingly suggest a longing for other places or a love of ephemeral beauty.[5]

In any case, noticing such things, generalising in this way, establishes retrospective traditions rather than identifying existing ones. Retrospective traditions may perhaps provide some satisfactions for the academic seeking connections but do they matter at all to writers? Is it possible to belong to a tradition without knowing it, or is this something of a joke like M. Jourdain finding out that he has all along been speaking prose? The 1986 conference provided an example of a kind of retrospective discovery for Liz Lochhead, who agreed that Marion Angus's 'The Blue

Jacket' (p.20), which she had not previously known, had an emotional affinity with her own 'Poem For My Sister' (p.154): of course, this is a small discovery, yet it at least gives the more recent poet a confirming sense of continuity. Specifically, however, some poets in this volume do pay implicit and explicit homage to a female tradition, although not generally a Scottish one. Allusions and tributes to male models are, however, probably more consistent but so is a certain suspiciousness about the oppressive weight of the male tradition.

Alice V. Stuart, in 'Wreath for E.B.B., 1806–1861', celebrates Elizabeth Barrett Browning and her 'singing sisters', Christina Rossetti, Alice Meynell and, most recently, Edna St Vincent Millay:

> What of this later age? One music only
> Rises in fountain jets of power like these,
> The New England voice of Edna St Vincent Millay
> Beyond Atlantic seas. (1963)

The unconquerable unmusicality of Edna St Vincent Millay's name has kept the poem out of the anthology but it remains an exemplary poem for me not only because of its sentiments but because it chooses for the 'later age' a poet who remained devoted to rhyme even as the Modernists were rejecting it. The Scottish women poets of the first half of the twentieth century tended to be formally conservative. The conservatism does not inhibit the determined appropriation of literary mothers. Yet it is always the lyric Barrett Browning that subsequent women poets tend to follow; that radical seizure of the epic for a woman's life and work that she achieved in *Aurora Leigh* is never taken on. Other mothers, Emily Dickinson and Emily Brontë, are not always explicitly recognised but certainly hover behind the work of a number of the earlier writers, notably Margaret Sackville.

Yet fathers are not spurned. There are a number of poems that celebrate admiration for Scottish male writers: for example, Norman MacCaig, Edwin Morgan (Liz Lochhead, p.156, and others), Hugh MacDiarmid (Lillias Chisholm), Sorley MacLean (Ciorstai NicLeòid, p.29, Meg Bateman), George Bruce (Sheena Blackhall), Alastair Reid (Liz Niven, p.183) and it has unfortunately not been possible to include all of these. Meg Bateman also celebrates Seamus Heaney (p.215); Edith Ann Robertson translated from the 'suddron' the work of De La Mare, Day Lewis and, most impressively, Gerard Manley Hopkins. It is everywhere obvious that all the poets in the pre-war period read Burns and some in the later period still feel rebuked by his genius, even if they express this comically: as Ellie McDonald, 'joukan atween thae/double deck buses, wishan tae hell I had wings', is wryly conscious that the worst that the heritage of Burns has to fear is a bit of pigeon-shit on the head of his statue, while she cannot even get off the ground (p.128). Alison Prince's three poems on women and poetry recognise the intimidating difference of the male tradition (p.122–124). On the other hand, Alison Kermack's debt to Tom Leonard is perhaps damagingly obvious (p.242).

The Gaelic poets composing within the sung tradition – Oighrig Dhòmhnallach, Carstìona Anna Stiùbhart, Curstaidh NicDh'àidh – have a different relationship to traditional models, a relationship conditioned by the community rather than even implicitly gendered. They are all working to approved models in genre, metre and diction that are known to and sustained by their communities. These works, tied to oral performance, cannot really find their full life on the written page. Self-disclosure and introspection are inappropriate in this tradition. The holding in check of indecorous self-expression is well illustrated in the Tiree lament of Oighrig Dhòmhnallach (p.1), where the poet's own grief never intrudes in such a way as to deflect the expression of family and community grief: it is perhaps the more intensely felt for this restraint. Ciorstai NicLeòid's poems form a striking exception to the work of these traditional poets of the first half of the twentieth century: her 'Litir chun a' Bhàird' ('A Letter to the Poet') to Sorley MacLean adopts Maclean's own modernist stance within its idiosyncratically personal voice.

THE SCOTTISH TRADITION

Questions similar to those provoked by gender may be asked about Scottishness. Do/should Scottish writers, variously defined, write differently from those identified with other places? Is there a national tradition at all? Robert Crawford and Mick Imlah identify three main characteristics of Scottish poetry. Weather, translation and, most typically, 'prejudice in Scotland's favour'.[6]

The women in this volume certainly confirm Crawford and Imlah's sense of translation as a special Scottish preoccupation and it is no doubt Scotland's peculiarly rich linguistic heritage that makes this so. It would have been possible – and it would be interesting to do it – to produce a volume entirely of translations and versions. None of the translations by women have achieved the fame of the great verse of Gavin Douglas or Edwin Morgan but Edith Robertson's translations of Gerard Manley Hopkins deserve it.

About weather, I am not sure: this is a modern collection and I have a sense that we have come too far from Henryson's 'doulie season' for it to have much force for these women. Those from the north-east, from Jacob to Blackhall, place their people in cold, often threatening landscapes but even these are rendered with love, for the last characteristic is everywhere in evidence. Scotland is much loved, even in its less attractive manifestations. The predilection in favour of Scotland that Crawford and Imlah remark is everywhere in evidence, sometimes to the extent of wilfully ignoring the deficiencies of the country, as in Nannie Wells's eroticising of Scotland as her lover (p.24). But the predilection in favour of Scotland does not derive from ignorance of other places. Scottish women poets have not been a stay-at-home bunch. In the first half of the twentieth century the writers were often children or wives of Empire. Violet Jacob's husband served in the British army and she accompanied him to India, Egypt and even England before she returned to Angus after her husband's death in 1937 and so much of her writing in Scots consisted of home thoughts from abroad that this often gives a special longing intonation to her use of the vernacular. Isobel Wylie Hutchison was a traveller in her own right, a botanist and explorer. In 1927, the year that saw the publication of *The Northern Gate* (from which the poems in this anthology are taken) also found Isobel Hutchison botanising in Greenland. Her first collection of poems was *Lyrics from West Lothian*; her last in 1935 was *Lyrics from Greenland*. For Jacob and Hutchison, however, the culture of other places remains 'other'; the desire to understand and love that 'other' is strong but the experience does not lead to any serious questioning of their own cultures. As the century progresses, however, a willingness to compare Scotland with other places does not automatically result in confirmation of the superiority of home. Scotland is increasingly seen more clearly either from afar or after a return from elsewhere – Gillies, Lochhead, Rose, Jamie.

The Gaelic poets included here have not been travellers, although a number – Carstìona Anna Stiùbhart, Màiri NicGumaraid and Mòrag NicGumaraid – have brought lowland experience back to their native places. And others of the new generation of poets claim both Highland and Lowland as home. Indeed, one might almost feel that Meg Bateman, a lowlander and learner, has gone to find in Skye the community that will validate her intensely personal voice. At the beginning of the century the traditional community poets worked within their long-established, secure and apparently relatively impermeable tradition, closely tied to musical expression; but the tradition has in a sense been retrospectively permeated and its exposure to the wider world offers new possibilities of reading.

PRINCIPLES OF ANTHOLOGISING

It seems unlikely, then, that we will stop discussing the pressures of gender and place on writing and so any anthology that increases the available evidence for the discussion has a value. But it would be a feeble defence of an anthology of poetry that it merely a little extended critical and theoretical debate. If poetry does not give us pleasure, if it does not delight us in the way Marion Lochhead identifies, then it can scarcely be defended. It will be evident to all readers of the poems in this anthology that some of them are better than others, by which I mean that some of them struggle with experience more intensely, offer deeper engagement with sound, language and meaning than others; but I would, nevertheless, contend that there are no poems in this volume that do not show their authors as involved in that tussle with words, in that endeavour to put the 'best words in the best order' of which Coleridge speaks.

Anthologies act both to recover and to remind and are themselves part of a constant process of publication and republication. They recover past poems that are forgotten simply because they are unavailable to the majority of readers. While it is unlikely that the second-rate will survive, it does not follow that what goes out of print is necessarily second-rate: it may be second-order while still forming the necessary bedrock without which a culture of poetry writing and reading could not survive at all. The recovery of even a small part of that bedrock allows us to construct a past readership as well as a continuing tradition. And anthologies remind us that what we admire now may not survive time's arrow, and certainly will not, if we are fickle readers and buyers – and so while buying new collections is our primary duty as readers, buying and reading anthologies is a way of consolidating and preserving poems.

But I would wish to confront directly the reader who may say that the poetry in this anthology is not of uniform quality, that much of it is not technically innovative and sometimes not even up-to-date. Tom Leonard in *Radical Renfrew* asks for a reappraisal of what we customarily admire in poetry, particularly in the academy. He insists in giving subject matter primacy over technical innovation but then he seems to sell the pass by insisting that the subject matter be radical. Is there not some kind of potentially dangerous censorship going on here? I have found this a great problem in compiling this anthology. I could have produced a more radical selection in both method and content than I have done but would it have honestly reflected what the women of its period were writing, and writing honestly? Of course, poetry that is merely servile to received forms and ideas can be of little interest to us and some of the writers that I have included cannot escape such criticism of some of their poems; yet, even in the case of poets who have a too easy recourse to exclamation marks and 'poetic language', there are often at least a few poems that demand more serious consideration, that reveal an intense, personal engagement with words. Indeed, it has been the capacity of the poetry of the first half of the twentieth century to surprise that has struck me most. It has been startling to be told that there is a 'little extra streak of Hell/In Ayr' (p.11) or to find such a witty, gentle and relieved refusal of the romantic position as Hutchison offers when she passes the lovers in the lane (p.49).

Of course, attachment to tradition for the Gaelic community poet is not servility but piety. And within that tradition the skill is in the reworking of known metrical models or in the verbal dexterity that is brought to the advancement of community values. These values may be expressed as edification, as in Catriona NicDhòmhnaill's hymns, or humorously and satirically, as in Curstaidh NicDh'àidh's Parliament of Fowls (p.84) or elsewhere in her wry description of the advance of consumerism in her 'Bachelor's Song'.

We have, then, chosen to represent almost a hundred poets in this anthology. The alternative was to restrict ourselves to the dozen or so poets who are already widely known. Yet a sterner selection would not at all represent the sheer quantity of poetry that was being published and not all of it by small presses that have gone out of business. We decided, therefore, to try to show this quantity at the risk of exposing unevenness of execution. Moreover, it needs no anthologist to tell the reading public that Liz

Lochhead changed the face of women's poetry in Scotland or that Kathleen Jamie is a fine writer in any gathering, national or international. The anthologist's task seems properly to go a bit outside what everyone knows already. A number of the poems that have been included may strike the reader as remarkably formally conservative, although we have generally excluded those that still adhere to mid-nineteenth-century diction well into the twentieth. But there is no doubt that Scottish women's poetry is at least until the middle of the twentieth century more formally conservative than the productions of men of the same period. Marion Angus's 'Alas!, Poor Queen', a somewhat over-anthologised piece, is sometimes compared to early Pound but such a comparison cannot be sustained throughout her work, and her vernacular poetry is in any case probably more innovative, albeit in its manipulation of older forms, than her English poetry.

Veronica Forrest-Thomson stands out as quite exceptional: her formal innovations derive in part from her contempt, as a critic, for discussions of poetry that merely paraphrase the prose content, the story, of the poems and so she writes unparaphrasable poems that refuse to provide a story. But some apparently more conventional strategies also tantalise with half-told story, as in the allusive methods of the ballad. Indeed, commitment to the ballad does in part explain and mitigate a kind of conservatism and here we find some quite remarkable manipulations of traditional form – Angus, Jacob, Cruickshank, Adam, MacArthur. Throughout the century evocation of the ballads allows poets the impersonality that protects them from senti-mentality and self-absorption. The impersonal voice of the folk, which nevertheless remains intimate, even visceral, allows a number of women access to a harder and more challenging poetry. But apart from these exceptions we have to wait for Liz Lochhead for a modern craft that consistently comes close in its awareness of the new to the male writers. After her, generalisation is less easy.

ASKING FOR PERMISSION

Drawing her analogy from the children's game of 'Mother-May-I', which she herself played as a child, Kathleen Jamie explains how her own writing has laid claim to new ground:

> Each new development in our writing begins when we seek permission to approach it; to approach a new area of experience. We ask permission, that is, to blunder into a delicate place. We ask permission to assume 'ownership', and appropriate to ourselves whatever it is our writing is moving toward. How much of history or nationship may we assume to ourselves? May we plunder the past? Reveal the secret histories of our lovers, and families? Be intellectual? Be a poet at all? It's a courtesy, which at times hardens into a moral question, this 'May I?'[7]

Perhaps the best way to put the dilemma for the older poets is that in certain areas they either failed to enter the game, never asked for new permissions, or, having asked, kept being refused permission by 'Mother'. But 'Mother', Jamie points out, in the game is 'one of us', a peer temporarily elevated to an authority figure, and so in the end the poets have mainly themselves to blame if they are unadventurous. Of course, social and political pressures have been adduced but the bottom line is self-permission and this needs a kind of courage and aggression that many of the older poets would have thought unfeminine. It turns out, however, that Kathleen Jamie feels that she has moved past the position that she identified as marked by permission-seeking.[8] It may well be that this request is an interim stage in the development of the writer, one which perhaps many less self-conscious writers are scarcely aware of, just as it is one that many less adventurous writers have never reached.

BECOMING PROFESSIONAL

Jamie's interrogation of her craft is typical of the professionalism of contemporary women poets in Scotland and elsewhere. The twelve living female poets who contribute to *Contemporary Women's Poetry* and the nine who contribute to *Strong Words* are writing about their *work* in every possible construction of the term.[9] But the relative conservatism of earlier poets is not a consequence of lack of professional commitment. Beginning in 1929 and continuing through the 1930s, Marion Lochhead wrote a series of articles on Scottish women writers for the *Bulletin*. The *Bulletin* was, of course, a conservative newspaper and the ideologies of the women that were celebrated didn't rock many boats. Nevertheless, these were no twinset-and-pearls pieces: they are characterised by attentiveness to the specificity of the texts dealt with; they are, as Violet Jacob says in her letter of thanks to Marion Lochhead, 'so singularly lacking in claptrap or sentimentality'. And the demands they place on their readers exceed those of most such pieces today. On Margaret Sackville, Lochhead writes:

> A short poem, to be memorable, must be the very essence of thought and beauty . . . The brevities of poetry are nearly always sad or ironic, partly because

of their associations with great epitaphs and valedictions, from those in the Greek anthology down, partly because great emotions fall naturally into brief utterances. (11 April, 1929)

Marion Lochhead's papers in the national Library contain a number of letters from the writers she contacted that also demonstrate serious involvement with writing and with issues of gender and place.[10] Margaret Sackville worries about whether having a Scottish mother is sufficient credential; Naomi Mitchison says that she's 'much interested in the Scottish renaissance people, and attempts to understand MacDiarmid'; Helen Cruickshank typically modestly worries that her verse has not earned her the title of 'woman writer', far less of 'poet'; and Willa Muir pinpoints the gender dilemma: 'Perhaps it could be summarised by describing me as half a "stickit" scholar, with scholarly and temperamental leanings, and half a temperamental woman: if I were whole-heartedly one or the other life would be much easier for me. I drive too many incompatible horses in my team.'

BATTLES OF THE SEXES – AND SOME ALLIANCES

If we have a strong sense that these pieces and the newspaper that they were published in belong to a silenced era, we have Douglas Dunn to confirm that sense: 'Earlier in the century women poets were prominent – Rachel Annand Taylor, Violet Jacob, Marion Angus and Helen Cruickshank being the best known. Until the 1960s, however, literary women might have been discouraged by a conspicuously male-centred poetic country.'[11] And the male poets were not merely dominant, they were argumentatively so. In November 1959 the Scottish Arts Council supported the publication of a volume of new Scottish poetry, *Honour'd Shade*, edited by Norman MacCaig to celebrate Burns's bicentenary.[12] The *Scotsman* reviewer quite mildly remarked that this collection of poems from 27 male poets, most of whom he admired, seemed to have odd exclusions and might have been called the 'Rose Street Anthology', from the street of pubs in Edinburgh reputedly frequented by its contributors. This provoked a fairly acrimonious correspondence, which lasted for over a month and featured MacDiarmid, Douglas Young, Sidney Goodsir Smith, Hamish Henderson and, in the younger generation, Stewart Conn. It contained more assertion than demonstration and was not strictly *about* poetry. Douglas Young protested the absence of women poets and hopes that '2 or 3 lady writers will prepare a representative collection of poems by Scotswomen of this century, many of whom do not frequent megalopolitan dram-shops' (21 November, 1959). As might have been expected, this brought down MacDiarmid's wrath:

> I do not agree with Mr Douglas Young about the bevy of Scottish songstresses today, and think that perhaps his regard for them is due to his objection to modernistic trends in poetry and determination to uphold superannuated kinds of verse. (24 November, 1959)

Perhaps an unfair charge against an anthologist who included 15 of MacDiarmid's poems in his own 1952 anthology.[13] Helen Cruickshank was unwise enough to involve herself in the controversy: her Scots poem accusing MacDiarmid of writing dictionary Scots with no real audience – 'Noo, wha dis Hughoc think he can impress/Wi's fremit learnin'?' Certainly not, replied MacDiarmid, those who 'ignore all the real problems raised in a lengthy correspondence in favour of an inane giggle which lets loose more than a whiff of sour grapes' (16 December, 1959). The last word, however, went to a woman: Alice V. Stuart's poem was published 19 December, 1959.

> Who honour best our Rabbie's Honour'd Shade?
> Not those who thrawn discursive verse parade,
> But those in whom the lyric impulse pressed
> To eager utterance. Their's a Sang at least.

Perhaps an inconclusive victory. And even Douglas Young, it must be said, did not manage in his anthology to include more than 16 women (as against 91 men) in the period from 1900 to 1951.[14] But Young was a constant advocate of women's writing: in 1953 he had written to Edith Anne Robertson that her *Voices* was 'a truly astonishing challenge to those who think the Lallans incapable of conveying thought (as E. Muir incautiously maintained in "Scott and Scotland" and incapable of expressing subtleties of feeling (as MacCaig too often assents). Moreover it does fill the gap I emphasised (in my Nelson anthology), when I remarked on the comparative lack of mystical verse in Scots,'[15] and in 1962 he writes to Bessie Bird MacArthur that *From Daer water* contains 'all well felt necessary poems'.[16] Bessie MacArthur also conducted a correspondence with William Soutar, who assured her that of the poems about her son's death, 'Last Leave' showed no emotional disharmony and 'Hight Gaed Oot' achieved a 'genuine ballad atmosphere'.[17]

   There is, then, a great deal of evidence after all that Scottish women writers worked together and learned from each other during the whole of the twentieth century. But there is evidence too of fruitful interaction with male writers. MacDiarmid himself was much more supportive, and not just in a patronising manner, than some of his more intemperate public statements would suggest.

SCOTS, CLASS AND *NOBLESSE OBLIGE*

Nevertheless, that very misjudged pawkiness of Helen Cruickshank illustrates one of the problems that poets have with Scots – the temptation to the quaint that hovers round the use of a language that has uneasy and sometimes only fitful connections with the spoken word. The other is the problem that MacDiarmid himself identified as *noblesse oblige*. He believes that Violet Jacob and even Marion Angus, like the eighteenth-century songwriters, write Scots from this motive. Now, there is a certain homogeneity among the writers in English and Scots of the first half of the twentieth century. Mostly they were middle-class or higher and mostly they were educated, sometimes highly educated. I have remarked Marion Lochhead's familiarity with the classics and her assumption of such familiarity among her readership. Many of them had a separatist education in girls' schools, whether day or boarding; they became school and college teachers or civil servants or they married members of the professional or landed classes. The subject matter of their poetry, then, tends to exclude working-class or even urban life. Their use of Scots, too, is a kind of tribute to the language rather than a question of speaking in their own tongue. Even Flora Garry, who probably originally spoke as she writes, leaves a set of quotation marks around most monologue and dialogue poems, even 'The Professor's Wife'.

I turn now to some specific concerns and themes – the natural world, public events, love and motherhood.

NATURE

Do women have and record a gendered response to the natural world? This question has occupied the imagination of writers and critics since at least the end of the eighteenth century. From the Romantics on, there have been a number of attempts to claim that there is a special female way of encountering and constructing the natural world. I have already suggested a peculiar attachment to wild geese and spindrift as figures of longing and loss but, of course, this is merely superficial. At a deeper level, I think women perhaps more modestly than men respect the otherness as well as the perceived beauties of the natural world. Indeed, the poets in this volume seem linked by their constant refusal to appropriate the natural world merely to explicate or comment on the human one; consequently the relationship between them is metaphysical in Roderick Watson's sense,[18] without nature itself ever being less than intensely observed, as in Nan Shepherd's 'The Hill' (p.53) or as in Anne Stevenson's 'With my Sons at Boarhills' (p.124), where the voices of her children:

> . . . return like footprints over the sandflats,
> permanent, impermanent, salt and sensuous
> as the sea is, in its frame, its myth.

PUBLIC EVENTS

Women poets have suffered a lot from men telling them that they should know their place and that their place is not in the public realm. Stick to love and domesticity, rhymes for children and ladies, and leave political and occasional poetry to men. Thus Mrs Barbauld was ticked off for daring to be unpatriotic in her '1811', told by Croker to get back to her knitting; Elizabeth Barrett Browning became suspect when she inserted herself into Italian political debates. And Gaelic female bards had in the past had quite precise specific permissions for subject matter. Of course, women have always challenged these demarcation lines: some of the popular seventeenth- and eighteenth-century clan bards, as well as Màiri Mhòr MacPherson herself, transgressed into the public sphere. And public poetry is increasingly not a male preserve; women are progressively being permitted public voices.

Yet women's responses to the two great wars of the last century have not been uniformly encouraging. The First World War tended to provoke rather unquestioning sentimental piety, which necessarily entails a kind of conventionality of language and form. The poems I include are not really representative of all the poems I read, in many of which worthiness stifled possible anger. Mary Symon's 'A Recruit for the Gordons' (p.12) doesn't question conventional constructions of heroism, any more than does Oighrig Dhòmhnallach's lament (p.1) but both poems get some of the sense of the pity and waste that the best First World War poems offer. As Symon's recruit, 'the heir o' brave langsynes', hears the 'dead lips' of fellow soldiers calling to him, we confront the truth that the voice of the poem is itself issuing from 'dead lips'. Mary Boyle's sonnets on her brother's death also accept the conventional notion of heroism but the loving specificity of all her verse gives the sense of waste a meaning of which Owen himself might not have disapproved (p. 33). Màiri NicDhòmhnaill's 'Crom-Lus Arrais' ('Arras Poppy') (p.118) is a more enigmatic evocation of how men's blood might make meaningful the soil on which it fell. And Margaret Armour and Margaret Sackville, in 'The Airmen' (p.21) and 'Foam and Earth' (p.35), lift both exultation (that 'lonely impulse of delight' that Yeats evokes) and pity above mere convention. Jean Guthrie Smith is, however, the only poet I encountered who took on board the horror that the return of the loved one might be something to dread rather than celebrate (p.10). Indeed, it seems as though most of the women did feel the force of Owen's exclusion ('Apologia pro poemate meo'), felt, that is, that they had no right to invade the horrors of the battlefield.

The second war provoked less in the way of direct engagement. We have Bessie MacArthur's moving poems in memory of her sons, one of which is included: they are the verbal equivalent of the stained glass window in Elvanfoot Parish Church commemorating her son Alastair's death. In 'Eight Gaed Oot' (p.46) the ballad atmosphere, which William Soutar remarked, provides the distance and impersonality without which the subject could not be approached. Once more, poems from this period memorialise the lost without tackling the darker issues of the war. Horrific death and persecution are written about in the poetry and prose of Jenny Robertson but restrospectively, examining a legacy, not a present nightmare (p.135). Similarly, one of the most moving engagements with love and loss in the Second World War is *A Flame in My Heart* written jointly by Kathleen Jamie and Andrew Greig. I have not included any of this poem sequence, since it seems not to lend itself to being extracted, but we should remark its function as a bridge between the generations, a tribute from the generation that lived through the Cold War to the one that suffered the preceding violence.

The Cold War, the legacy of earlier conflicts, was lived through by most of the women born between 1940 and 1970 – a remarkably long period, in truth. Alison Fell's 'Women in the Cold War' (p.139) charts the parallel sequences of public events and the events of the lives of ordinary women. Generally, poets from this period are more acutely aware of the intersection of private and public events as perhaps only Naomi Mitchison had been earlier. All Mitchison's poems are political in their insistence that all private acts have a larger public context and Liz Lochhead extends this perception in 'Mirror's Song' (p.155) to summarise how much the whole notion of the private feminine is a consequence of public history:

Smash me for your daughters and dead
mothers, for the widowed
spinsters of the first and every war
let her
rip up the appointment cards
for the terrible clinics,
the Greenham summonses, that date
they've handed us. Let her rip.

Lochhead's poem promises that women will henceforth take control of their destiny, a promise that is reiterated in the poems of most of the women who follow her. At the same time, Carol Ann Duffy, Jackie Kay, Janet Paisley and Angela McSeveney are in their different ways all conscious that some private lives are wholly determined by public events and public acts of gendering that the individual cannot control. A moving contrast between the two poems in this volume that invoke the sinking of the yacht, *Iolaire*, on its way to Lewis with its freight of returning servicemen, illustrates the complex relationship between private and public. Carstìona Anna Stiùbhart records the loss to the community in a poem that claims male territory, while Anna Frater's charting of the pain of her grandmother, who lost her father on the ship, has an affinity with the distinctive female voice of the Gaelic folk tradition. Thus the loss to the community is recorded over 70 years later in terms of its effect on a private destiny in a poem that employs a modernist technique and stance while simultaneously securing itself to traditional kinds.

LOVE

'Do you have a lot of love poems in your anthology? I suppose you do since they are all women' – this Lizzie MacGregor, librarian of the Scottish Poetry Library. And yet women have not always found it easy to write love poetry. Catherine Carswell wonders if love poetry is worryingly intimate and revealing:

> Do we as English readers feel perfectly comfortable when we read the love poems of the Brontës, or Christina Rossetti, or Mrs Browning, or the prose love confessions of a Marie Bashkirtseff, the married confessions of a Sophie Tolstoi?[19]

There must be something at least apparently confessional about love poetry or it doesn't seem authentic: the poet has to give herself away and not all women have found it easy to do this. 'The lyric has always reflected the nature of the relations between the sexes in Western culture, more accurately perhaps the lyric has surely had a central role in *constructing* those relations. Although the first love poet may well have been Sappho, lyrical poems of desire in the Western tradition are often discussed as though they were always written by men to women.'[20] And there may well be special difficulties for Scottish women, since the paradigmatic Scottish love poet surely remains Burns and he is not an easy model for women. The special authority of 'My Love is Like a Red, Red Rose' seems not really achievable by a woman. Even male abjection is usually turned into a kind of authority by Burns – 'Ae Fond Kiss' and 'Mary Morrison'. And the confident, full-throated ease of Burns's love songs has not produced anything similar from women.

The love poems of Violet Jacob and Marion Angus usually do focus on woman's love even when the speaker is male but the technique remains oblique; the trick is to provide women with hidden stories, narratives that insinuate the secrets of female desire and loss. Where, as with Rachel Annand Taylor, love is more directly expressed, its sincerity is compromised by its theatricality. Nan Shepherd, on the other hand, writes a plainer and more delicate love poetry and we may be struck by the gentle putting aside of resentment when love is over that characterises Hutchison's 'In the Lane' (p.49).

More recent poems show love in more varied forms: Liz Lochhead repeatedly turns abjection into a kind of equivocal triumph and Janet Paisley wittily appropriates menstrual muddles for empowerment (p.172). But the most important message that the younger poets offer is that it is the quality of our love and not the nature of our sexuality that matters; love, like the nation itself, should obliterate boundaries, be generous. Jackie Kay's love of her adoptive parents, always in evidence, informs her understanding of the suffering of Bessie Smith and that understanding opens into a wider compassion, indistinguishable from love for all who have have felt the ecstasy of passion and the pain of rejection ('The Red Graveyard', p.227).

The weight of traditional discourses of love is not any easier to bear in Gaelic and it crosses gender barriers. Contemporary women writers of love poetry have to find ways of reimagining the conventional imagery of the modern (usually male) romantic love song but the passionate disclosures of the older (usually female) folk tradition must also be encountered and, if possible, reworked, as in Meg Bateman's 'Leigeil Bhruadaran Dhìom' ('Letting Go of Dreams') (p.219).

MOTHERHOOD

This new openness to all kinds of love has also, I think, allowed in the course of the last hundred years an increasing celebration of motherhood. Women have always been expected to embody the best features of their mothers while casting aside the restrictions that have limited their mothers' lives: this is a difficult task and one the poets in this collection negotiate with loving tact. I think perhaps it is the awareness that there is much in the lives of their female forebears that they wish to reject that makes the younger poets celebrate the lives of their mothers and grandmothers with gentleness, wishing to preserve what was best in the customs and courage of the people who produced them. Thus Alison Fell, Liz Lochhead and Jackie Kay pay tribute to their grandmothers in 'Border Raids', and 'My Grandmother's Houses', and Jackie Kay's constantly expressed love of her parents shows that biological inheritance is not a necessary part of being a child.

Being a mother has also acquired new resonances over

the last century. There are an increasing number of poems about motherhood as the century goes on. Borrowing Jamie's phrase, more writers are asking, 'Mother, May I reveal my motherhood'. The tearing intimacy of motherhood is, however, absent from the poetry of the first half of the century and becomes increasingly a presence during and after the second war. Of course, more mothers actually lost their sons in the first war but women cannot all find a way of writing about this loss: Violet Jacob, for example, never did so directly. The first war also ensured that fewer women actually had children, since there was no acceptable way of choosing single parenthood: I came across, although I have not been able to include, a number of poems that regretted the loss of the opportunity to have a child.

New ways of writing about motherhood have not, however, simply depended on more women poets actually being mothers. One of the factors that have fuelled the daring of the younger writers has to do with a different, or at least modified, conception of motherhood. There has been a tradition in women's writing of relating female creativity to actual birth but the process of giving birth is no longer seen as an alternative form of creativity; instead, birth processes have proved harnessable to explain the peculiar mixture of pride and guilt, responsibility and horror, that attend creativity. In her Frankenstein poems and in 'An Abortion', which I have not included partly because it is so well-known, Liz Lochhead follows Mary Shelley's lead in thinking about the monstrosity of female creativity: if it is monstrous for Frankenstein to construct his monster it is monstrous for the female writer to construct *Frankenstein*, and hence the monster. Mary Shelley is doubly guilty as she sits down, in Liz Lochhead's poem, apparently serene in damped muslin, to give birth to her 'monstrous progeny' (p.152).

Other poets have engaged in a less oblique manner with

new perceptions of motherhood and its attendant gains and losses. Janet Paisley conveys the pain of stillbirth in 'Mayday' (p.172). Jamie's rendering of the new vision enabled by ultrasound particularly claims new territory: 'Oh whistle and I'll come to you, my lad, my wee shilpit ghost/summonsed from tomorrow' (p.234). The lines allusively invoke love story and ghost story and unite the otherworldly summons with the day-to-day, affectionate, vernacular 'shilpit'. The words are so few and are doing so much, are offering a new land to explore: the whole poem is a perfect example of that union of the 'demotic' and the 'metaphysical' that Roderick Watson finds characteristic of the finest Scottish poetry.[21] Gillian K. Ferguson's 'Scan' is more limited in its range of reference than Jamie's poem but 'the new blood' ('Everything is more', p.245) that the child represents is a new blood for poetry too. Gillian Ferguson in 2002 won a Creative Scotland Award to develop a project called 'The Poetry of Cloning', which will explore the 'context of mapping the human genome'. A number of journalists found this risible but I think they were wrong, for Ferguson will surely be following Wordsworth's recommendation in his celebrated Preface to *The Lyrical Ballads.* (1802) that it is the duty of the poet to 'be at the side of the man of science' carrying 'sensation into the midst of the objects of science itself'.

Standing back now and trying to get something of the whole picture of *Modern Scottish Women Poets*, the most pressing feature seems to be a developing sense of plurality as far as both gender and Scotland are concerned. Being a woman is a question of multiple experience, not of limitation. Violet Jacob's respectable woman may still lament the life of the 'jaud' but the 'jaud' herself has been empowered, given a voice in the poetry of Carol Ann Duffy, Jackie Kay, Tracey

Herd and many others. And Meg Bateman has brought to the Gaelic tradition a new radical female voice. Being Scottish, however, is a matter of a series of acts of inclusion; not a drawing of boundaries but persistent crossing or removal of barriers. Where the travellers of the first half of the century tended to use their encounters with otherness as a confirmation of their own ethnicity (and sometimes, in accordance with the custom of the day, of the superiority of their native culture), today's travelling poets are open to otherness as a way of mingling and muddling, rather than differentiating and setting apart. This tendency has forced new linguistic strategies. I have already remarked the element of *noblesse oblige* in the employment of Scots by some of the earlier poets. The Scots of Liz Lochhead and of Kathleen Jamie signals a richer linguistic inheritance that privileges neither English nor Scots. Kathleen Jamie used Scots in her poetry for the first time when she was travelling in Tibet at the time of Tiananmen. In 'For Paola' (p.231) and 'Sang o the blin beggar' and 'Xiahe', Jamie writes in Scots: 'A'm far fae hame,/I hae crossed China'. The Scots acts not nostalgically to effect a return but rather to enable an understanding of the local elsewhere. Kate Clanchy too invokes both the 'jaud' and far places: 'Slattern', which celebrates a careless multiplicity of self, has a lovely Scotticism to confirm a self that is at once fragmented and controlled:

> I leave myself about, slatternly,
> bits of me, and times I liked:
> I let them go on lying where
> they fall, crumple, if they will.
> I know fine how to make them walk
> and breathe again.

'You know fine how to' followed by some injunction about getting a grip has echoed through the childhood and adolescence of many a Scottish girl. Clanchy seizes the cliché and transforms it, giving a new force to 'fine'. And 'The Bridge Over the Border' (p.241) uses the notion of bridges to turn a journey to her Scottish home into a memory of love, which in turn allows a vision of promise, always reachable and always just out of reach.

This increasing emotional and linguistic openness seems to confirm a group of poets who are at last self-empowered, have replied 'Of course, you may' to their own requests for permissions.

Dorothy McMillan

A Note on Gaelic Poetry

It was not the original intention of the editors to make any distinctions between the poems in Gaelic and poems in English and Scots. This principle is followed in the order of appearance of the poets, which is simply chronological by birthdate, as far as that is known. Similarly, commentary on the Gaelic poems is incorporated with the other material in the Introduction. Yet, it will not quite do overly to elide difference, since the poems in Gaelic necessarily exist in a different poetic environment. First of all, they have, with two exceptions ('Cum Sinn Dlùth' and 'Màiri Iain Mhurch Chaluim', translated by Ronald Black and Anne Frater respectively), been 'translated' by Michel Byrne: the intention here has been not so much to downgrade the English versions provided by some of the poets themselves as to privilege the Gaelic in a special way. One result of this, however, is to stress even more firmly that these poems are only fully available to Gaelic speakers. The writers of the poems are all bilingual and the younger writers, as Christopher Whyte points out, 'to a greater degree than any previous generation . . . exist in a bilingual world'.[22] One of these, Meg Bateman, is a learner and the arrival of learners is, along with the 'return to mythology' and the 'refeminisation' of Gaelic verse, according to Ronald Black, one of 'the three distinct trends in the last quarter' of the twentieth century.[23]

Only Gaelic speakers will encounter all of the poems in this volume wholly on their own terms, for whether or not we think of Scots as a distinct language, it cannot be claimed that it is one that it is as difficult for non-native speakers to learn as is Gaelic. This is, then, a privilege of sorts for Gaelic speakers and it is one that is perhaps due to those whose tongue has survived rigorous attempts to extirpate it.

Dorothy McMillan and Michel Byrne

NOTES

[1] Catherine Kerrigan, ed., *An Anthology of Scottish Women Poets* (Edinburgh: Edinburgh University Press, 1991). Recent national anthologies include: Douglas Dunn, ed. *The Faber Book of Twentieth-Century Scottish Poetry* (London: Faber & Faber, 1992); Roderick Watson, ed., *The Poetry of Scotland: Gaelic, Scots and English* (Edinburgh: Edinburgh University Press, 1995); Robert Crawford and Mick Imlah, eds, *The New Penguin Book of Scottish Verse* (Harmondsworth: Penguin, 2000); and for Gaelic poetry Ronald Black, ed., *An Tuil* (Edinburgh: Polygon, 1999); Christopher Whyte, ed., *An Aghaidh na Sìorraidheachd/In the Face of Eternity: Ochdnar Bhàrd Gàidhlig/Eight Gaelic Poets* (Edinburgh: Polygon, 1991).

[2] Gillean Somerville-Arjat and Rebecca E. Wilson, eds, *Sleeping with Monsters: Conversations with Scottish and Irish Women Poets*: research and interviews by Rebecca Wilson (Edinburgh: Polygon, 1990); Ian A. Bell, ed., *Peripheral Visions: Images of Nationhood in Contemporary British Fiction* (Cardiff: University of Wales Press, 1995); Douglas Gifford and Dorothy McMillan, eds, *A History of Scottish Women's Writing* (Edinburgh: Edinburgh University Press, 1995); Christopher Whyte, ed., *Gendering the Nation* (Edinburgh: Edinburgh University Press, 1995); Vicki Bertram, ed., *Kicking Daffodils* (Edinburgh: Edinburgh University Press, 1997); Alison Mark and Deryn Rees-Jones, eds, *Contemporary Women's Poetry: Reading/Writing/Practice*, with a Preface by Isobel Armstrong (London: Macmillan, 2000). Other collections on Scottish Women's Writing include: Aileen Christianson and Alison Lumsden, eds, *Contemporary Scottish Women Writers* (Edinburgh: Edinburgh University Press, 2000).

[3] Robert Crawford, *Identifying Poets: Self and Territory in Twentieth-Century Poetry* (Edinburgh: Edinburgh University Press, 1993)

[4] Suspicion about notions of a special 'feminine' language is now common at least among British and American writers and critics: 'It is no longer tenable to hold that there is a specifically "feminine" language, and with the disappearance of this essentialism has also come a sense that the politics of gender have become progressively more complex' – Isobel Armstrong, 'Preface', Alison Mark and Deryn Rees-Jones, eds, *Contemporary Women's Poetry* (London: Macmillan, 2000).

[5] Happily, it is also possible for the anthologist to *unload* the dice. Thus we have tried to avoid over-anthologising by reproducing only the most famous of the writers' poems. Anthologies always carry the danger of keeping poets in memory by reducing the poems they are known for to two or three. And so readers will not find here Violet Jacob's 'Tam i' the Kirk' or Helen Cruickshank's 'Shy Geordie', Liz Lochhead's 'Revelation' or Kathleen Jamie's 'The Queen of Sheba'.

[6] Robert Crawford and Mick Imlah, eds, *The New Penguin Book of Scottish Verse* (Harmondsworth: Penguin, 2000), pp.xxvi–xxix.

[7] Kathleen Jamie, 'Holding Fast – Truth and Change in Poetry', in W.N. Herbert and Matthew Hollis, eds, *Strong Words: Modern Poets on Modern Poetry* (Newcastle-upon-Tyne: Bloodaxe, 2000), pp.277–78.

[8] So she said at a poetry reading at Glasgow University, 19 March 2002. On the same occasion, Jamie suggested that fidelity to forms is a male characteristic and, while this is historically clearly not true, since women writers have generally worked more closely with traditional forms, it might well be a feeling that more recent women writers share. That is to say, for some women the challenge of difficult metrical forms requires a kind of aggression that, whether or not actually gendered, is certainly not self-effacing – Eleanor Brown's poems come into this category.

[9] W.N. Herbert and Matthew Hollis, eds, *Strong Words: Modern Poets on Modern Poetry* (Tarse: Bloodaxe, 2000).

[10] All the letters are taken from MS 26190, NLS.

[11] Douglas Dunn, ed. *The Faber Book of Twentieth-Century Scottish Poetry* (London: Faber & Faber, 1992).

[12] *Honour'd shade:* an anthology of new Scottish poetry to mark the bicentenary of the birth of Robert Burns; selected and edited by Norman MacCaig (Edinburgh: Chambers, 1959).

[13] Douglas Young, ed., *Scottish Verse, 1851–1951* (Edinburgh: Nelson, 1952).

[14] Douglas Young, ed., *Scottish Verse, 1851–1951*.

[15] MS 26984, NLS.

[16] MS 27429, NLS.

[17] MS 27429, NLS.

[18] Roderick Watson, ed., *The Poetry of Scotland: Gaelic, Scots and English* (Edinburgh: Edinburgh University Press, 1995).

[19] Catherine Carswell, *Lying Awake* (1950; Edinburgh: Canongate, 1997), p.123.

[20] Barbara Johnson, *The Feminist Difference* (Cambridge, MA; London: Harvard University Press, 1998), p.114.

[21] Roderick Watson, ed., *The Poetry of Scotland: Gaelic, Scots and English*, p.xxxiii.

[22] Christopher Whyte, ed., *An Aghaidh na Sìorraidheachd/In the Face of Eternity*, p.vii.

[23] Black, *An Tuil*, p.lvii.

EDITORS' NOTE

The dates after the poems normally mark their first appearance in a collection of the poet's work or first appearance in a magazine, journal or anthology, if uncollected.

Oighrig (nì 'Illeasabaig) Dhòmhnallach/Euphemia MacDonald (1842–1936)

Cumha do Iain Dòmhnallach
(a mharbhadh san Fhraing sa bhliadhna 1917)

Thàining naidheachd don dùthaich
Dh'ùraich mulad as ùr dhuinn is bròn,
Nach bu mhaireann am fiùran
A bha measail is cliùiteach na dhòigh;
Leam is duilich ri innseadh,
Thu bhith d' chàradh gu h-ìosal fon fhòd,
Fad od chàirdean 's od dhìlsean,
'S fad on dachaidh 's an tìr thug dhuit lòn.

Tha do phàrantan lèirte,
'S beag an t-iongnadh an ceum a bhith mall,
On as fìrinn an sgeula
Gun do spìonadh a' gheug às a bonn:
Thàinig saighead bhon nàmhaid,
Chuir a gaithean gu làr thu, 's b' e 'n call;
'S iomadh òganach sàr-mhath
Chaidh an là ud gu bàs anns an Fhraing.

Tha do pheathraichean brònach,
'S tha do bhràithrean fo leòn 's tu gan dìth;
'S tu gun dèanadh an còmhnadh.
Bha thu tuigseach is eòlach 's gach gnìomh;
Nuair a ghlaodhte thar chàich riut
Air an raon latha bhlàir 's anns an strì,
'S tu gun seasadh an làrach,
Eadar sinne 's an nàmhaid gar dìon.

Bu tu fhèin an duin' uasal,
B'e sin teisteas an t-sluaigh ort gu lèir;
Bha thu faic'llach ad ghluasad,
Agus measarra, stuama da rèir;
Bha thu smearail mar shaighdear,
Agus iriosal, coibhneil am beus:
'S mise dh'fhaodadh a ghràitinn
Gur e fìrinn tha 'm dhàn 's nach e breug.

'S iomadh cliù ort ri innseadh
Nach bi mise cur sìos ann am dhàn;
On a dh'fhalbh thu 's nach till thu
Dh'fhàg thu cridheachan ìosal aig pàirt;
Ach cliù don Tì chaidh a cheusadh
'S a choisinn dhuinn rèite le bhàs,
Gun do shaor E dha fhèin thu
Le chorp naomh thoirt mar èirig nad àit'.

'S iomadh aon a tha duilich
Bhon a chual iad mu bhuille do bhàis,
Gun do chrìochnaich thu 'n turas
Nuair a thuit thu le tubaist sa bhlàr:
Seo 'n cogadh thug cìs dhinn,
Ged is fheudar bhith strìochdte nar càs;
Tha ar beatha neo-chinnteach,
Air a coimeas san fhìrinn ri sgàil.

1932

Lament for John MacDonald
(killed in France in the year 1917)

News has reached our shores
and awoken fresh sorrow and grief,
that the sapling has died
whose manner was admired and esteemed;
it pains me to report
that they lowered you into the soil
far from your family and devoted
and your home in the land that sustained you.

Your parents are distressed,
small wonder their step is so slow,
since the story is true
that the branch from its root has been torn:
from the enemy came an arrow
that felled you with its dart – great the loss!
Many splendid young men
met their death that day in France.

Your sisters are sad
and your brothers are wounded without you;
it's you would advise them –
you were wise and insightful in all matters;
when called on over others
on the field of war and in action,
it was you'd hold the ground
between us and the enemy, our protection.

You were truly a gentleman,
as the verdict of the people bore witness;
your behaviour was attentive,
and measured and moderate with it;

a fighter most valiant,
you were kindly in manner and modest:
I can say with assurance
that my song tells the truth and no falsehood.

There is much of your renown
that I cannot put down in my poem;
it leaves many hearts raw
that you are gone and will not be returning;
but the Crucified be praised
who gained our atonement by His death,
He released you for Himself,
His sacred body a ransom in your stead.

Many persons are hurting
since they heard of the blow of your death;
how you ended your journey
as in ill-fated combat you fell:
this war's tax is grievous
but resigned we must be to our plight –
our lives are uncertain,
and likened in Scripture to a shadow.

Violet Jacob (1863–1946)

The Wild Geese

'Oh, tell me what was on yer road, ye roarin' norlan' wind
As ye cam' blawin' frae the land that's niver frae my mind?
My feet they trayvel England, but I'm deein' for the
    north—'
'*My man, I heard the siller tides rin up the Firth o' Forth.*'

'Aye, Wind, I ken them well eneuch, and fine they fa'
    and rise,
And fain I'd feel the creepin' mist on yonder shore that lies,
But tell me, ere ye passed them by, what saw ye on the way?'
'My man, I rocked the rovin' gulls that sail abune the Tay.'

'But saw ye naethin', leein' Wind, afore ye cam to Fife?
There's muckle lyin' yont the Tay that's mair to me nor life.'
'My man, I swept the Angus braes ye haena trod for years—'
'O Wind, forgie a hameless loon that canna see for tears!—'

'And far abune the Angus straths I saw the wild geese flee,
A lang, lang skein o' beatin' wings wi' their heids towards the sea,
And aye their cryin' voices trailed ahint them on the air—'
'O Wind, hae maircy, haud yer whisht, for I daurna listen
    mair!'

norlan': northern   *straths*: river valleys
siller: silver   *haud yer whisht*: be silent
loon: lad

1915

The End o't

There's a fine braw thistle that lifts its croon
    By the river-bank whaur the ashes stand,
An' the swirl o' water comes whisp'rin' doon
    Past birk an' bramble an' grazin' land.
But simmer's flittit an' time's no heedin'
    A feckless lass nor a prideful' flow'r;
The dark to hide me's the grace I'm needin'.
        An' the thistle's seedin',
            An' my day's owre.

I redd the hoose an' I meat the hens
(Oh, it's ill to wark when ye daurna tire!),
An' what'll I get when my mither kens
It's niver a maiden that biggs her fire?
I mind my pray'rs, but I'm feared to say them,
I hide my een, for they're greetin' fast;
What though I blind them – for wha wad hae them?
The licht's gaen frae them
An' my day's past.

Oh, wha taks tent for a fadin' cheek?
No him, I'se warrant, that gar'd it fade!
There's little love for a lass to seek
When the coortin's through an' the price is paid.
Oh, aince forgotten's forgotten fairly,
An' heavy endit what's licht begun,
But God forgie ye an' keep ye, Chairlie,
For the nicht's fa'en airly
An' my day's done!

birk: birch
redd: tidy
meat: feed
biggs: builds

gar'd: made
forgotten fairly: completely forgotten
airly: early

1921

The Jaud

'O what are ye seein', ye auld wife,
I' the bield o' the kirkyaird wa'?'
'I see a place whaur the grass is lang
Wi' the great black nettles grawn fierce an' strang
And a stane that is clour'd in twa.'

'What way div ye glower, ye auld wife,
    Sae lang on the whumml'd stane?
Ye hae nae kin that are sleepin' there,
Yer three braw dochters are guid an' fair
    An ilk wi' a man o' her ain!

'There's dule an' tears i' yer auld een
    Tho' little eneuch ye lack;
Yer man is kindly, as weel ye ken,
Yer fower bauld laddies are thrivin' men
    And ilk wi' a fairm at his back.

'Turn, turn yer face frae yon cauld lair
    And back tae yer plenish'd hame;
It's a jaud lies yont i' the nettle shaws
Whaur niver a blink o' the sunlicht fa's
    On the mools that hae smoor'd her name.'

'Her hair was gowd like the gowd broom,
    Her een like the stars abune,
Sae prood an' lichtsome an' fine was she
Wi' her breist like the flowers o' the white rose tree
    When they're lyin' below the mune.'

'Haud you yer havers, ye auld wife,
    Think shame o' the words ye speak,
Tho' men lay fast in her beauty's grip
She brocht the fleer tae the wumman's lip
    An' the reid tae the lassie's cheek.

'Ye've lived in honour, ye auld wife,
    But happit in shame she lies,
And them that kent her will turn awa'
When the Last Day braks tae the trumpet's ca'
    And the sauls o' the righteous rise.'

'Maybe. But lave me tae bide my lane
At the fit o' the freendless queyn;
For oh! wi' envy I'm like tae dee
O' the warld she had that was no for me
And the kingdom that ne'er was mine!'

jaud: hussy	*shaws*: stalks
bield: shelter	*mools*: mosses
clour'd: split	*smoor'd*: covered over
glower: stare intently	*havers*: nonsense
whumml'd: overturned	*fleer*: scornful remark
ilk: each	*happit*: wrapped
dule: sorrow	*lave me to bide my lane*: let me be
lair: grave	

1921

Donald Maclane

The ling for bed and the loan for bield
    And the maist o' the winter through
The wild wind sabbin' owre muir an' field,
There's lang, lang drifts on the braes I've speil'd,
    O Donald Maclane, wi' you!

Fu' mony trayvels in sun and rain
    Wi' a sang for the gait they treid,
But the blythest gangers step aye their lane,
No twa thegither but ane by ane,
    When gangin's their daily breid.

A dancin' ee and a daffin' tongue,
    A voice i' the loanin' green—
Aye, fules think lichtly when fules are young
Tae pu' the nettle and no be stung,
    An' it's nocht but a fule I've been.

A crust for meat an' a curse for cheer,
    The wecht o' a heavy hand;
A skirl o' pipes i' the mornin' clear,
The rose-hip reid wi' the fadin' year
    And the breith o' the frozen land.

There was nane tae see when I set ma face
    Till a road that has ne'er an end,
There's a door that's steekit and toom's the place
That minds ma ain o' a black disgrace
    And an ill that they canna mend.

Ma feyther's bent wi' his broken pride
    And the shame that he'll no forgie,
But the love o' mithers is deep an' wide,
And there's maybe room for a thocht tae hide
    An' a prayer for the likes o' me.

Play up, play up noo, Donald Maclane,
    And awa' till oor rovin' trade;
For the wild pipes gie me a he'rt again
In a breist sae weary that whiles there's nane,
The wailin' pipes and the bairnies twain
    That are happit intill ma plaid.

ling: heather
loan: common field
bield: shelter
speil'd: climbed
gait: road
treid: tread
gangers: travellers/tinkers

their lane: alone
daffin': jesting
loanin': meadow
steekit: shut
toom: empty
happit: wrapped

1927

Jean Guthrie Smith (*fl*. 1922)

Ayr

Ayr, black Ayr,
Whose chimneys smutch the blue south sky there,
You have your harbour with its busy shipping,
And massive bard-sung bridges arching fair,
Hot trams that hurtle through the summer's glare,
Flat fields beyond, the tawny river slipping.
In Ayr
Cracked windows mock each other,
And backstreet doors gape open;
Misery, torpor and despair,
Folly to drug, and hopelessness to smother
The minds of men
In Ayr!
There must be gold to spare,
For there is many a house
With flowerbeds boasting this year's richest roses;
Clean curtained casements gleam through well-pruned
    boughs;
And purr of car discloses
Some have a hearty share
Of wealth in Ayr.
Dulled looks the faces wear,
With sullen eyes,
Of those you meet
Along the torrid street,
As if life's stagnancy were bad to bear:
We know there is no earthly Paradise,
No town of dreams,
No islands of delight;

All cities have their blot; and yet there seems
A little extra streak of Hell
In Ayr.
Ah well,
There are wrongs everywhere,
And strong men live to set them right;
But no one seems to care
In Ayr!

1922

The Soldier's Wife

My warrior comes from France to-night
And I, so long disconsolate,
Once more the well-beloved of Fate,
With work-scarred hands go quick to light
The red fire in the polished grate,
To set the chairs and china straight;
Turned young again, with youth's delight
In form and colour, scent and sight,
With happy dreams intoxicate;
I have a home again – a mate.
The centre of a world blown bright,
I wait – and wonder while I wait
My warrior come from France to-night!

. . . . . . And two doors down the street, alone
A woman lies, unreconciled
To grief, whose heart beat like mine own,
Whose love came back, yet came not, grown
A stranger to her and her child.
She only said he had 'gone wild,

Clean wild': and with her life turned stone
She watched this man, not hers, and smiled.

. . . . . . And yet another tries to break
Pain's barrier of silence, wears
Her sorrow like a rose to shake
To life his dead, dead laughter; cares
For naught but this, to hear him make
The old, dear jokes; yet cannot wake
For all her eagerness and prayers
The silent boy who stares and stares . . . . . .

I wait – and wonder while I wait.
My lamps are lit, my door ajar;
He nears, and yet he seems as far
And further than he was of late.
Like flower to flower and star to star
Were we: and yet how strange things are
To wait – and wonder while I wait!

1922

Mary Symon (1863–1938)

A Recruit for the Gordons

I'm aff! The halflin gets my crib,
    An' keeps the chaumer key;
The morn aul' Mains can dicht his nib,
    An' scoor the lift for me.

I've listed! Dang the nowt an' neeps!
    I'm aff to fecht or fa';

I ken, withoot their weary threeps,
   They're mair than needin's a'.

Wi' Huns upon wir thrashel-stane,
   An' half the world red wud,
Gweed sax feet ane o' brawn an' bane
   Is nae for plooman dud.

An' sae I paumered back an' fore,
   Practeesin' in my kilt,
An' Sownock fae the bothy door
   Kame-sowfed a martial lilt.

They leuch till howe an' hill-tap rang –
   I steppit saft mysel', –
For aye anaith my bonnet sang
   Bit things I couldna tell –

The bonnet wi' the aul' 'Bydand'
   That sat upon my broo –
An' something stirred, grey Mitherland,
   In my puir hert for you,

As aye an' aye the plaidie green
   Swung roon my naked knee,
An', mairchin' there anaith the meen,
   Lord sake! That wasna me,

The eat-meat sumph that kissed the quines,
   An' took a skyte at Eel;
I was the heir o' brave langsynes,
   A sodger, head to heel.

Ay me! 'At never shot a craw,
 Nor killed a cushey-doo –
But bleed's aye bleed, an' aul' granda
 Did things at Waterloo.

. . . . . .

I'm aff the morn . . . There's nane'll ken
 O' ae broon curly head,
That ees't to lie aside my ain
 In Mains's stoupet bed:

It's laich, laich noo, in Flanders sod,
 An' I'm mairchin' wi' the drum,
'Cause doon the lang La Bassée road
 There's dead lips cryin' 'Come!'

halflin: young lad; *crib*: bed; *chaumer*: sleeping place for farm servants; *dicht his nib*: rub his nose; *scoor the lift*: search the sky; *listed*: enlisted; *dang the nowt and neeps*: damn the cattle and turnips; *threeps*: nagging; *thrashel-stane*: door-step; *wud*: mad; *gweed*: good; *dud*: clothes; *paumered*: stamped; *bothy*: hut; *kame-sowfed*: 'to sowf through a comb covered with paper, a primitive but not uncommon musical effort'; *howe*: valley; *Bydand*: crest of the Gordon Highlanders; *eat-meat sumph*: idle oaf; *quines*: girls; *took a skyte at Eel*: got drunk at Yule; *craw*: crow; *cushey-doo*: wood pigeon; *ees't*: used; *stoupet bed*: poster bed; *laich*: low (as in low-lying ground); *La Bassée*: the Battle of La Bassée was fought October–November 1914; losses were heavy.

1933

Marion Angus (1866–1946)

Mary's Song

I wad ha'e gi'en him my lips tae kiss,
Had I been his, had I been his;
Barley breid and elder wine,

Had I been his as he is mine.

The wanderin' bee it seeks the rose;
Tae the lochan's bosom the burnie goes;
The grey bird cries at evenin's fa',
'My luve, my fair one, come awa'.'

My beloved sall ha'e this he'rt tae break,
Reid, reid wine and the barley cake,
A he'rt tae break, and a mou' tae kiss,
Tho' he be nae mine, as I am his.

lochan: little loch   *burnie*: stream

1924

At Candlemas

Lang syne at Candlemas
At first cam o' the mune,
I, a bit lassie,
Hame-gaun fae the toon,
Fell in wi' a stranger
Frail as ony reed,
Wi' a green mantle
Hapt aboot her heid.

Haste, I wad haste me,
The whinny road along,
Whinny, crookit road
Whaur the grey ghaists gang.
Wi' her een fu' o' spells,

Her broo runkled sair,
She micht weel be the witch
O' the Braid Hill o' Fare.

Here cams Candlemas,
A wan deein' mune,
Eh! bit I'm weary.
Cauldrife wis the toon!

Yon's a blythe bairnie
Soople as a reed,
Rinnin' wi' a hankey
Tied aboot her heid,
Hastin', hastin',
Limber-licht fit,
Doon the crookit road
Whaur the grey moths flit.

Quo' she, 'Ye'r sma'-bookit,
Yer broo's runkled sair,
Er' ye the auld witch
O' the Braid Hill o' Fare?'

lang syne: long ago	*runkled*: wrinkled
cam: coming	*cauldrife*: chilly
hame-gaun: on the way home	*limber-licht fit*: light-footed
hapt: wrapped	*sma'-bookit*: shrunken
whinny: overgrown with gorse	

1924

The Fiddler

A fine player was he . . .
'Twas the heather at my knee,
The Lang Hill o' Fare
An' a reid rose-tree,
A bonnie dryin' green,
Wind fae aff the braes,
Liftin' and shiftin'
The clear-bleached claes.

Syne he played again . . .
'Twas dreep, dreep o' rain,
A bairn at the breist
An' a warm hearth-stane,
Fire o' the peat,
Scones o' barley meal
An' the whirr, whirr, whirr,
O' a spinnin'-wheel.

Bit aye, wae's me!
The hindmaist tune he made . . .
'Twas juist a dune wife
Greetin' in her plaid,
Winds o' a' the years,
Naked wa's atween,
And heather creep, creepin'
Ower the bonnie dryin' green.

braes: hills
claes cloth..
dune: done
greetin': weeping

1924

Think Lang

Lassie, think lang, think lang,
Ere his step comes ower the hill.
Luve gi'es wi' a lauch an' a sang,
An' whiles for nocht bit ill.

Thir's weary time tae rue
In the lea-lang nicht yer lane
The ghaist o' a kiss on yer mou'
An' sough o' win' in the rain.

Lassie, think lang, think lang,
The trees is clappin' their han's,
The burnie clatterin' wi' sang
Rins ower the blossomy lan's.

Luve gi'es wi' a lauch an' a sang,
His fit fa's licht on the dew.
Oh, lass, are ye thinkin' lang,
Star een an' honey mou'?

lea-lang: long and wakeful   *sough*: sigh

1924

The Wild Lass

Hameward ye're traivellin'
In the saft hill rain,
The day lang by
That ye wearied o' the glen;
Nae ring upon yer han',

Nae kiss upon yer mou' –
    Quaiet noo.

There's fiddlers an' dancin'
An' steps gaun by the doors,
Bit nane o' them s'all fret ye
In the lang nicht 'oors.
O, Peace cum on the wind,
Peace fa' wi' the dew,
    Quaiet noo.

Cauld was the lift abune ye,
The road baith rough and steep,
Nae farrer s'all ye wander
Nor greet yersel tae sleep,
Ma ain wild lass,
Ma bonnie hurtit do'o –
    Quaiet, quaiet noo.

lift: sky   *greet*: cry
abune: above   *hurtit*: hurt
farrer: farther

1927

The Can'el

She's ta'en her can'el frae the boord
    Wi' hands baith slim an' sma',
A gowden rose it bloomed and floo'red
    An' flamed atween us twa.

She's pluckt ma hert frae oot ma breist
Wi' hands as white as faem,
She's pluckt ma hert oot o' ma breist
An' warmed it at the flame.

Syne, when the can'el flickered laigh
Wi' her twa hands she's ta'en
Ma hert, and at the dawnin' grey
Gi'en it me back agen.

can'el: candle   *laigh*: low
faem: foam

1927

The Blue Jacket

When there comes a flower to the stingless nettle,
   To the hazel bushes, bees,
I think I can see my little sister
   Rocking herself by the hazel trees.

Rocking her arms for very pleasure
   That every leaf so sweet can smell,
And that she has on her the warm blue jacket
   Of mine, she liked so well.

Oh to win near you, little sister!
   To hear your soft lips say –
'I'll never tak' up wi' lads or lovers,
   But a baby I maun hae.

'A baby in a cradle rocking,
   Like a nut, in a hazel shell,
And a new blue jacket, like this o' Annie's,
   It sets me aye sae well.'

maun: must   *sets*: suits

1931

Margaret Armour (18?–1943)

The Airmen

Have you heard those birds of the morning
   That rise with the lark's first flight?
Have you seen those birds of shadow
   That pounce with the owl at night?
They swoop where hell is flaming,
   They soar in heaven apart.
They fly with the swallow's swiftness,
   And fight with the eagle's heart.

Have you seen their glinting feathers?
   They are off to the Fields of Fate,
Where the flowers all wear scarlet,
   And the rivers red are in spate.
To prick new names of glory
   On valour's ancient chart,
They fly with the swallow's swiftness
   And fight with the eagle's heart.

Margaret Armour (18?–1943)

Have you heard their thrumming music?
　　It drones to the cannon's boom
And the wailing whizz of the shrapnel
　　Like an undersong of doom.
Wherever in loudest chorus
　　The deafening thunders start,
They fly with the swallow's swiftness,
　　And fight with the eagle's heart.

And though some of the first and fleetest
　　Have flown away to the west,
And sunk on the seas of twilight
　　With a wound in their shining breast,
The others know that, homing,
　　In the end all birds depart,
And they fly with the swallow's swiftness,
　　And fight with the eagle's heart.

Have you seen those birds of the morning
　　That rout the carrion crow?
Have you seen those birds of shadow
　　That pounce on the stoat below?
Till Hell recalls its legions,
　　And Death lays down his dart,
They'll fly with the swallow's swiftness,
　　And fight with the eagle's heart.

1954

My Voysey Wall-Paper

I have two gardens for my ease,
Where skies are warm and flowers please;
With skilful mastery each designed
Is fair and perfect of its kind.
In one the tulips every year
Flame April out and disappear;
And roses red that garland June
Are worn but for a summer's noon.
It is a garden, flower and leaf,
Where lovely things are very brief.

Upon a wall my other grows,
And changes not for heat or snows.
Its tulips do not flaunt and die,
But, dreaming, watch the spring go by.
In pensive grey, like musing nuns,
They hold no commerce with the suns.
There leaves in order are outspread
Which ruffling winds shall never shed.
The roses are the magic blue
That in the faery gardens grew,
Not fashioned for themselves alone,
But for the common beauty grown.

They shall not wax, they shall not wane,
They shall not flush to fleet again,
But quaintly, in their quiet place,
Shall charm me with unaltered grace,
And fresh for ever, flower and shoot,
Shall spring from their eternal root.

1954

Nannie Katharin Wells (1875–?)

Scotland My Lover

There are mountains that are more to me than men,
There are rivers that are more to me than love,
There's a rock where my soul takes cover.
Wild winds on a maddened world have driven,
Lifted me up to the bare hills above,
        Scotland, my Lover.

Here is a lover who will never change.
In storm and stillness, every lightning mood,
New ways of loving I'll discover,
A living sureness nothing can estrange.
Your grief and joy will be my daily food,
        Scotland, my Lover.

Ours is the love of lovers born to belong,
Our hearts sing the same music, beat as one.
Our glass of 'the water of life' brims over,
Our thrice-rich, flowering native song,
Prodigal and gay. And, when my song is done,
        I'll lie with you, my Lover.

Clear northern skies lit childhood's innocence.
The day's darg over, dew under my feet, bare
on the cool grass, stars blaze and hover.
O still make love with me, far from the decadence
of this dire century, of love's despair,
        Scotland, my Jewel, my Lover.

1958

From the Altar-Squint

There is no Youth in Hell.
They are all adult and tired
of doing well.
The ground is barren and idle-wild,
Nothing is left to be desired.
I miss the Child.

They have sickened of Love.
The needle stimulates the indifferent heart
for an hour, just time to prove
the futility of caring. They depart
into disgust – or move
into a more degraded art.

The clever-selfish intellect
leaves every mind defiled,
the radiance of the perfect
withered, or sardonically smiled
away; all gentleness and joy in sore neglect.
I miss the Child.

1958

Rachel Annand Taylor (1876–1960)

A Minor Tragedy

She was a woman, yet a child and poet,
And an ambiguous angel. Could he know it?
He shamed the woman, slew the smiling child,

And broke the angel's burnished wings and wild,
And crazed the poet. Well! She did not show it,
Or showed it most improperly in speech
That could not flatter, wheedle, or beseech.
Even her tears were like white blood with pride
And reticence. So he was justified.

1909

To a 'Georgian'

If you go seek for 'copy' in the street
It is base inessentials that you meet.
You take a perverse pleasure in the unsought
And evil noise, the squalors that are fought
With bitter gaiety by the scornful poor,
The people that so mockingly endure.
But I will signify what might befall
If you indeed were Beauty's seneschal.
You could find, up abominable stairs
Where dangerous holes admit the fœtid airs,
A woman in her narrow perfect room
Like a Madonna dreaming of her doom,
Her head against the casement, calm, content:
Or in some other hopeless tenement
A handsome youth with sombre haughty eyes
Burning through all God's wickedness and lies,
Since his bright desperate womenfolk are sewing
Upon the floor worthless rude sacks, not knowing
When sacred Food might succour (Seraphim
Of tragic holy love, no work for him!)
Or, in the corner of a two-roomed place,

A little child, locked fast in Shakspere's grace
Of music and imagination – well! –
Waking to the World-politic from that spell.
(If that same child be of Apollo's clan,
She'll never be a sordid 'Georgian'.)
Beauty is beauty, whether her white feet
Go flickering down the dark dramatic street,
Or on the violet, silver-hung hill-side
She walk alone, the wild deer for her guide,
Or in pierced palaces of long ago
She finger her ball of amber. For I know
Better than any what wild wonders be
Within the Keeps of Lady Poverty.

1909

The Kirkin' Goon

'What for sud ye gang in the loanin' green
   When ilka body's hame?
I mind ye were a bonnie thing,
   But ye're nae mair the same.'

'Oh! I never hae worn my kirkin' goon
   Though I kent my bridal gear.
Sae thole my riddle as well ye may
   Sin' ye maun spy an' speir.

'And I rarely loe the loanin' green
   Whan nane can fach wi' hovers,
And I rarely loe the burn that rowes
   Ayont wi' its warlock clavers.

'For oh! though I kent my bridal gear
I had nae kirkin' goon.
Sae ye're daft if ye keek in my fremit een,
There's a broken hert tae droon.'

what for: why; *loanin'*: meadow;
kirkin' goon: gown worn at first
church ceremony after marriage;
thole: put up with; *speir*: ask; *rarely*:
especially; *loe*: love; *fash*: annoy;
havers: nonsense; *warlock clavers*:
witchlike chatter; *gear*: things; *keek*:
look; *fremit*: strange; *een*: eyes

1923

Catherine Carswell (1879–1946)

V

i

In word, in act, this man was slow and faltering,
In gainful deeds feeble while he had breath.
But being swift in love, sure, never altering,
He triumphs and grows eloquent in death.

ii

This man was reckoned wise:
Perhaps he was
Because
To love and suffering he closed his eyes.

iii

He has his faults. Not one of these I'd spare.
They make of him, as Shakespeare says somewhere,
A man for whom one must sincerely care.
It is his virtues that are hard to bear.

iv

To be alive is vulgar, you have said.
And you, my love, are usually right.
But have you thought, my love, that it is quite
As vulgar, if not more so, to be dead.

1950

VI

On the stale platform I saw a porter suddenly dancing.
A station porter clapping his hands and springing.
Soiled, heavy body on small feet retiring advancing
To the music of a weary harmonica and pale soldiers
   singing.

1950

Ciorstai NicLeòid/Christina MacLeod (1880–1954)

Litir Chun A' Bhàird

'Ille chòir, mar thubhairt thu
Gu cuimir ann ad dhàn
Thug thu don òighe biothbhuantachd
Le caomhalachd do ghràidh;
Ach ise, thug i 'n tuilleadh dhuits'
Mar ultach luchdt' le gràs;
Chan e a-mhàin dhuit biothbhuantachd
Ach doimhneachd tuigs' air cràdh.

Nam biodh do ghràdhs' air abachadh
Air achadh pailt a gràidhs'
Dh' fhaodadh diasan tachairt riut
Gun thoradh suas gu 'm bàrr,
Do bhuain gun cuirte 'n adagan
Mar bhuain an fhir nach b' fheàrr
'S na Gàidheil thruagh bhiodh falamh di;
Cha sin a dheònaich Dàn.

1951

A Letter to the Poet

Dear lad, as you expressed it
with eloquence in your poem,
you gave the girl immortality
through the tenderness of your love;
but she gave so much more to you,
a load weighty with grace;
for you not mere immortality
but a truer understanding of suffering.

Had your love grown ripe
on the rich field of her love,
you might have found the ears of corn
were hollow to their tip,
your harvest gathered up in stooks
no better than a lesser man's,
and the sorry Gaels deprived of it;
that is not what Fate commanded.

The reference is to Sorley MacLean's *Dàin do Eimhir* (1943), and in particular to Poem XIX 'Thug mise dhut biothbhuantachd' ('I gave you immortality').

Dia

Chan eil eagal orm roimh Dhia –
Dia a' Bhiobaill 's Leabhar Cheist;
Dia a' cheartais; Dia a' ghràidh;
Dia dan eòl gach snàth sa bheirt.
'S aithne Dha a h-uile truaighe
Bha fuaighte riut od bhreith;
'S aithne Dha a h-uile truaill
Air 'n tug thu buaidh fad rè do bheath';
'S aithne dha a h-uile strì
Agus dìcheall rinneadh leat,
'S ged a thuit thu minic sìos,
Mar a leum thu suas gun mheat'.
Lìogaire a shlìobas làr
Nach aidich càil ma bhios e 'n cùil,
Saoilidh e gun car e Dia
Mar a bhriagas e gach sùil.
Abair thusa ri do Dhia –
'Faic mi Dhè mar dhealbh thu mi.
Ged nach d' rinn mi mar bu mhiann
Bha mi fiachainn anns gach nì.'

       *   *   *

Dia a' cheartais, Dia a' ghràidh,
'S aithne Dha mo chàs gach àm;
Chan eil eagal orm roimh Dhia.
M' eagalsa – 'Bheil Dia ann?'

1951

God

I have no fear of God –
the God of Bible and Catechism;
the God of justice; the God of love;
the God who sees each thread in the loom.
He knows every woe
sewn onto you since birth;
He knows every corruption
you have vanquished through your life;
He knows your every struggle,
every effort you have made,
and however many times you fell
how you leapt up undeterred.
The sneak who crawls along
and when cornered won't confess,
imagines he can outwit God
like he lies to every face.
Turn to your God and say–
'Lord see me as you made me:
I may not have done as you desired
but you know I tried in all things.'

      *   *   *

The God of justice, the God of love,
He knows my plight at every twist;
I am not afraid of God.
My only fear – 'Does God exist?'

As-creideamh

Creideamh ghabhas tlachd an gruam
Luchd-ciùil ga gluas'd gu osannaich,
Falbh air fàth 's na h-uile smuain

Mus caill e duais na biothbhuantachd;
Ach eagal bàis na eallach cruaidh,
Taobh thall na h-uaigh dha doicheallach.
Mas sin do chreideamh b' fhèarr gach uair
As-creideamh sluaigh tha onarach.

1951

Non-belief

A creed that pleasures in gloominess
whose singers turn music to sighs,
running to monitor every thought
lest it lose them eternity's prize;
the fear of death a grievous weight,
the beyond-the-grave a thing of dread.
If that's your creed, better indeed
the non-belief of honest men.

Mary Elizabeth Boyle (1881–1974)

V

Sometimes I hear your footstep on the stair,
A curious way you scuffled slippered feet,
And am inclined to run halfway and meet
You on my threshold, Waiting in my chair,
Grow cold, whilst thinking were you really there,
There were no pause before you came to greet.
A laugh, an extra scuffle, movement fleet
To silence protest, light pull of my hair

To tilt my face, so eyes could laugh at eyes;
The mirror would reflect two faces gay.
Instead it shows a woman staring, blank,
Whose ears are traitors, telling wished for lies,
Whose eyes are blinded, looking far away
Unto last August, when her youth's sun sank.

1916

Margaret Sackville (1881–1963)

Flanders – 1915

The men go out to Flanders
    As to a promised land;
The men come back from Flanders
    With eyes that understand.

They've drunk their fill of blood and wrath,
    Of sleeplessness and pain,
Yet silently to Flanders
    They hasten back again.

In the Low-lands of Flanders
    A patient watch they keep;
The living and the dead watch on: –
    Whilst we are sound asleep.

1919

Foam and Earth

'Oh! when will ye come home?'
'Never, never, never, never, never,
We have become brown earth – earth and blown foam.'

  'But we who sit at home
Through all the days, the long blind days, without ye
All day, each day, knowing ye cannot come,
That ye are now nothing but earth and foam,
How shall we live, and what shall we become?'

  'White, drifting foam, brown earth,
Is all your sons (brave dust made dear for ever!)
Earth and foam, ye gave us birth,
Foam and earth which come not home –
Nor would ye know us should we come.'
'Come ye not home?' – 'Your sons shall come home never.'

1919

Fame

The laurel crown
   Above my head
Has fallen down,
   Its leaves are dead:

And no one ever
   Comes this way,
Even to sweep
   The leaves away.

1923

The Stranger

A little Joy,
So light of wing,
Perched on my window-sill
To-day.

I knew a lovelier
Joy last Spring.
And drove that stranger
Joy away.

1928

Edith Anne Robertson (1883–1973)

The Scots Tongue

Gin I'm a livan tongue loe me;
Saebins we'll hae mair bairns:
Gin I'm a deid tongue nae call for keenin,
Ye'll find me wi the gods
Ayont the reaveries o Time:
Yon are the gowden tongues!

loe: love　　　　　　　　　*reaveries*: thefts
saebins: so that　　　　　*gowden*: golden
keenin: mourning

1955

The Granderie of God

Erd is dirlan with the granderie of God.
   It will bleeze to a kything like shell-gold's shakken foil:
   It gedders til a granderie, weel-preasit like ooze of oil.
What way than div men nae mair mind his rod?
Generations hae trod, hae trod, hae trod;
   And aathing's smeared with trade, blad, blain with toil,
   And cleed in human smudge and reek: plene soil
Lies bare, feet fond to kiss the dews, go shod.

Nay, for aa yon, nature bydes aye in fleur;
   Bydes aye the fondest freshness deep doon things;
And gin day's last lichts hint the black West cour,
   Be-east, O dawkenin, by yon brown break springs –
For that the Hailie Ghaist ower Erd's bent floor
   Broods laich, plume sunlit, – And O luik ye! The
      gowden wings!

                      1968

God's Grandeur
by Gerard Manley Hopkins

The world is charged with the grandeur of God.
   It will flame out, like shining from shook foil;
   It gathers to a greatness, like the ooze of oil
Crushed. Why do men then now not reck his rod?
Generations have trod, have trod, have trod;
   And all is seared with trade; bleared, smeared with toil;
   And wears man's smudge and shares man's smell: the
      soil
Is bare now, nor can foot feel, being shod.

And for all this, nature is never spent;
    There lives the dearest freshness deep down things;
And though the last lights off the black West went
    Oh, morning, at the brown brink eastward, springs –
Because the Holy Ghost over the bent
    World broods with warm breast and with ah! bright
        wings.

1918

Inversnaid

Thon shade-shed burnie, horse-back broon,
Wheelmagig rock-ower hurlan doon,
Coopt and coomed in the flisk o his faem
Fluchts, syne laich til the loch wins hame.

A skimmeran wind-ba of fáwn-fróth
Twists and twindles ower the broth
Of a pule sae pik-dark, féll fróunan
It rouns and rouns Wanhope til drownan.

Brockit with dew, droukit with dew
Are the howes of the braes the burn threeds thru;
Heather-cowes and bracken fern,
And the bead-bonny ash that sets ower the burn.

Whaur would this warld be, scant
Of weet and of wild-like days. Tak tent
Case-be we scaithe yon maikless sweet
Green wilderness, aneath our feet.

1968

Inversnaid
by Gerard Manley Hopkins

This darksome burn, horseback brown,
His rollrock highroad roaring down,
In coop and in comb the fleece of his foam
Flutes and low to the lake falls home.

A windpuff-bonnet of fáwn-fróth
Turns and twindles over the broth
Of a pool so pitchblack, féll-frówning,
It rounds and rounds Despair to drowning.

Degged with dew, dappled with dew
Are the groins of the braes that the brook treads through,
Wiry heathpacks, flitches of fern,
And the beadbonny ash that sits over the burn.

What would the world be, once bereft
Of wet and of wildness? Let them be left,
O let them be left, wildness and wet;
Long live the weeds and the wilderness yet.

Til My Ain Hert

My ain hert lat me nae conter aye, lat
Me efterhend til my glum sel byde kind,
Mair love-fraught: nor fore-and-back this torkit mind
Whackan twa-fauld, sae whackan ball and bat.

I claucht at conforts I can nae mair get at
By graipan roun onconfort, nor e'en nicht-blind
Can win, thro their mirk, day; nor drouth can find
Drouth's aa in aa, in aa a wardle's wat.

Saule, sel, here's my avisement, quait, quait!
Adone, puir jaded Jack-ma-sel, lowse awhile!
Gie confort ruit-room, everie joy maun spate

In God's guid time, in God's guid kennin. Heaven's smile
's nae wry smile, – cud be shy smile – sae skies gangrel gait
Foilzies mirk bens – lichtens a loesome mile.

1968

My Own Heart
by Gerard Manley Hopkins

My own heart let me more have pity on; let
Me live to my sad self hereafter kind,
Charitable; not live this tormented mind
With this tormented mind tormenting yet.

I cast for comfort I can no more get
By groping round my comfortless, than blind
Eyes in their dark can day or thirst can find
Thirst's all-in-all in all a world of wet.

Soul, self; come, poor Jackself, I do advise
You, jaded, let be; call off thoughts awhile
Elsewhere; leave comfort root-room; let joy size

At God knows when to God knows what; whose smile
's not wrung, see you; unforeseen times rather – as skies
Betweenpie mountains – lights a lovely mile.

Helen B. Cruickshank (1886–1975)

Wild Geese

The earth frostbound, an azure sky,
A far-off, unfamiliar cry;
Look! Flashing in the sunlight high
A wondrous sight!
With stretching necks and beating wings
The wedge of tameless, urgent things
Drives thro' the air, and ceaseless sings
In rapid flight.

As swift, as wild, is loveliness,
Whose winged visions wound and bless
The mind that struggles to express
The passing bright.
So, thrilled and shaken by their cry
I saw, far up the echoing sky,
The gaggle of wild geese go by
And pass from sight.

1934

In Glenskenno Woods

Under an arch o' bramble
    Saftly she goes,
Dark broon een like velvet,
    Cheeks like the rose.

Ae lang branch o' the bramble
   Dips ere she pass,
Tethers wi' thorns the hair
   O' the little lass.

Ripe black fruit, an' blossom
   White on the spray,
Leaves o' russet an' crimson,
   What wad ye say?

What wad ye say to the bairn
   That ye catch her snood,
Haudin' her there i' the hush
   O' Glenskenno Wood?

What wad ye say? The autumn
   O' life draws near.
Still she waits, an' listens,
   But canna hear.

een: eyes   *snood*: hair-ribbon

1934

Sea Buckthorn

Saut an' cruel winds tae shear it,
Nichts o' haar an' rain
Ye micht think the sallow buckthorn
Ne'er a hairst could hain;
But amang the sea-bleached branches
Ashen-grey as pain,
Thornset orange berries cluster
Flamin', beauty-fain.

Daith an' dule will stab ye surely,
    Be ye man or wife,
Mony trauchles an' mischances
    In ilk weird are rife;
Bide the storm ye canna hinder,
    Mindin' through the strife,
Hoo the luntin' lowe o' beauty
    Lichts the grey o' life.

saut: salt
haar: sea mist
hairst: harvest
hain: protect
dule: sorrow

trauchles: burdens
weird: destiny
luntin': blazing
lowe gleam

1934

The Price o' Johnny

'Oh, what's the price o' Love?' I said,
    A-counting out my money.
Old Life the Salesman shook his head.
    '"Twill cost a deal, my honey!
Have none o' it,' he said to me,
'You're better far to keep your fee,
    And think no more o' Johnny.'

'Nay, but I must have Love!' I cried,
    'While yet my cheeks are bonny.'
Old Life the Salesman sadly sighed,
    A-picking up my money.
My peace, my sleep, he took from me,
Down to the very last bawbee,
    To pay for love o' Johnny.

My cheeks that were sae rosy-red
  Are paler noo than ony.
The joy I used to ha'e is fled,
  And cares are mony, mony.
'Twas true, what Life the Salesman spoke,
I bocht a dear pig-in-a-poke
  When I bocht love o' Johnny!

bawbee: halfpenny

1934

Hope Mirrlees (1887–1978)

A Skull

1

I wish my library had got a skull!
(All libraries should have *grave* furniture) –
Whose, whether that of poet, king, or trull
Would not affect its erudite allure,
Like Latin in its logical bone-structure,
And which time's *accidence* cannot annul.

2

St Jerome, in the wood-cut reassures
His study's fitness by a skull, and one
Lies in the closet where a dean endures
A lover's and a poet's doom – poor Donne!
Does Love's gold hair comfort his skeleton? . . .
Good God! Suppose the skull I owned was *yours*!

3

Beside the globe in its pale rosewood frame
Upon the Georgian table it would lie,
Saying, 'Remember that you too must die' –
Just that. And in the past did I not often blame
The coldness of the sculptured ivory,
The living eyes that never said my name!

4

But gazing on a skull resolves the stress
Of tuneless years in chords of baroque art,
Articulated richly to express
The grammar of assent learned by Mozart –
And suddenly my not unfaithful heart
Is sick with an unearthly tenderness.

1976

Margaret Winefride Simpson (1888–1971)

Rhyme for Two

O' it's a'e wish for Winter
Whase he'rt is hard an' cauld,
But anither wish for Simmer
When a' the flooers unfauld!

A'e thocht for the snawdrift
That lingers on the hill,
But anither for the sunlicht
When the haughs lie warm an' still!

It's a'e wish for the feck o' fowk
The hale wide warld through,
A'e thocht aye for a' the lave,
But anither thocht for you!

For the true he'rt has a treasure
But twa can haud or hain,
An' the leal he'rt has a secret
That's shared by nane but ane:

Sae it's a'e wish for the feck o' fowk
The hale wide warld through,
A'e thocht aye for a' the lave,
But anither thocht for you!

haughs: meadows   *hain*: protect
feck o' fowk: most folk   *leal*: loyal
lave: rest

1937

Bessie J.B. MacArthur (1889–1983)

Eight Gaed Oot

Eight gaed oot ayont the faem,
Eight gaed oot and fower cam' hame.
Eight gaed oot in royal flicht,
Jewell'd wings athort the nicht:
Fower cam' hame at brak o' daw,
But fower cam' never hame at a'.

*For the other members of a Catalina
aircraft shot down while protecting
the North African convoy, and for
Alastair.*

ayont: beyond   *athort*: across
faem: foam   *daw*: dawn

1943

For a Modern Ophelia

Lovely and fair she lies,
Tranquil and mild,
Hands on her bosom crossed
Like a tired child.

Mourn for her tenderly,
Yet be at rest,
Wearing her memory
A flower in your breast,

Sure that her spirit white,
Free from all pain,
Flowerlike, shall blossom
In beauty again.

1962

Wings

Whinchak an' shilfie
Fleein' roun aboot,
Steerie blue-bonnet
Joukin' in an' oot,

Wee broon lairock
Soarin' as it sings,
God was shairly lauchin'
When he gied them wings.

whinchack: whinchat
shilfie: chaffinch
steerie: bustling

blue-bonnet: blue tit
joukin': dodging
lairock: lark

1962

Isobel Wylie Hutchison (1889–1982)

In Front of March

Here is a list of inconsidered things
Whose names recall a thousand Scottish springs.
The buxom elm-flower in her satin kilts,
The red-tailed willow-catkin that uptilts
Her fingers for the other catkin's pollen;
The golden saxifrage all wet and fallen
With one foot in the burn. The dusty yew
That flecks with powdered gold the drop of dew
Caught like a diamond on the gravestone mosses,
Where upright in the vivid spongy bosses
The spore-case like a bright torpedo's laid
On her thin prop. In a wet woodland glade
I know too where the rare white butterbur,
The spotted lungwort, ay – and tulip, stir
At breath of March; but these are very shy
Of Scotland, and I will not tell – not I –
That place. Yet know that omphalodes too
Grows there, as blue as God has made His blue,

And Star of Bethlehem all milky white
Like Venus in the soft green sunset light.

1927

In the Lane

I met two lovers in the lane
  Sheepish and shy,
I met two lovers in the lane
  And passed them by.

Oh! It's a lovely thing to be
  A lover or his lass,
And it is lovely to be free
  And look and pass.

1927

Maimie A. Richardson (*fl.* 1926–37)

And Yet

I have no bitter places in my life,
All but the little things have passed me by.
My heart can neither hate nor love o'er much,
My path is smooth, well ordered and content,
Like a neat garden, where the flowers stand
Straight in a row, most pleasing to the eye.
No passion flowers grow there, nor any weed,

Only sweet blooms, but not too colourful.
I pity those I see who go distraught,
Beating their wings against the bars of life . . .
. . . But sometimes when at dusk I go alone,
And see two lovers wander hand in hand,
Mute and content, with dreaming look, their eyes
Wrapt, almost holy, as an angel's wings
Had brushed them passing by. Or when I see
A mother smile upon her sleeping babe,
My eyes grow hot and wet – I know not why.

1926

Forgotten

You are forgotten, little wife, who loved me;
I could not keep my faith when you were dead:
So many lids drooped shy beneath my glances –
– So many lips were red.

1929

Willa Muir (1890–1970)

The Farmer's Wee Lassie
Lo Filho del Poyson

The farmer's wee lassie has gotten a man;
She's gotten a man, says she.
Oh ay, she's gotten a man,
As kind as a man can be.

The lassie's owre young to ken how it's done,
says he.

He's ta'en her hand, sae kind and humble;
Bonny bride, says he,
We'll gang together to the kirk,
so keep you close by me.
Mind your wee feet and dinna tumble,
says he.

He's ta'en her hand, sae kind and humble;
Bonny bride, says he,
We'll dance together on the green,
so keep you close by me.
Mind your wee steps and dinna stumble,
says he.

He's ta'en her hand before the folk;
Bonny bride, says he,
We'll sit together at the board,
so keep you close by me.
Mind your wee mou' and dinna choke,
says he.

He's ta'en her hand sae kind and humble;
Bonny bride, says he,
We'll sleep together in the bed,
so keep you close by me.
Mind your wee – Oh mind yoursel' & dinna fumble,
says she.

mou mouth

1931

Wendy Wood (1892–1981)

Original Sin

Whit can it ken
O' sin – new born
that disna ken at a'?
It shrinks frae edgelessness an' cauld
And seeks close warmth an' food;
It disnae greet fer wickedness
Nor toss its taes fer gude,
Wi' burdened minds
We cannae keek
Until a bud's unfurled,
Whit richt hae we tae maggot it
Wi' crime o' all the warld?
Whit can it ken
O' sin – new born
That disnae ken at a'?

ken: know   *keek*: look
taes: toes

1967

Nan Shepherd (1893–1981)

Loch Avon

Loch A'an, Loch A'an, hoo deep ye lie!
Tell nane yer depth and nane shall I.
Bricht though yer deepmaist pit may be,

Ye'll haunt me till the day I dee.
Bricht, an' bricht, an' bricht as air,
Ye'll haunt me noo for evermair.

1934

The Hill

So it may be a hill was there,
    Blue, tremulous, afar.
I looked and thought the gleam was air,
    And thought the morning star

Might tremble thus and thus resolve
    Its fire in common light,
Content, while world and sun revolve,
    To vanish from the sight.

So hard it was that morn to tell
    If earth or heaven I saw,
I knew not how on earth to dwell
    Nor how from heaven withdraw.

For vanishing within my thought,
    And stealing back to view,
Earth mingled so with heaven, they wrought
    One universe from two.

1934

Half Love

No, love me not: not on my hungry breast,
   Nor mouth, nor mouth by your mouth made aware,
   Not on my pulses' tumult, not my hair,
Not on my body be your love confessed.
But still by eager thought be I caressed,
   Trouble me still with longing, love from far,
   Still be to me the burning of a star
In heaven perceived but yet on earth possessed.

So coward I cried, broken and spent with loving,
   Broken and spent with half-fulfilled desire.
I am too weak and mortal for your having
   Who fear to flare not burnish in your fire.
O star, O star from utmost heaven removing,
   How can I hold you in my arms entire?

1934

Naomi Mitchison (1897–1999)

The House of the Hare

At the time I was four years old
I went to glean with the women,
Working the way they told;
My eyes were blue like blue-bells,
Lighter than oats my hair;
I came from the house of the Haldanes
Of work and thinking and prayer
To the God who is crowned with thorn,
The friend of the Boar and the Bear,
But oh when I went from there,

In the corn, in the corn, in the corn,
I was married young to a hare!

We went to kirk on the Sunday
And the Haldanes did not see
That a Haldane had been born
To run from the Boar and the Bear,
And the thing had happened to me
The day that I went with the gleaners,
The day that I built the corn-house,
That is not built with prayer.
For oh I was clean set free,
In the corn, in the corn, in the corn,
I had lived three days with the hare!

1978

Living in a Village

Living in a village is walking
Among snare wire, being
The bulge-eyed rabbit, ware of
The light heart, dancing gossip-stoats, the blood-lipped,
Biding their time.
Living in the Big House is being
The big stag, the twelve-pointer,
Watched on, edible, spied and lied to,
From burrows, runways, witch-twisted bushes, and most
From the hoodies' rock where the observant, the cautious,
    the hungry hoodies
Feed upon small game still, hoping for bigger,
And bide their time.

1978

Buachaille Etive Mor and Buachaille Etive Beag

Those two had shepherds, hunched above their sheep,
Dreaming of blood and pain and the long sleep
In their too certain circumstance of when:
Two black shepherds and myself and the Glen.

If you speak ill of the shepherds, speak it low;
Wait for the winter, they say, wait for the snow,
Wait for the night of the Campbells, the day of the fox,
The frayed rope and the boot that slips on the rocks.

1978

XIII. Work and Love

The months and the years pass
Quickly, as good years can
For a blithe and sober man
With a daughter like a small rose
And a lamp lit in his heart.
And the anger of Scotland grows,
The need and anger of Scotland.
And I must take my part.

One man and another
Passing the sleeper, cries
Alba, Alba, Alba!
Will you stop your dreaming at last,
Wake out of a smother
Of old dreams and old lies?
As when Tom Johnston passed
Through the sleep of Carradale

And we turned uneasily.
Then back to sleep for some
But the County Council for me
With work and fighting to come.

The old scar skins over
But the shape of the cut stays,
As stays the strength of the promise,
As stand the hills of Scotland
To the end of the years and days.
And you, Donnachadh Bàn,
For her green and comely veil,
Have planned and planted a forest.
And myself, the laird and writer,
Neither did I fail
Over building of roads and houses
And a harbour for Carradale.
And each looks to the other
For the heart-word of praise.
It is work and love for the mending
Of an often broken promise:
After ill and false intending
Of all the centuries past,
Faith between Highlands and Lowlands.

At last and at long last
There will be getting and spending
For the sake of Alba, our mother,
There will be hope and life,
The pibroch over the hill
And the fiery cross of good will,
And I see my poem's ending
And the cleansing of the knife.

1978

Kate Y.A. Bone (1897–1986)

Skeletons of Honesty

Skeletons of honesty linger in my garden,
Brittle as the thought of death, frail as fickle flowers.
Bullfinches that eat my buds do not ask for pardon,
Should I then forgo regrets, enjoying summer hours?

Skeletons of honesty linger in December
Soon the lusty winds of Spring will blow them all away.
My regrets are rooted firm, and I must still remember
Thoughts that were not honest, words I did not say.

Skeletons of honesty now give way to seedlings,
Leaves appear and rosy flowers, rejoicing those who come.
I can leave my dead regrets while merry thrush sings,
Shall I then forget them? Shall my mouth be dumb?

Skeletons of honesty linger in my garden,
Dead but graceful in their death, purely dressed in white.
There may still be mercy for those who ask for pardon.
Skeletons of honesty shining in the light.

1971

Margot Robert Adamson (1898–?)

At the Turn of the Year
On the Hogg Monument by St Mary's Loch

The night is swift on Ettrick now,
  The snow is white upon the hill,
The broken brackens weakly bow –
  Late dawn and early dusk are chill –

And shadowed by enduring pines
  The Ettrick Shepherd's votive stone
Watches the meeting of the lochs,
  And muses with his dog alone.

For him the troublous days are o'er,
  The thresh of thought and change and mind;
And by St Mary's quiet shore
  He communes with the endless wind.

Across the grey-green border hills
  He sees the light and shadow run,
The hurry of the misty rains,
  The brown bent's glitter in the sun.

Too human quarrel and mistake
  No longer harry him or grieve:
He only sees the rainbows wake
  Among the hills about Altrieve.

The garland of his mountain song
  Enwreathes him with immortal dew,
The larks above his head prolong
  The music that his spirit knew,

And where his troubled spirit trod
　His carven memory may see
Hill flowers that blossom in the sod
　And breathe of immortality.

1928

The Passing of the Wild Geese

Heather and birch and pine,
Three idle words, three idle things;
And all the autumn's gold
And all the rain-blown springs!

Last night when skies were still,
Slept, sunk in deepmost night,
Beneath the sinking moon
The wild geese passed in flight.

Their whirring, beating wings
Flew southward through the dark,
Deep stillness after them:
Only the soul might mark

The changing of the year,
The coming breath of cold.
Along the Grampian slopes
The birches will be gold.

Snow upon Eskdalemuir
And, where wild pigeons brood,
The aspens all in flame
Fringing the Ord Bain wood

Will burn in scarlet leaves.
The clearing glows at night,
Cairngorm is crowned with snow.
The whirring wild geese' flight

Went by in solitude
'Neath a low orange moon.
The summer hush has gone,
The wind will change its tune.

Heather and birch and pine,
Three wild and lovely things,
And all the taste of them
Swift on those passing wings!

1928

Alice V. Stuart (1899–1983)

Rencontre

She walked to the music of her own mind's making,
The tall, spare spinster in the cheap, drab coat,
And her pale lips, faintly moving, their divine thirst were
    slaking
At the gods' own Hippocrene, where bright bubbles float.

As I passed her in the half-light, on a waft of wind I
    caught the
Words once shaped by mortals beyond all mortal ken.
With Shelley and with Shakespeare she walked, with
    godlike Milton,
This poorest, palest, shabbiest of the daughters of men.

I looked at the girls, with their silken curls tossing,
Their redder lips than nature, their bright eyes of desire.
Oh, brief is your springtime (I thought) my blossomy
    darlings,
But hers the authentic, the undying fire.

And I kissed the nearest blossom (was she Daphne? was
    she Chloë?)
And as betwixt my fingers her soft curls stirred
My thoughts were far from her, my thoughts were on the
    highway
Where walked the lone, gaunt spinster with the immortal
    word.

1944

The Dark Tarn

Slipping my self
As a bather strips his clothes,
Nightly I plunge
Into the dark tarn, the lone,
Ebon, glassy, deep,
Sunk beneath cliffs of sleep.

I stumble to it drowsily
Up mazy slopes of dream,
Then plunge, plunge and am
Lost, immersed, drowned,
Beyond reach of sight or sound,
Of consciousness my spark
Dowsed, douted, quenched in the dark.

Slowly emergent
To the cheerful light,
The sunstream from on high,
This not-I, once more I,
Day's traffickings, day's loves
Resumes with sense and sight.

But some day, ah, some day
As yet outwith my ken,
I shall sink to unplumbed deeps
Beyond dredging net of men,
From that underwater world of timeless sleep
Never to rise,
Never to rise to upper day again.

1953

Sleeping Penelope

*(The marble monument to Penelope Boothby, 1785–1791,
Ashbourne Church, Derbyshire)*

She lies like a plucked snowdrop, white as she
Whom the glass coffin sheltered from the breath,
The perishing airs of our mortality,
    Serene in a sleep like death.

Her soft cheek dints the pillow: lightly curled
Are the nestling hands by her chin, while round her bare
Small feet the hem of her muslin gown is swirled;
    Her lips seem to take the air,

She sleeps as on a mattress, in the chill
Half light of the transept, and around her tomb

Run the deep-cut words, in several tongues that tell
    Grief for untimely doom.

'Sorrows for Penelope' her father wrote,
Seeking through verse to immortalise his child,
And the shipwreck of his hopes in this frail boat:
    His love, loss, anguish wild

Still speak to the world in this fair snowdrop maid
At rest on her pillow: touch her gently; she
May wake from the tranced sleep in which she is laid, –
    Young sweet Penelope!

1963

Christine Grant Millar Orr
(1899–1963)

The Loud-Speaker

1

There is no space: turn the loud-speaker on!
The escaping trains that shriek by Arthur's Seat,
The tinker's bagpipe down the windy street,
The deep-throated sirens from the Forth are gone.
London's without the window; Mayfair, Kew,
Stars at the Spaniards, crowds at Charing Cross,
Lights that in bacchanal beauty wheel and toss,
Underground, River, petrol-stench, and you.
We are not pent, as children by a nurse
For petty faults each in a separate room;

We are blindfold merely, touching hands through gloom
In this same little cell of the universe.
There is no space: for sonorous, lo, Big Ben
Annihilates distance on the stroke of ten!

2

There is no time: the round mechanical
Of the dial registers not changed hours in the heart.
The years I have lived are of myself a part,
Past minutes present still, stored, salvaged all.
Each record I may recapitulate
On my brain's gramophone, every nursery tune,
Each madrigal of our enchanted noon,
Often rehearsed nor ever out of date.
Self changes not; still as at seven I'm shy,
As twenty passionate, as eleven bold,
At odds with the world. Grows any spirit old?
Stares not a questioning child from every eye?
There is no time: his pendulum's still when we
Embracing trespass on eternity.

3

They have so frightened us with empty breath,
With names that have no substance, Space and Time,
Phantasms and words – how if we reach and climb
To find the emptiest word of all is Death?
Time, Space do us confine in loneliness
Not half so much as personality –
Webbed motive, battling mood – hides you from me;
How if this Death divide us even less?
God never fathered myth. Space, Time's a lie –
How if the mightiest enemy of love

Be found a lie all other lies above?
How if our souls from prison loosed shall cry,
When Space, the paper-barrier, perisheth,
And Time's poor clockwork's dumb: *There is no Death!*

1928

Flora Garry (1900–2000)

The Professor's Wife

I wis a student at King's.
Ma folk hid a craft in Glenardle.
'Learnin's the thing,' they wid say,
'To help ye up in the wardle.'

They vrocht fae daylicht to dark.
Fine div I min' on ma midder,
Up ower the queets amo' dubs,
Furth in the weetiest widder,

Swypin the greep in the byre,
Forkin the crap on the lan',
Treetlin wi water an aess an peats,
Aye a pail in her han'.

I wis a student at King's.
O the craft I nivver spoke.
Peer an prood wis I
An affrontit o ma folk.

An fyles on a still Mey nicht
I wid tak a daaner roun'
By Spital an College Bounds
To the lythe o the Aul' Toon.

An I wid stan an glower
In at the windows wide
O the muckle hooses there
Faar the professors bide,

At caun'le-licht an flooers
Shinin silver an lace,
An, braw in a low-neckit goon,
The professor's wife at her place.

'Fine,' says I to masel,
'Fine to be up in the wardle,'
An thocht wi a groo, on the brookie pots
In the kitchen at Glenardle.

'Learnin's the thing,' says I,
'To help ye up in the wardle.'
I wed a professor come time
An gid hyne awa fae Glenardle.

I bide in a muckle dark hoose
In a toon that's muckle an dark,
An it taks me maist o the day
To get fordl't wi ma wark.

Traachlin wi sitt an styoo.
Queuein for maet for oors,
A body his little time or hert
For caun'le-licht an flooers.

Ma hans are scorie-hornt,
An fyles I fin masel
Skushlin ma feet, as ma midder did
Oot teemin the orra pail.

The aul' folk's lyin quaet
In the kirkyard at Glenardle.
It's as weel; they'd be gey sair-made
At the state noo-a-days o the wardle.

'Learnin's the thing,' they wid say,
'To gie ye a hyste up in life.'
I wis eence a student at King's.
Noo I'm jist a professor's wife.

craft: croft; *wardle*: world; *vrocht*: worked; *midder*: mother; *queets*: ankles; *dubs*: muddy water; *widder*: weather; *swypin*: sweeping; *greep*: gutter; *crap*: hay; *treetlin*: plodding on; *aess*: ashes; *peer*: poor; *fyles*: sometimes; *daaner*: wander; *lythe*: peacefulness; *glower*: stare; *muckle*: big; *faar*: where; *groo*: shiver of disgust; *brookie*: sooty; *gid*: went; *hyne*: far; *get fordl't*: get on with; *trachlin*: toiling; *sitt*: soot; *styoo*: dust; *maet*: meat; *scorie-hornt*: work-roughened; *skushlin*: scuffing; *teemin*: emptying; *orra pail*: household pail; *sair-made*: distressed; *hyste*: lift; *eence*: once

1974

Janetta I.W. Murray (*fl.* 1922–52)

Chinese Print

A sage at ease beneath a spreading tree
Complete with learned scroll and line and hook,
Some pomegranates and a pot of rice
A beaker and a flagon;

Before him slowly flows a tiny brook,
Behind him lurks among slim bamboo shoots
A lizard maybe or maybe a dragon.

For twice a thousand years he has sat so
Or even more, and thought on thought, or nought
Weighing the infinite of mere man's nonentity,
Letting the years slip past his unbaited hook;
His scroll is still unrolled,
And still rolls on the tiny brook.

Never a breeze has ruffled herb or tree;
Ripe pomegranates and a pot of rice
Are still in hand; beaker and flagon
Offer as ever potent consolation;
The scroll is still unrolled, the brook rolls on,
And bright-eyed, still, among green bamboo shoots
A lizard lurks or maybe it's a dragon.

As I consider this contented sage
I wish that he were I or I were he,
Prisoners exchanged, a sane to a mad age.
No, that's not fair; I would not wish that he
Should lose such golden calm to take my place,
Blown out of blissful quiet to endure
The misery of our distraught humanity:
I could not bear to see fade from his face
The contemplative calm of days gone by.

And so instead of such exchange I'll wish
To step into the picture, sit with him
Complete as he with rod and line, and fish,
Fish patiently with neither bait nor hook
Idly and endlessly in the tiny brook,

The tiny brook that slips so quietly
Across the picture by the tasselled scroll
Heavy with wisdom he's not cared to unroll
Complete with pomegranates and a pot of rice,
Beaker and flagon, is his paradise.
I'll choose to share with him that joke that he
In every smiling wrinkle seems to be
Savouring, and from deep-carven wrinkles it appears
Has been enjoying for two thousand years.

1952

Marion Cleland Lochhead (1902–85)

To a Minor Poet

Others may lead us to heaven-bordering heights
    Of being, where angelic hosts have trod,
May rend the veil that hides the holy place,
    Or show, as in a glass, the face of God.

But you can only tell of homely things,
    A darling countryside, a child at play,
Of little pleasures and timidities,
    The change and current of a quiet day.

Yet, the magnificence of God Who made
    The hills is seen in the small flowers and grass,
And, o'er the humble landscape of your song,
    The winds of the eternal spirit pass.

1928

Painted Things

I love painted things –
   Bright wooden toys and boxes, coloured beads,
Shawls like a peacock's plumage, scarves like wings
   Of birds that flaunt and flutter: all that breeds
Delight and thoughts fantastic. I love glass,
   Deep-tinted, amethystine, fire-red, gold,
That throws dim, changing luminance as I pass,
   And shifts, deploys like tapestries unrolled –
I love all these
   Gay fantasies; but more I love the grey
Austere walls of cathedrals, the bare trees
   That stand unmoved, with light and song away.

1929

The Choice

The story-teller came,
   And sat by the fire:
'Now what is the tale
   That your hearts desire?'

The lads and girls prayed
   For a tale of woe
Of the darksome land
   Where all bright things go;

But the old folk there
   Who had suffered long,
And were near their passing,
   Craved a happy song.

1929

Dorothy Margaret Paulin (1904–?)

The Cynic

I saw two lovers in the street to-night
    Close-leaning, radiant in the rosy mist
    Of dreaming; eyes that shone and lips that kissed –
All the poor ecstasy and cheap delight
Of love avowed and dying: and between,
   Gaudy and thin, illusions each did build
   To hide the other's nakedness, and gild
The shoddiness with dreamlight's glamoured sheen.

Ah, Love! speak not of loving yet awhile.
   As dawn is perfect for a moment's space
    Nor all our striving or bewildered tears
Can grasp it or delay; so neither smile
   Nor kiss can cherish love's awakening grace
    That fades and changes down the after years.

1936

In Spring

The sun has warsled clear o' the wintry clood,
  An' the larks are liltin' abune the whunny broo,
But the wee sma' gouden sang that a fain hert sung
  Is by wi', noo.

The burn fa's singin' doun by the sca'd hillside,
  An' the wild bees drone day-lang on the thymy brae,
But the foolish hert, ower torn wi' luvin', is dumb,
  Sangless an' wae.

This wild rose, lyin' sun'ered upon the gress
   In its waxen beauty, was nane mair frail nor sweet
Than the luve yon foolish hert laid doun afore
   Ane's heedless feet.

warsled: struggled; *whunny broo*:   *gouden*: golden; *by wi'*: over; *sca'd*
furze-covered brow of the hill;   scarred; *wae*: sad; *gress*: grass

1939

Dorothy Seward Walton (*fl*. 1934–52)

The Golden Thread

When Theseus lonely in the labyrinth
Of Ancient Crete, his sword unsheathed for war,
Sought out and slew the monster minotaur,
He cherished through the fight the unwound thread
That back to life and love and Ariadne led.

I think that when he heard the breathing beast
And felt the poisoned air grow dark with fear
His heart was smirched and changed as he drew near
And brute excitement flamed in him so hot
The bobbin almost slipped his hand, forgot.

We fight it now, the hidden primal beast:
We must fear nothing, nothing except that change
Which could so softly rot our hearts, estrange
All of us from our time. We must keep hold
For our returning, of that thread of gold.

1952

Sisters

Love of sister for sister
Stands a safe stanchion for the groping hand,
  Stays fixed and uncorroded
In the flux of life, the shifting sand.

  Slow as coral builded,
of betraying flesh forever free,
  Stripped bare, bone shining
It endures beneath the illusory.

  Secret eyes of sisters
To the same airs opening at birth
  See through darkness to each other
Rayed as radium in the hidden earth.

  Behind the mask age-wrinkled
Behind the blurring, the false difference
  They still see the cameo outline
Young, clear-cut, of morning innocence.

1952

Kathleen Raine (1908–2003)

The Locked Gates

Everywhere the substance of earth is the gate that we
    cannot pass.
Seek in Hebridean isles lost paradise,
There is yet the heaviness of water, the heaviness of stone

And the heaviness of the body I bring to this inviolate
    place.
Foot sinks in bog as I gather white water-lilies in the tarn,
The knee is bruised on rock, and the wind is always
    blowing.
The locked gates of the world are the world's elements,
For the rocks of the beautiful hills hurt, and the silver
    seas drown,
Wind scores deep record of time on the weathered
    boulders,
The bird's hot heart consumes the soaring life to feather
    and bone,
And heather and asphodel crumble to peat that smoulders
    on crofters' fires.

1952

The Well

The poem I wrote was not the poem
That sang in my own voice
Out of the past a phrase of Gaelic song,
And with the song rose scent of birch, and birds
In skies long set, ancestral gloaming,
As love and grief rose up from the beginning
And joy from lives long gone,
And I knew all they and the song had known.

When I, a child who spoke with a northern tongue
Telling of a land of birch and heather,
Dipped my country dipper in a stone well,
Sand-grains danced where the spring rose so clear,

Its water seemed a place purer than air
I could not enter, though I dipped my hands in,
And saw my face reflected in its cold brim,
And filled my buckets and carried the water home.

The poem I wrote was not the poem that in a dream
Opened a well where water flowed again.
I cleared dead leaves away with my hand,
But inextricable weeds had grown
Rooted in the ancestral fountain;
And yet the water flowed
Pure from its inexhaustible hidden source,
And all to whom that water came . . . .
In my dream I bathed a new-born child
And washed away the human stain.

An exile I have drunk from the Castalian spring,
But not such water as there rose.

1965

Olive Fraser (1909–77)

On a Distant Prospect of Girton College

Here the snow beats her flowers of fate
On my soul's gate.

Here the redbreast weeps again
For the world of men.

Here the child cries, cries wild,
Ever for the lost child.

Here the maiden lays her down
Her shroud her wedding gown.

Here does heavenly Plato snore,
A cypher, no more.

Here Herodotus goes by
At many knots, silently.

Here sits Dante in the dim
With Freud watching him.

Here does blessed Mozart seem
Alas, a sensual dream.

Here I could curse the hearts that shred
The great roses of the dead.

Here does holy innocence crave
A convent or a grave.

Here does Love lose his wings
Where women are female things.

Here is virginity thought to be
A state of the flesh only.

Here, my blood, muffle thy drum
Lest the hangman come.

Here, my muse, as we had died,
Sleep or be crucified.

Here's not thy Parnassus bright
But Hecla's icy light

O here do never, never come
Pure spring, perfect autumn.

1943

The Unwanted Child

I was the wrong music
The wrong guest for you
When I came through the tundras
And thro' the dew.

Summon'd, tho' unwanted,
Hated, tho' true
I came by golden mountains
To dwell with you.

I took strange Algol with me
And Betelgeuse, but you
Wanted a purse of gold
And interest to accrue.

You could have had them all,
The dust, the glories too,
But I was the wrong music
And why I never knew.

26th January, 1971

Nobody will come

Nobody will come, my love,
In the winter's rain.
In the dingy-sheeted bed
Turn to me again
Lie we close in silence bound
'Til we both are underground.
Nobody will come tonight.
Nobody will ever
Step below the church's wall,
Cross the flying river
To separate yourself and me
Desperate faithful poverty.

3rd August, 1974

Helen Adam (1909–92)

Kiltory

Kiltory rode hunting through deep woods and green.
In the kingdom o' Scotland his like ne'er was seen.
Wherever he hunted, by valley or steep,
The hearts o' the youthful like fountains wud leap.

There's many a bonnie lass making sad mane,
'Kiltory has left me at day-break alane.
Oh! why mun he leave wi' the first light o' day?
Kiltory rides hunting though love bids him stay.'

Lord Rand's wanton lady, where hill waters flowed,
Caught sight o' Kiltory as hunting he rode.

She saw him jaunt past at the blue break o' day.
'If yon were the huntsman, I'd fain be his prey!'

On the brink o' the river Kiltory rode by.
In the first light o' sunrise his face she did spy.
'Gin I were a falcon tae come at your call,
Frae ramparts o' heaven tae your fist I wud fall.'

Lord Rand, frae the Indies, fetched home for his dame,
Rare diamonds like water, and rubies like flame.
'For diamonds and rubies I care na',' she said.
'I would that Kiltory were laid in my bed.'

'Oh! what will content ye, my dear lady gay?'
'Alane wi' Kiltory content I wud stay.
I crave for the finest o' a' Earth's delights,
Tae lie wi' Kiltory for ten starry nights.'

Kiltory rode hunting in the forest sae green.
And ever behind him, Lord Rand rode unseen.
He saw the sun glint on Kiltory's brown hair.
'Ye micht ha' lived lang gin ye were na' sae fair.'

The woodlands were lonely. Lord Rand took a dart,
And struck doun Kiltory cleft clear through the heart.
When evening drew late, tae his lady he said,
'The huntsman, Kiltory, is laid in your bed.

Come hither, my lady, lie doun wi' your dear.
A rival sae braw I ha' reason tae fear.
Come lie wi' your true love for ten starry nights.
I'll grudge ye nae hour o' your stolen delights.'

Tae the dead man he flung her. He nailed up the door.
'Kiltory, I wish ye the joy o' your whore!'

Awa in the woodlands the wild throstles cried,
And the waters ran red on the brant mountain-side.

The waters, at morning, run red on the steep.
The wild throstles cry, and the young lassies weep,
For never again, at the blue break o' day,
Will Kiltory ride hunting while love bids him stay.

1964

Janet Caird (1913–92)

Ageing

It crept up gradually; no dramatic leap,
but was there curling round legs
hindering steps,
laying a lethargic paw over fingers,
brushing fur across eyes.

One learns to live with it.
It sits on the hearth
purring cosily,
but the claws dig deep
and the bite is mortal.

1977

Janet Caird (1913–92)

The Sisters

In that walled and happy garden
the sisters spend their days;
play round the cypresses;
skip down paved walks;
dip fingers in the pool
where agéd carp
circle, circle.
A golden age of childhood passes;
with bright threads and shining needles
they duplicate the garden;
sit by the pool, fish into thought,
the water troubled, the carp
circling, circling.
Comes a clear day of sun and little clouds
stippling the sky defined by marble walls
where fruit-trees spread their arms in crucifixion.
Irked by the garden-prison's peace
they drop the threads; the needles glint.
They prowl, they peer
in shaded corners, carved pavilions.
'An axe or shears?'
'Hands suffice.'
'Here is the gardener's tool-chest.'
'Here is a tree well-fruited.'
The lid is raised;
the apple snatched.
Clouds smother the sun; the wind
is a tornado; it lashes
the pool to emptiness; the carp
gasp and are dead; the trees
bend and break; the needlework is rags.
Too late the box is shut;

too late the core spat out.
Through havoc to the riven wall
hand-linked the sisters run.

1983

At the Bus Stop

Do not walk too proudly past the bus stop,
blonde hair swinging,
long legs striding,
eyes so confident.
Do not walk too proudly past them
as they wait
with plastic bags, wearied feet, frizzy hair, drooping
   lips, crumpled brows –
do not walk too proudly;
for these are veterans;
they have come through; they know.
Not saplings, upright, slender, but
trees the wind has twisted, sculpted,
pinpoint significance in a landscape –
you must not walk so proudly.

1988

Curstaidh NicDh'àidh/Christina Mackay (1914–2001)

Coinneamh nan Cearc mun Ghràn

An àm a' Chogaidh bha biadh chearc uabhasach gann. Chan fhaight' e gun choupons. Dhòirt, turas, poca mòr gràin air starsach fear dhe na marsantan.

Thuirt coileach Eàirdsidh Belaig 's e toirt crathadh air a
    sgiath
''S còir dhomh fios thoirt seachad gur e fìrinn tha san sgeul
Thuirt eireag Dhòmhnaill 'ic Alasdair 's cha chanadh ise
    breug,
G' eil sìol mòr air starsach Ailein, 's sinne fannachadh gun
    bhiadh.'

Cha robh gob sa bhaile nach do thuig dè bha e gairm
'S gu grad chaidh iad gu siubhal cheart cho ullamh ri
    luchd-airm,
Dh'fhàg cuid dhiubh blàths nan neadan 's thog iad orra
    mach le fonn,
B'ann aig Crois an Rathaid chaidh a' Phàrlamaid air bonn.

'Se seann chearc bhàn le Ailig bha na ceannard air a' chùirt
'S a dh'innts le beagan glagadaich dè 'n t-adhbhar iad
    bhith cruinn,
'Feuch am faigh sinn ceartas thoirt a-mach dhuinn fhìn 's
    dhar cloinn,
Sìol mòr a' dol a dholaidh 's sinn gun ghonag thèid nar
    broinn.'

Sin labhair coileach Lomax, 'Tha mi mionnaichte gur fìor,
'S mi bha thall 's a chunnaic e 's nach fhac a leithid riamh,
Air m' onair tha mi 'g innse dhuibh gun d'fhàs mo
   chìrean blàth
Nuair chunnaic mi na sìleanan, cho prìseil air an làr.

''S gu deimhinn tha mi 'g ràdh ribh gur e gnothach nàir a
   th' ann
Mar dh'fhàgadh air an làr e fo na sàilean, 's e cho gann.
Nan togadh iad air seibheal e 's a shiabadh air ar feadh
'S iomadh giaban 'n Cille-Pheadair a bhiodh riaraicht às a
   leth.'

Ghearain cearc a' Mhinisteir, 'Cha bheir mi tuilleadh ugh,
Chan fhad a bhios aon it' annam – mo chìrean air fàs
   dubh,
Tha m' ìnean fhèin air dìreadh is gu dearbh chan
   iongnadh leam
A' sgrìobadh smùrach lofaichean 's buntàta mosach
   pronn.'

Bha cearc-ghuir an t-sagairt ann is sianar aic' a chloinn,
Mhionnaich i gu daingeann nach deach gràinean riamh
   nam broinn,
'Chan fhaigh sinn ach min-choirce còmh' ri fras na
   cuiseig ruaidh,
'S bheirinn mo chnàimh-pòst airson dòrnan de ghràn
   cruaidh.'

Bha gèadh le Raghnall Iain Shaoir ann 's thug e iteag às a
   sgiath,
'Nach toir sibh dhomh "particulars" gun cuirinn
   "statement" sìos,
M' anam-sa nuair bhruidhneas mi bidh fios air rud no dhà,

Ach feuchaibh g'eil an fhìrinn ann – chan fheumte m'
  fhaighinn ceàrr.'

Bha cearcan Ghearraidh-Sheilidh ann an comann beag
  dhaibh fhèin,
Bha pailteas anns na h-iodhlainn a chumadh iad gun èis;
'S ann chruinnich iad aig a' cheàrdaich 's chuir iad
  fiathachadh gu càch
Nan tigeadh iad dhan Union gun 'claimeadh' iad an gràn.

Bha bantam dubh le Niall ann 's chuir e fiaradh beag na
  cheann,
'Nach gòrach leam ur diugadaich 's gun choupons agaibh
  ann,
Ged bhiodh an sìol sin còipte fa chomhair ur dà shùil
Cha robh chridhe aig ur sgròbain dhol na chòir gun
  chead a' bhùird.

'Ach innsidh mi dè nì sinn 's bidh sinn cinnteach às ar duais:
Cuiridh sinn fios-cabhaig thun a' chlèirich Calum Ruadh,
Canaidh sinn mas math leis ugh air Inid 's eun air Càisg
Gu faigh sinn cead le sgrìobhadh dhol gar dìnneir dhan
  tòrr ghràin.'

1979

The Hens' Convention on the Grain

During the war chickenfeed was awfully scarce, and
impossible to obtain without coupons. On one occasion a
huge sack of grain was spilt in front of the house of one
of the merchants.

Said Belag's Archie's cockerel, as he gave his wings a shake,
'I really ought to tell you that the story's not a fake –
Donald MacAlastair's chick has said – and she wouldn't tell a
    porky –
that there's good fat grain on Alan's steps, while we grow faint
    with hunger.'

Not one beak in the village failed to understand his crowing
and as smartly as foot soldiers they at once took to the road,
some left their warm and cosy nests and marched off in good cheer,
and at the village crossroads the Parliament convened.

It was one of Alec's elderly white hens that took the chair
and explained with some brief clucking the reason they were there:
'Let's demand that justice be dispensed to our broods and to
    ourselves,
There's good grain going to waste but not a morsel in our bellies.'

Then Lomax's cockerel spoke up: 'I can swear that it's no lie –
I've been and I have seen, and I have never seen the like,
upon my word I tell you that it warmed my very crest
to see spilt on the ground so many precious beads of grain.

And in all truth let me say it's an unspeakable disgrace
that it's left there to be trampled underfoot when it's so scarce.
Were they to lift a shovel and among us have it scattered
many gizzards in Kilfedder would be filled to satisfaction.'

The minister's hen lamented, 'Not one egg now can I lay,
I soon won't have one feather left – my comb has gone all grey,
my nails have grown to such a length, and it's really no surprise,
when all they have to scrape on are crumbs of bread and measly
    mash.'

Curstaidh NicDh'àidh/Christina Mackay (1914–2001)

The priest's own brooding hen was there, a mother to six chicks,
and she swore blind they had never had a single grain to pick,
'All we can find is oatmeal and the shower off docken stems,
and I'd give my very wishbone for a fistful of hard grain.'

A goose of Joiner Iain's Ron took a feather from his wing,
'Now please give me particulars and I'll get a statement down;
without a doubt when I get heard we'll learn a thing or two,
but I mustn't be found wrong, so tell me only what is true.'

The hens of Garryhilly were in a combo of their own,
since they had an abundance in their yards to keep them going;
they met up at the forge and sent an invite to the rest
that if they joined the Union they'd put a claim in for the
    grain.

A bantam cock of Neil's was there and he cocked his head a tad,
'Since you've not one coupon between you, all your squawking is
    quite mad –
even if all that grain was cowped under your very nose
you wouldn't dare go near it without permission from the Board.

But I'll tell you what we'll do so that our prize can be assured,
we'll send an urgent message to the clerk, one Calum Ruadh.
We'll tell him if he likes his egg at Shrove and his Easter hen
we need a written permit now to feast on the heap of grain.'

Editor's note: verses 4–6 omitted.

Carstìona Anna Stiùbhart/Christina Ann Stewart (1914–83)

Eachdraidh na h-*Iolaire*

Bha còmhlan den a' chabhlaich
Air slighe dhachaigh anns a' Chaol,
'S bha 'n *Sheila* cus ro luchdaichte
Le cudthrom bathair's dhaoin'.
Sin thàinig fios le òrdugh
Gheata mhòr a cur fo aont
A ghiùlaineadh na seòldairean
Do Steòrnabhagh an gaoil.

Bha an oidhche gruamach iargalt ac'
Le siantan agus gaoth
Ri tighinn teann bhon iardheas orr'
'S na chliathan an Cuan Sgìth.
Cò am fear am measg nan ceudan ud
A dh'iath e air a smaoin
Gun robh a thuras crìochnaichte,
Na shìorraidheachd cho dlùth?

Bha ceithir bliadhna luasganach
A' bhuairidh air an cùl
A chaidh seachad iarganach
Air cuantan agus raoin,
Ceartas air a riarachadh
Le buaidh ga toirt air daors',
'S a' Ghearmailt fo a riaghladh ac'
Le fallas dian an gnùis.

Is iomadh cridhe mànranach
Bha bualadh blàth le mùirn

Ri sgioblachadh nam fàrdaichean
Airson sàir ris an robh dùil
Tilleadh dhachaidh sàbhailt
Bhon a' bhlàr thuca len saors',
'S a' choinneamh bhiodh cho aoibhneach ac'
Air oidhche na bliadhn' ùir.

Roimh sgarachadh nan tràthan
Chaidh an gàirdeachas mu sgaoil
Nuair bhriseadh sgeul a' ghàbhaidh ud
Le guth a' bhàis gach taobh.
Cha tug i mach an t-àite
Chaidh an àirde oirr' anns a' Chaol,
A' chala anns an fhàire
'S i sàbht' air Biastan Thuilm.

Nach bu dorch an neul
A bha còmhdach grian gach sgìr'
Le dubhachas is cianalas,
Le tiamhaidheachd is glaodh,
Dìlleachdain is dàimhean
Is banntraichean gun mhaoin,
'S a' chosgais bh' air a' chunntas ud
Na an t-suim cha tèid am prìs.

Teaghlaichean le tuill annta
Ri caoidh na bha dan dìth
A chunnaic crìoch na h-aimhreit
Agus bonntachadh na sìth.
Làraich lom na muinntir sin
Nach togadh ceann an tìm,
Is ged a b' fhaisg am fonn orra
Nach d' fhuair am bonn air tìr.

Cha deachaidh 's cha tèid àireamh
Gu bràth don àite 'n call,
Cha ghleachd gàirdean làidir
Ris a' bhàs a thig na àm.
An Niseach còir a dh'fhàg
Cuid de 'làmhan anns a' chrann,
'S bha fear na mheadhan teàrnaidh innt'
A shnàmh aist' leis a' bhall.

Nach iomchaidh do na h-àil
Iomradh sàr fhir ghleidheadh beò
A dhìon sinn bhon an nàmhaid
'S a choisinn blàir na h-Eòrp'.
Na dorsan ged a ràinig iad
'S an tràigh bha gràdhaicht' leò,
Nach daor, nach daor a phàigheadh
A' chàin le Eilean Leòdhais!

1978

The story of the Iolaire

A contingent of the Navy
was in Kyle bound for home,
but the Sheila was overladen
with her weight of men and cargo.
So the order then was given
that a large yacht should be leased
to carry back the sailors
to their beloved Stornoway.

The night was black and eerie
and relentless stormy squalls
bore down on them from the south-west,

and the Minch rose up in walls.
Among those several hundred men
did it enter the thoughts of any
that his journey might be at an end,
and eternity so near him?

Four years they had behind them
of turbulence and trauma,
years painfully put by
on battlefields and oceans;
justice was dispensed
and oppression overcome,
and Germany was brought to heel
by the hard sweat of their brow.

So many hearts were songful
and beating warm with joy
as hearths were cleaned and tidied
for the heroes who they thought
were returning safe and sound
from the war, at last released,
to be joyfully reunited
on the night of the New Year.

Before the early hours of dawn
their cheerfulness had died,
as news broke of the tragedy,
death's voice on every side.
She never made it past the place
on which they'd set her course in Kyle,
and when dawn rose on the harbour
she was split on the Beasts of Holm.

The darkness of that cloud
smoored the sun in every parish
with black despair and mourning,
sorrow and cries of anguish,
orphans and dependants
and widows without a penny,
the cost of that number or its sum
cannot be estimated.

Families now depleted
grieved for the men they'd lost
who'd lived to see the peace declared
and the ending of the war.
The empty places of those men
who would return no more,
who came so close to their native ground
but never got a foot ashore.

The loss to the place has never been
and never will be counted;
strong arms cannot fight off Death,
it comes at the time appointed.
The good Ness man who clung to the mast
and left the skin of his hands,
and the one who made rescue possible
when he swam the hawser to land.

It is surely fitting that descendants
should cherish the name of heroes
who defended us from the enemy
and won the war in Europe.
Although they reached the gates
and the shore they loved most truly,
how high, how high the tax
that was paid by the Isle of Lewis!

Editor's note: verses 3–4 omitted.

Dorothy Dunbar (1915–

Arunculea

Arunculea is my name,
A name that's not unknown to fame,
I lumber round a circus ring,
I lumber round and round the thing . . .
I put my two front feet on little boxes,
I stand on little boxes
I dance on little boxes,
I lumber round and round the thing,
The thing they call a circus ring,
And yet, I'm not unknown to fame.
Arunculea is my name.

My name was famous long ago,
Upon the mountains capped with snow.
I lumber round and round the thing,
The thing they call a circus ring.
I put my two front feet on little boxes,
I stand on little boxes,
I dance on little boxes,
And yet I'm not unknown to fame.
Arunculea is my name.

My forebear carried Hannibal;
She was a famous animal!
I put my two front feet on little boxes,
I stand on little boxes,
I dance on little boxes.
Across the Alps with Hannibal . . .
She was a famous animal.
I lumber round and round the thing,

The thing they call a circus ring,
And yet, I'm not unknown to fame.
Arunculea is my name . . .

Elma Mitchell (1919–2000)

Thoughts after Ruskin

Women reminded him of lilies and roses.
Me they remind rather of blood and soap,
Armed with a warm rag, assaulting noses,
Ears, neck, mouth and all the secret places:

Armed with a sharp knife, cutting up liver,
Holding hearts to bleed under a running tap,
Gutting and stuffing, pickling and preserving,
Scalding, blanching, broiling, pulverising,
– All the terrible chemistry of their kitchens.

Their distant husbands lean across mahogany
And delicately manipulate the market,
While safe at home, the tender and the gentle
Are killing tiny mice, dead snap by the neck,
Asphyxiating flies, evicting spiders,
Scrubbing, scouring aloud, disturbing cupboards,
Committing things to dustbins, twisting, wringing,
Wrists red and knuckles white and fingers puckered,
Pulpy, tepid. Steering screaming cleaners
Around the snags of furniture, they straighten
And haul out sheets from under the incontinent
And heavy old, stoop to importunate young,
Tugging, folding, tucking, zipping, buttoning,

Spooning in food, encouraging excretion,
Mopping up vomit, stabbing cloth with needles,
Contorting wool around their knitting needles,
Creating snug and comfy on their needles.

Their huge hands! their everywhere eyes! their voices
Raised to convey across the hullabaloo,
Their massive thighs and breasts dispensing comfort,
Their bloody passages and hairy crannies,
Their wombs that pocket a man upside down!

And when all's over, off with overalls,
Quickly consulting clocks, they go upstairs,
Sit and sigh a little, brushing hair,
And somehow find, in mirrors, colours, odours,
Their essences of lilies and of roses.

1987

This Poem . . .

This poem is dangerous: it should not be left
Within the reach of children, or even of adults
Who might swallow it whole, with possibly
Undesirable side-effects. If you come across
An unattended, unidentified poem
In a public place, do not attempt to tackle it
Yourself. Send it (preferably, in a sealed container)
To the nearest centre of learning, where it will be
    rendered
Harmless, by experts. Even the simplest poem
May destroy your immunity to human emotions.

All poems must carry a Government warning. Words
Can seriously affect your heart.

1987

Màiri M. NicGhill-eathain/
Mary M. MacLean (1921–

Am Blàr-Cath

Feuch, trilleach ro gharbh is borbachd cogaidh,
Le marbhteachd gunn' agus lann;
Cluinn gearain is caoidh is daoin' a' plosgail
Le osnaich ghuineach 's iad fann:
Tha 'n lasair le fuaim a' ruagadh thairis
Air bruaich is carraig is gleann –
Gur gairisneach, uamhalt' 'm bruaillean sgreamhail,
'S gur cruaidh mac-talla nam beann.

Tha lèirsgrios an t-slèibh neo-shèimh mar ghailleann –
Ghrad-thrèig an talamh a chiall;
Tha 'n cruaidh-chath le reubainn, sèist is creachadh
A' beucadh thairis, gach ial:
An e seo da-rìribh brìgh na cruinne –
Sgrios, mì-rùn, ainneart is pian?
A bheil mòr-roinn an t-sluaigh air ghluasad uile
Le fuath is fuileachd gun rian?

Ged bha 'n òg-mhadainn chaoin a' sgaoileadh thairis
('S bu chaomh i sgaradh nan tràth),
Bha cneatraich is gaoir, bha aog is casgradh
Air raointean coimheach a' bhlàir:

Bha ceatharnaich ùr 's an cùl ri talamh
Fo chuibhreach daingeann an sàs
Bhiodh, mus tuiteadh an duibhr' o chùirt nam flaitheas,
An dùsal maireann a' bhàis.

Air dhomh amharc mun cuairt, bu chruaidh an sealladh:
Gach truaghan lag agus leònt'
Nan sìneadh cho fuar, grad-bhuailt' ri talamh,
'S iad truaillte, salach gu leòr;
An taice ri craoibh ri m' thaobh bha balach
Le chiorraman lag agus breòit' –
Bha athchuing na ghnùis 's a shùil gam tharraing
'S gam ghairm gu fantainn na chòir.

Bha sgleò air a shùil, 's a' taomadh tro mhalaidh
Bha driùchd neo-fhallain a' bhàis;
Bha acaid a chreuchd a' reubadh anam,
An t-eug ga tharraing an sàs:
Bha luasgan a chlèibh gu geur a' casadh –
A mheud chan aithris mo dhàn –
Ach bha bhuadhan gu lèir gun ghèilleadh fhathast,
'S rium fèin gun d' labhair e, 'g ràdh:

'A charaid, dèan èisteachd rium car tamaill
Mus tèid mi don chadal bhios sìor;
Tha solas na grèin' dhomh fèin a' laighe,
Mo reult a' cromadh san iar;
'S e 'n gunna dubh caol rinn smùr de m' aitreabh –
Tha 'm ball' air a leagadh na smàl,
'N taigh talmhaidh ag aom', tha 'n aonta seachad,
'S bidh 'n t-aog a' togail a' mhàil.

'Ach ma tha e an dàn gun tàrr thu fhathast
A làmhan frioghail luchd-fuath,
'S gun tèid thu ri d' bheò an còir mo dhachaigh,
Thoir an t-soraidh mu dheireadh seo uam:
Dèan inns' do m' luchd-gràidh a dh'fhàg mi 'n Uibhist
Gu robh iad gu tairis nam smuain,
'S ged tha mi 'n seo brùit' is ciùrrte buileach,
Tha rùintean m'anam gan luaidh.

''S ma bhios iad fo ghruaim le smuairean aithnicht'
'S na deòir a' frasadh on sùil,
Dèan aithris gu luath gun d' fhuair mi cobhair –
Gun d' bhuannaich m'anam cairt-iùil;
'S nuair dh'fhuasglar an snaidhm tha daingnicht'
    fhathast,
Gu tairis gan ceangal san t-saogh'l,
Gun coinnich sinn shuas, gach buaireas thairis,
An comann neo-sgaraicht' nach sgaoil.'

Le cromadh na grèine thrèig an anail
'S bha chèis ud falamh gun dàil,
'S chaidh a chàradh leis fhèin san rèidhleig thana
Gun bhrèid no anart no càil;
'S bidh 'm preasarnach uain' air uaigh mar phlaide,
Le suain gun airsneal na blàths,
'S cha dèan buaireas an t-sluaigh no fuaim a' bhatail
A shuaimhneas bhriseadh gu bràth.

1999

Màiri M. NicGhill-eathain/Mary M. Maclean (1921–

The Battlefield

See the terrible disruption and barbarity of war,
the savagery of guns and blades;
hear the moans and the groaning and the panting of men,
their gasps of pain as they fade:
the roaring flames sweep all in their way
over slope and glen and cliff,
horrific and chilling their loathsome tumult
and brutal the echo of the hills.

The blasting of the mountain is fierce as a cyclone –
the earth has taken leave of its senses;
every second the roar of war surges forward
with plundering, siege and pillage
Is this the true nature of our universe –
malice, violence, pain and destruction?
Is most of humanity completely possessed
By hate and unbridled bloodshed?

Though the tender young morning drifted across
(and how gently it dispelled the darkness!),
there were cries and groans, there was death and slaughter
on the foreign fields of battle:
fresh young fighters, their backs to the earth,
lay trapped in immovable shackles
who, before night descended from the court of the heavens,
would sleep in death's permanent shadow.

As I gazed around, it was a cruel sight:
every pitiful wretch weak and wounded
stretched out in the cold, thrown to the ground
in grievous filth and defilement;

propped against a tree nearby was a boy
weak and disfigured with injuries –
his face pleaded, his eyes drew me in
and begged me to remain beside him.

His eyes were clouded, and there seeped through his brow
The noxious sweat of the dying;
The piercing pain of his wounds tore his spirit,
As death drew him into its clutches:
The heaving of his chest grew ever more strained –
My poem cannot paint his labour –
But his senses had not all deserted him yet,
And he made to address me, saying:

'My friend, listen to me a while
Before I sink into sleep forever;
The light of my sun is fading now,
My star in the west is setting;
the slender black gun has shattered my dwelling –
the wall is reduced to rubble,
My earthly home is collapsing, the lease has expired,
And death now demands its rental.

'But if you are fated yet to escape
From the furious claws of the hating,
And should you ever again be near my home,
Bear these my farewell greetings:
Tell all the loved ones I left in Uist
That I thought of them with fondness,
And lying here broken and mortally wounded,
For them is my soul's deepest longing.

'And should they be cheerless and visibly grieving,
Should the tears stream from their eyes,
Quickly assure them I found my salvation –
My soul has acquired its compass;
And when the knot is loosened which as yet holds firm
And still binds them gently to the world,
We shall meet up above, every torment behind us,
Reunited in indissoluble friendship.'

As the sun sank low his breathing faded,
And that body was soon just a shell,
And he was buried alone in a shallow grave
With no shroud or linen at all;
but the shrubs' green foliage will drape his tomb,
And he will sleep serene in their warmth,
And neither tumult of people nor turmoil of battle
Will ever disturb his repose.

Editor's note: Composed ten years after the death of the poet's step-brother at St Valéry, 1940.

Elise McKay (1922–

Arrested Development

Daffodils won't bloom in my garden.
They simply bud and there it stops.
No use giving them pep talks,
encouragement, that sort of thing;
for there they sit, slim-sheathed in green,
delicately understating the spring,
while all along the road, gardens burst

with burgeoning blooms, with fulsome frills,
over-ripe, abandoned, trumpeting their wares.
I know why mine won't open up,
turning their heads to catch a subtler tune;
sweet, schizoid buds – missing so much –
too proud to boast, too cold to bloom.

1984

No Answer

I tore your letter up,
like all the others; after all
letters are only words,
and words have failed before.
It was not unkindly done.
I know you've nothing else
to give; and I have less.

But words can fail,
unseen, unheard;
small lost perfections,
celebrating what must die.
Don't think of this.
I tore your letter up.
One should not look for
permanence in words.

1988

Kathrine Sorley Walker (*fl*. 1945–

Scottish Legacy

Tough roots, unfelt, unseen in daily life
(magnetic is the land, as are hill, bush and tree)
draw back the wandering heart to influences
deep in the past, absorbed without clear thought
but all pervasive.
So buried are these roots, so overlaid
with later, more accountable, allegiances
they rarely stir; but when they do
they have great power. Within a landscape
is strange potency. Does it derive
from the long line of generations
whose human dust, mixed with the burial earth,
scattered in ashes on the hills and glens,
speaks to me, in this land, of love of place,
kinship and ancestry?

Through the cold centuries my fathers lived
knowing this northern country.
They knew the drift-deep snow, the moors icebound,
the waves whipped high in storm. Cold dawn, cold day,
the white-cold winter night,
the moon frost-rimmed, the stars and snowflakes bright.
They tilled the armoured earth, sailed the steel sea,
and toughened flesh and spirit to resist
winter's high tyranny.
From their strong stock I sprang, thin-blooded, weak,
sapped by the heat of Indian infancy.
Bitter to me the sleet and stinging rain,

torment the chill that lay beneath my skin
deep in the ice-dipped marrow of each bone.

To winter they bequeathed me – he, their friend,
always my enemy. Yet there were days of summer heat,
high in the hills and on the open heath,
drawing the scents from juniper and ling,
wild rose and golden gorse. And I, as they,
was blessed with such delights.

So the long skein of genealogy is spun
that ends in me. So is the history unrolled
that chronicles quiet, far from famous, lives,
each to itself important, as mine to me.
They are my people, blood-linked by marriage nets
spread across families of diverse kinds.
Their varied backgrounds, traits, abilities,
merge in my temperament as, within this earth,
by right of legacy, winters and summers lie –
the contrasts and the complements of life.

1999

Catrìona NicDhòmhnaill/
Catherine MacDonald (1925–

Cum Sinn Dlùth

A Rìgh nan Dùl dan lèir gach neach air thalamh,
    Bi-sa dlùth nuair dh'iadhas duibhre dhorch' –
Tha stoirmean garbh' na beatha cruaidh rin giùlan

'S tha solas geal an dòchais doirbh ri lorg:
Cum sinn dlùth, cum sinn dlùth,
Cum sinn dlùth fo dhìon 's fo sgiath do thròcair chaoimh.

Tha sinn cho fosgailt' do gach seòrsa cunnairt,
    'S cò tha foghainteach fa chomhair deuchainn cràidh?
Ach bi-sa dhuinn nad sgiath 's cuir sinn nad fhasgadh
    'S gun gabh ar cridhe fois, 's ar n-earbs' nad ghràdh:
Cum sinn dlùth, cum sinn dlùth,
Cum sinn dlùth fo dhìon 's fo sgiath do thròcair chaoimh.

Nuair dhùmhlaicheas an dorchadas mun cuairt dhinn
    'S nach lèir dhuinn 'n ceum a tha for bonn,
Thoir òirnn bhith suidhe sìos gu socair stòlda,
    Ciùinich Fhèin am bruaillean tha nar com:
Cum sinn dlùth, cum sinn dlùth,
Cum sinn dlùth fo dhìon 's fo sgiath do thròcair chaoimh.

Tog ar sùilean trom' a-rithist suas gad ionnsaigh,
    Sgap na sgòthan chum 's gum faic sinn solas iùil,
Nochd thu fhèin tron chlèith o chùl a' bhalla
    'S cluinneamaid do ghuth ag ràdh, 'Thig leam.'
Cum sinn dlùth, cum sinn dlùth,
Cum sinn dlùth fo dhìon 's fo sgiath do thròcair chaoimh.

Is thèid sinn leat, a dh'ainneoin dragh is àmhghair
    Ged bhiodh an t-slighe dorcha mar tro cheò –
'S Tu an caraid 's dlùithe leanas ruinn na bràthair,
    Truasail, dìleas thar gach duine beò:
Cum sinn dlùth, cum sinn dlùth,
Cum sinn dlùth fo dhìon 's fo sgiath do thròcair chaoimh.

'S nuair thig an t-àm san ruig sinn ceann na slighe
    'S a chì sinn sealladh soilleir air gach nì a bhà,

Tuigidh sinn an sin do Làmh a smachdaich;
   Ach gus a-sin, ar n-ùrnaigh théid an àird':
Cum sinn dlùth, cum sinn dlùth,
Cum sinn dlùth fo dhion 's fo sgiath do thròcair chaoimh.

1987

Hold Us Close
(Translated by Ronald Black)

O King of the Elements who sees every person on earth,
   Be Thou close when impenetrable darkness surrounds us –
The wild tempests of life are difficult to bear
     And the bright light of hope is hard to detect:
Hold us close, hold us close,
Hold us close protected by Thy gentle mercy's wing.

We are so open to each kind of danger,
     And who is strong enough to face the test of pain?
But be to us a shield and give us Thy protection
     To let our heart find rest, trusting in Thy love:
Hold us close, hold us close,
Hold us close protected by Thy gentle mercy's wing.

When the darkness intensifies around us
     And we cannot see the path that's underneath our sole,
Make us sit down with stoic ease,
     Calm Thou the panic in our breast:
Hold us close, hold us close,
Hold us close protected by Thy gentle mercy's wing

Raise our drooping eyelids up again to Thee,
     Disperse the clouds to let us see a guiding light,

Show Thyself through the wattle from behind the wall
And let us hear Thy voice saying, 'Come with me.'
Hold us close, hold us close,
Hold us close protected by Thy gentle mercy's wing.

And with Thee we will go, despite trouble and anguish,
Though the way may be dark as if through a mist –
Thou art the friend that stays closer to us than a brother,
Compassionate, loyal beyond any person alive:
Hold us close, hold us close,
Hold us close protected by Thy gentle mercy's wing.

And when the moment comes for us to reach our journey's end
And when we clearly get a sight of everything that's been,
Then we'll understand Thy Hand that chastised;
But till then, it's our prayer that will arise:
Hold us close, hold us close,
Hold us close protected by Thy gentle mercy's wing.

Trusgan Na Fèin-Fhìreantachd

'S ann agam a bha 'n trusgan
A bha cofhurtail mum dhruim:
Trusgan na fèin-fhìreantachd,
Gun sracadh air 's gun tuill,
Gam chòmdachadh gu h-iomlan
O là gu là gun tàmh –
Cha robh gainne tomhais air,
'S e ruigheachd gu mo shàil.

Cha tàinig e nam inntinn
Gu robh dad sam bith air ceàrr,
'S chan iarrainn trusgan eile

Ged a bha e sean a' fàs;
Is e bha geal nam shùilean
Is dèanamh air bha brèagh' –
Is e mi fhìn a rinn e,
Is bha e gu mo mhiann.

Ach mhothaich mi aon latha dha,
Gu robh e tana fàs,
'S gu dearbha bha e loireach
Nuair a sheall mi ceart 's gach àit';
'S nuair bhuaileadh dath na Grèine air
'S ann litheach bha a dhath:
Thilginn 'n uair sin dhìom e,
'S gun e còrdadh rium ro mhath.

Cha bhiodh seachdain air dol seachad
Nuair bhiodh e orm a-rìs;
Cha robh e dad nas cumhaing'
Agus dh'fhalbh dheth an dath lì:
Bha e ga mo mhealladh,
Cha robh agam aon a b'fheàrr
Gus an d'fhuair mi o dheagh Charaid
Brat de dh'obair ghrinn le snàth'id.

Seo far bheil an trusgan
Nì a' chùis 'son cùirt an Rìgh;
Cha cheannaich òr no airgead e –
Is tiodhlac e gun phrìs.
Fhuair mi o m' Fhear-saoraidh e
'S tha gu leòr dhiubh na thaigh-stòir,
'S chan fhacas aon cho fialaidh ris
Is chòmhdaich mi le deòin.

Trusgan na fèin-fhìreantachd,

Faigh cuidhteas e gun dàil –
Tha fàileadh fuaraidh saoghalt' dheth
'S cha dìon e aig a' bhàs.
'S e fìreantachd an t-Slànaigheir
An còmhdach sa bheil blàths;
'S am bàs le fhuachd cha mhill e thu,
'S tu 'n coltas Chrìost a' fàs.

1987

The Apparel of Self-righteousness

Mine was an outfit
that was comfortable to wear:
the apparel of self-righteousness,
without a hole or tear,
it covered me completely
throughout each and every day –
it lacked nothing in material,
as it reached down to my heels.

It never once occurred to me
there might be something wrong,
I had no wish for another suit,
though mine was getting old;
I thought its cut was elegant,
it was resplendent in my eyes –
I had made it with my very hands
and it was just as I desired.

But then one day I noticed
how it was wearing thin,
it was in fact quite shabby

when I inspected every inch;
and when the Sunlight caught it
its colour seemed to fade:
and I would cast it off then,
no longer quite so keen.

But before the week was out
I'd be wearing it again;
it was no longer constricting
and the faded look was gone.
It really had me in its spell,
I had no suit to match it,
till from a good Friend I received
a beautifully sown mantle.

That, now, is the apparel
for appearing in the court of Heaven,
which no gold can buy or silver –
tis a gift beyond all value.
It was given me by my Saviour
and He has plenty in His storehouse;
than Him none is more generous,
He unhesitantly clothed me.

The apparel of self-righteousness,
get rid of it at once –
it has a cold and worldly smell
and won't protect at death.
The righteousness of the Saviour
is the raiment that will warm you;
and as you grow in the image of Christ
chill death will not destroy you.

Anne Turner (1925–

Medusa

The ageing woman combs her hair
much as she did when, in her prime,
fashion and custom captured her.
And all her thought reflects that time.

Thought reflects that time for her
is a hair-spring; is defeat
spiralling within the coils
of static movement, self-deceit.

Movement, self-deceit, surrounds
the car, the clothes, the views expressed.
One moment between youth and age
matured, and prophesied the rest:

prophesied the rust, the dust –
the last mutations in her veins.
She struggles, prisoner of whims
which no platonic lust sustains.

Must so stains the well-dressed act
that *why* is lost beneath what seems.
A ghost virginity presides
wistfully over dyes and creams.

Cries and dreams, corroding cares,
wrinkle the mask to mock despair:

a myth that shames the mirror where
the ageing woman combs her hair.

1970

Cairstìona Anna NicAoidh/
Christina A. Mackay (1928–

An Druidheachd

Ri soillse na gealaich ùir
Bha Bliadhn' Ùr air a breith
Ceud-ghin na Dà-Mhìle.
'S bha tostachd dhìomhair dhomhainn do-thuigse
A' cur druidheachd air linne 's air lianag
A' mùchadh a-mach gach gluasad
Fiu 's gach tarraing-anail.

Ach shaoileam gun d' dh'fhidir mi sanais fann
A' sìoladh tro lìonanaich nan iomadh bliadhna.
Sin chuala mi fad às
Ri soillse gealaich eile
Gairm-maidne a' choilich,
Caithream is ceilearadh chloinne
Gu aon-ghuthach a' guidhe 'BLIADHNA MHÀTH ÙR
    DHUIBH'
Aig uinneig bhiùganach gach bothan.
'N sin cur ʼʼʼ ʼʼʼ ʼʼʼ char sna claisean.
A' draghadh, 's a' mireag ri chèile.
Oir bha an ceann-uidhe air fàire.
Luach-saoithreach aig crìoch na slighe!
TAIGH DHÒMHNAILL SEÒLADAIR!

Gu cur air a shlàint leis an 'fruit wine'
Bhon a' chupan-uighe letheach.
'S an cèic! . . . (criomag bho chriomag, cho slaodach!)
A thàinig air a' phost à Glaschu
Bho chlann-nighean na muinntireas!

2001

Enchantment

By the light of the new moon
a New Year was born
first child of the Bimillennium.
And a deep, mysterious, unfathomable silence
spread its sorcery over field and water
stifling every movement
every intake of breath, even.

But I thought I could make out a distant whisper
filtering through the tangle of the long years.
And then I heard far away
by the light of another moon
the cockerel's morning call,
the excited sing-song of children
shouting as one 'HAPPY NEW YEAR'
at the glinting windows of every bothy.
Then rolling in the ditches.
Pulling each other and horsing around.
For their goal was in sight.
The reward at the end of the road!
DONALD THE SAILOR'S HOUSE!
To be drinking his health with 'fruit wine'
out of half-filled eggcups.

And the cake! . . . (pulling off each crumb, so slowly!)
come with the Glasgow post,
from the girls in service!

Màiri NicDhòmhnaill/
Mary MacDonald

An Teine Beò

Ceanglaichean
Air an teannachadh
Le làmhan cruaidh a' chosnaidh

Tughadh
Sìoman fraoich
Ga chumail dìon

Àrd-doras
Leac bhuinn
An doras fosgailte

Chan eil mo chasan cinnteach
San dubhar

Ach tha èibhleagan dearga
Air leac an teintean
An teine beò!

Am beannachadh

Is i a' tionndadh
Laisir an teine
 na h-aodann

Blàths an teine
na sùilean

Agus tha mo chridhe
A-nis
Cinnteach.

1985

The Living Fire

Rafters
Secured
By hands toughened with toil.

A thatch roof –
Ropes of heather
Keeping it firm

A lintel
A threshhold
The open door

My steps are not hesitant
In the gloom

But there are red embers
On the hearthstone
The living fire!

The greeting

As she turns round
The glow of fire
in her face

The warmth of fire
in her eyes

And now
In my heart
No hesitation.

Crom-Lus Arrais

Bhuain mi crom-lus
An achadh arbhair
Faisg air Arras.
Fàilidh, dearg
Na bu deirge le
Todhar fala nam mìltean

'N ann an seo a thuit e?
Esan a bha mi sireadh.

Chum mi am flùr
Gu socair, maothail
An cuachadh mo làimh –
Buille chràitich mo chridhe
A' plosgartaich 's a' crith
Nam bileagan
Nis a' crìonadh.
Carson a spìon mi thu?
A dh'altram mi thu greis bheag
'S do fhreumhan fighte gu bràth
An duslach Arrais.

1985

Arras Poppy

I picked a poppy
In a cornfield
By Arras.
Delicate, crimson
Of a deeper crimson
From the blood of thousands.

Was it here he fell?
Him that I was seeking.

I held the flower
Gently, tenderly
In my cupped hand –
My heart's painful beat
Pulsing and trembling
Through the petals
Now wilting.
Why did I pluck you?
Nurse you for a short moment
When your roots are forever woven
In the dust of Arras.

Margaret Gillies Brown (1929–

Scottish Woman

I am this century's Scot,
One whose native tongue

Was borrowed from the south
By forebears – language heard
From the moment of birth
Rich with the roll of sound,
Rivered in consonants,
Vowel-round as the hills I wake to.
I speak in idioms
Strange to the southern ear,
Unaware that I do.

I am a Scot, be in no doubt,
Have no other ancestors
Save a French fisherman
Tossed on a wild shore
Before union with England.
I live through my country's history
Breathe through its rugged land
As it breathes through me.
Know its strengths and weaknesses,
Storms, dourness, its glorious
Clearness and cleanness,
Leanness of winter sheep,
Fatness of summer cattle;
Its darkness, enveloping mists and moods,
Mourning, rejoicing.

I know its people –
The tillers of the ground,
Men who weld steel
With dangerous flashes,
The carpenters loving the wood
That they work with,
The fishermen risking their lives
Against breakers:

Women renouncing, when they conceive,
A separate existence,
Teaching the children, nursing the sick,
Cleaning, cooking, sewing
Making life smoother and rounder.

Scotland –
I know its birds and trees
Wild flowers and animals,
Red deer on the hill, roe deer in the woods,
The hare with no home.
How the land lies sweetly in summer,
Triumphant in autumn, in banners of gold,
Bleakly and whitely in winter,
Vibrant in spring.

I've been child of its urban arms,
Child of its country airs,
Know its various faces,
Been nursed in its round hollows,
Nurtured at the breast of its hills
Shaped by its angry stormings.

1988

Rhoda Bulter (1930–94)

A Letter ta da Minister's Wife

Dear Mistress MacDougall, A'm writin dis nott,
Ta see if I can explain,

Dat I meant nae herm da picnic day,
Whin I said you wir gyaan wi da men.

You see Leezie o da Toogs yaal'd ower ta me,
Dat hit wid a been a fine shance,
For you ta geng hame idda trap wi her,
For shö hed ta geng right by da Manse,

Weel, I kent you wir bidin ta clear up da haa,
Wi da men an da boys wirkin dere,
An at someen wid gie you a lift hame da rod,
Whin you tidied awa aa da gear.

Sae redder as shout at da pitch o me voice,
In answerin Leezie again,
I telt peerie Hendry ta rin ower an say,
Dat you wir gyaan wi da men.

Very leekly dir someens at heard whaat he said,
Wi da crood at wis staandin dere,
An eekit bits on, sae da story wis spread,
Aboot Mistress MacDougall's affair.

Bit niver you leet whaat fok spaek aboot,
For if dey hed sense dey wid keen,
At dir nane at wid geng wi da minister's wife,
Laek mesel, I doot your day is been.

Bit if you sood slacken your stays, so ta spaek,
An geng oot some night fur a opree,
I keen eence-an-ower-weel whaat hit can be laek,
An da hidmist ta spaek wid be me.

I might even come wi you if you löt me keen,
Jöst ta see whaat hit's laek ower da fence;
Sae gödnight ta you eenoo, tak care o yoursel,
Your very dear freend, Aggie Spence.

peerie: little   *eence-an-ower-weel*: only too well
eekit: added   *eenoo*: at the moment

1980

Alison Prince (1931–

Women and Poetry 1

Often, on reading what a man has said
In poetry, I am astonished by
His confidence that no-one will ask why
He wrote down figments flitting through his head
Like bubbles in the stream of consciousness.
My female caution checks such blobs of thought
And scrutinises them – and, being caught,
They burst, as bubbles will. Their emptiness
Confirms my doubt. How rash I would have been
To show such insubstantial things! And yet,
If I could cry, Oh, look, look! – and forget
My fearfulness, their lustre might be seen.
Are we too real, my sisters? Should we share
The male ability to trust the air?

1994

Women and Poetry 2

Tread carefully, a child upon the hip,
A hand in yours. Beware the turning stone,
The deep gap between sedge-clumps, the wind-blown
Grasses, smooth as fur, where foot may slip
Down to a covered hole. Know your terrain,
Accept it, understand it, fit your skill
To leaf and bark and water, watch the hill
For cloud-change, find a shelter from the rain.
The men plan strategies, their eyes alight
With dreams. As sky and tree-branch interlace,
So they with us, like air in earth's embrace,
A match of equal opposites by night.
No groundlings they, their thoughts like comets fly –
But, lacking earth, they would not know the sky.

1994

Women and Poetry 3

Sometimes they are magnificent, the men,
Flying to God with slender sticks and string
To infiltrate the heavens on frail wing
Like Icarus, who built a mad machine
Of hope and wax-held plumes, challenged the sun
And died for his conceit. They challenge still,
In folly and magnificence. They kill
Themselves and us, rather than leave undone
The do-able. And we should aim as high,
Fire poem-bullets at the public mind,
They say. But do we want to? Will we find
Contentment in this urge to do and die?

> Ishtar, Osiris, Mary, pray for me,
> That I may not forget simply to Be.

1994

Anne Stevenson (1933–

With my Sons at Boarhills

Gulls think it is for them
that the wormy sand rises,
brooding on its few rights,
losing its war with water.

The mussel flats ooze out,
and now the barnacled, embossed
stacked rocks are pedestals for strangers,
for my own strange sons,
scraping in the pool,
imperilling their pure reflections.

Their bodies are less beautiful than
blue heaven's pleiades of herring gulls,
or gannets, or that sloop's sail
sawtoothing the sea as if its
scenery were out of date, as if its
photographs had all been taken:
two boys left naked in a sloughed off summer,
skins and articulate backbones,
fossils for scrapbook or cluttered mantelpiece.

If you look now, quickly and askance,
you can see how the camera's eye
perfected what was motion and chance before
it clicked on this day and childhood snapshot,
scarcely seen beside
hunched rugby stripes and ugly uniforms –
shy, familiar grins in a waste of faces.

My knee joints ache and crack
as I kneel to my room's fire, feeding it.
Steam wreathes from my teacup, clouding
the graduate, the lieutenant, the weddings,
the significant man of letters, the politician
smiling from his short victory . . .

Faces I washed and scolded, only
watched as my each child laboured from his own womb,
bringing forth, without me, men who must
call me mother, love or reassess me
as their barest needs dictate, return
dreaming, rarely to this saltpool in memory,
naked on a morning full of see-through jellyfish,
with the tide out and the gulls out
grazing on healed beaches,
while sea-thrift blazes by the dry path,
and the sail stops cutting the water to pieces
and heads for some named port inland.

Their voices return like footprints over the sandflats,
permanent, impermanent, salt and sensuous
as the sea is, in its frame, its myth.

1977

Lillias Scott Chisholm (Lillias Forbes) (*fl.* 1966–

Scotland

In faur-aff France I lie
This land o' fantaisie –
An' a' nicht-lang my hert
Girns for its ain countrie.

The dowie mirk hings doon,
But still I hear an' see
The birlin' o' yon burn
The munelicht on the lea! –

The yin like luve's ain lamp
Tae licht me ower the sea,
The tither like a tide
Wad win the hert o' me!

faur-aff: far-off   *mirk*: darkness
girns: complains painfully   *birlin'*: whirling
dowie: dreary   *tither*: other

1966

La Grande Jatte

I stop – my eye lingering over
'La Grande Jatte'
Drawn some way into Seurat's heat-crazed
Sunday afternoon parade . . .
My interest, however, not totally engaged:

But you, my friend, you with your penchant
For Proust, for La Belle Epoque,
For bosoms panting under camellias,
Sad histories of love . . . You, I suspect,
More readily seduced into the scene,
See yourself slotted into this promenade,
Nostalgia wafting over you like some sickness
For this spent fin de siècle your generation lost.

Heat hangs about this canvas,
Suspended from the crowns of trees,
Filters by way of languorous laden boughs,
Oppresses parasols, oozes unseen down pale veiled brows
Of inflexible, corseted women:
Their faceless escorts
Easing a plump finger round a sweaty neck:
While you, with evident collusion
Wish yourself fixed amidst these violet daubs.

On reflection would you really
Enjoy these starched outings?
The whalebone biting at your ribs
The jibe from that cheap coquette lolling nearby
Assailing your ear out of the seeming afternoon calm:
Your husband stretched prostrate on the bank
In his dreams considering your next paltry allowance
His hand, even in sleep, fast round the taut purse-strings.

1998

Ellie McDonald (1937–

Flying Lessons

Back an forrit atween the turrets o the Central Library
a wheen o halliket herring gulls gae soopan an skreichan
wi a din like tae wauk the deid. Their littluns, teeteran
alang the ledges, watch fair bumbazed, as grown-ups
jouk an weave an tummle catmaw through the air.
Tak tent, tak tent, nae second chancies here,
nae canny rocks tae divie aff, nae seaweed slides
tae safety. Ye'll only need tae hyter aince
an doun ye'll blatter on the tap o Rabbie's heid.
But gin ye think life's easier for me
tak a bit keek owre. That's me, joukan atween thae
double deck buses, wishan tae hell I had wings.

forrit: forward; *atween*: between;
wheen: several; *halliket*: wild and
noisy; *soopan*: sweeping; *skreichan*:
screeching; *wauk*: wake; *bumbazed*:
confused; *jouk*: dodge; *tummle
catmaw*: somersault; *tak tent*: take
care; *hyter*: stumble; *blatter*: clatter;
keek: glance

1991

On Not Writing Poetry

This is yer Muse talkin.
Ye're on yer final warnin.
Nae mair sclatchin i the kitchen,
nae mair hingin out the washin,
nae mair stour soukin.
This is yer Muse talkin
fae the wyste paper basket.

I kent it wis a bad idea
makin weemin poets.

sclatchin: messing about	*wyste*: waste;
stour soukin: sweeping up (hoovering);	*kent*: knew

2000

Tessa Ransford (1938–

The Poet's Daughters

The poet has brought her daughters
to the Commonwealth Literature Conference
and they have brought their knitting.

The knitting is pink and large:
soft balls of wool skewered by needles
lodge casually on a velvet chair
behind the dignitaries.

Bright as Jane Austen's heroines
these young girls miss nothing
behind their chattering needles:

speeches, introductions,
the huffs behind the puff,
poets whose standing
is not on their dignity,
whose words are their own fulfilment.

Eminent names here
could be shattered one day

by a slight chance recollection
of one of these girls, reminiscent,
looking up as she does
from her knitting.

The guillotine rises, falls.

1988

In the Royal Botanic Garden

After the sculptures have been removed to the New Scottish
Gallery of Modern Art in John Watson's School, 1985

'That was Henry Moore's *Reclining Woman*' –
    He pointed out a shape of yellowed grass
    where the large recumbent stone
    had welcomed clamb'ring children,
    tentative caresses.
'And there stood Epstein's *Christ*
    Christian soldier-like
    sentinel of the city
    watchman who never slept.'

I looked toward the trees beside the path
where first I saw that figure,
the city spread before him;
and always, looking up,
I'd know a stab of stern respect:
he could have bowed down
to have the kingdoms of this world.

'Once a girl rose from the lily pond –
    a nymph with head inclined,

as all below her and around
diverse fishes glinted.'

These figures now have been transplanted,
plucked as no gardener would do,
no soil taken with them,
no attentive placement
to placate their genius.

We feel their absent presence
where once we used to meet them,
sense the exile they must know
in having left their Eden,
and the loss we find
in this unpeopled garden.

1994

Blake's Wife

My love walked in a wild domain
I followed him as best I could
beyond the boundaries of the brain
half credible, half understood.
He hardly slept, strange music played
he wrote, dreamed, painted.

In love I pitied, helped him work
on copper plates, the ink and fire.
We cooled it down in printed books
of prophecy or soul's desire.
'The lark an angel on the wing'
purest line engraving.

His *spectre* visited for days
and silent brooded on the house.
I waited, made his soup, his clothes
until he found a form in chaos.
I gathered fragments he had scattered:
Job, Dante, Milton uttered.

I rocked no babies at the breast:
this child I had was child enough.
Like Mary I was chosen, blessed
to bear this spirit through his life.
'Jerusalem in every man'
this grain of sand in Albion.

My love walked in a wild domain
I followed him as best I could
beyond the boundaries of the brain
half credible, half understood.
We turned our trials into art
hammered the work upon the heart.

1998

Jenni Daiches (1941–

Reading by a Window

My finger catches the edge of a page,
and through the glass half-grown boys
play shinty, calling like crows, spinning
the ball across the grass. The paper
flutters the peaceful print. I am greedy

for words, cram and taste them, loose
them, reckless, into the bloodstream. A boy
pivots on his heel, an arm wide
as a wing. The water behind his head
blends cloud and supple islands.

Gulls balance above the boys'
swooping awkwardness. History
wheels. With my book open in my hands
the glass reveals a rehearsal of the past,
of boys shouting and turning, a boat
braced on the loch. For boys have run
on this shore since stories began, and wind
has driven the sails of the herring hunters.

The page settles, now cradling the tranquil
print. But the words are restive, shake
the window, call like boys or crows.
Spindles of smoke roll on the shore,
blurring the fire and the salt-bleached wood.
Under a diffident sun the boys
throw their bodies on the ground. The page
traps their breaking voices, suddenly
holds them hostage for the coming story.

1995

Carradale

We walked to the sea. I thought,
she has walked to the sea a thousand
times. Over the fence,
among the fat lambs,

through dark rhododendrons,
down the rough path bound
with broom and perfect thistles.
My hand disregarded.

The curved shore accepted
the restless water. I thought,
she has seen the almost still
ripple a thousand times.

And Ailsa Craig, far out,
afloat, a cone of mirror
glass, misting over
as if eyes were warm breath.

The beaded rim of sea
fretted at our feet. I said,
the tide is on the ebb,
but she knew better than I

the way the earth turns.
She said, I cannot join
the fishing as I used to do.
And we walked back, along

the pitted path, over
the fence, and she broke off
the last ragged petal
of rhododendron as we went.

1995
'She' is Naomi Mitchison.

Jenny Robertson (1942–

Black Houses, Ardnamurchan

Displaced from green glens
by the greed of their landlords,
they lived here beside
a seascape of islands,
burrowing close to bog and rock
in a huddle of houses
where women tended hearth, cradle, deathbed,
bore peats, boulders, bairns, buckets of water.
Men laid well-set lintels, fashioned space
for fire, for hinges; wrestled with rock,

turned windswept ground into lazybed:
their speech, their resourcefulness despised by their
   landlords
whose calculated rapacity swept them still further
in shiploads.
No funerals here for them, no names in the kirkyard.
Only the stones they once fitted together
stand empty and roofless,
a lament without language,
harsh as the cry of seagull and raven.

1989

Old Communist

His life has shrunk to a single room
among tall birches in a housing block.
His daughter, grand-daughter share their home,

divide their living-space to let him have his own
filled with the mindings of an ordered life
when men led women in bed and dance.
He went to war in Leningrad, Murmansk.
A year he hid in gloom
of forests; hands and well-drilled wits tracked tanks;
eighteen, then, prepared to die.
The leader, Lenin, broods above his bed.
This is no Peter to forswear or run away
though cock-crow heralds an uncertain day
and President, media, the young betray
his iron dream. Alert amidst the loss
his blue eyes laugh as with his guests
he downs a bottle, glass by glass.
A photograph? He smiles, combs back the hair
waving banner-bright about his head.

Among snores and slow talk on an endless train
with paper he has cut for cloths I spread
my table – with his salt eat fragrant bread.

1994

Sally Evans (1942–

Looking for Scotland

The rolling field
waved, brown over the bright
hedges. Her colander
burned with the fruit,

gooseberries, a few red,
to give a green jam
mixed with elderflower.
Brunton Turret
was not far away.
The white and brimming miles
of Roman Wall,
the North Tyne river.
How far away?
A mere ten years,
yet in those ten
how many muses
came and died?
Putting sugar to fruit
she still walks strong,
though her friends perished
and her friends' loves have gone.
She left the slopes
of black-ripe legend
for the feared country
it barred out.
Her friends' muses perished,
year upon year of jam
scattered with elder florets
were consumed like rhyme,
yet the memory of it
fell like fruit in time,
like bush and hedgerow fruit
she rolled, rich as the past,
rich as what perishes
into the bladed field
and does not come again,
no, does not come again

> until the earth is worked
> and stores of song may spring.

1996

Alison Fell (1944–

Border Raids
(for my grandmother)

Fierce pins plough her hair
You can tell by the angry drag
of the net
that once she was beautiful,
envied and glad of it
The nightingale of the county,
electrifying the village halls

She told me she wore winged hats
tall as gladioli,
and the hanging moon sang with her,
and how they clapped and horded
at her doors

When she went,
she went like the old bunch, cursing,
blue as smoke,
you could almost smell the burning
(Oh, they were a wild lot, the Johnstones,
border raiders,
horse stealers setting the Kirk alight
and all their enemies inside)
With her heart tattered

as a tyre on the road
she begged for morphine
and to be done with it,
to be gone among the gliding dead

She glints now in the gooseberry bushes,
her broom hisses out at low-dashing cats
In the night she slaps up her window
and hurls hairbrushes

1984

Women in the Cold War

Outside, time and famous dates passed –
Korea Suez Cuba Algeria all cannoned by
casually as a slap on the back.
In the butcher's and the grocer's,
not a word of them. No, only talk of
the sun, snow, seasons;
stillbirths, new banns posted;
the harvest, the Gala,
the Foot and Mouth which closed farm roads,
the Compensation.
As for violence, we had our own –
a thousand cattle burned in pits
a labourer, demented, raped a child
fine swimmers drowned in the loch's depths.
And most Saturdays some girl's wedding
brought the women clattering
down the High Street – they'd bang
on doors along the way and put up the cry,
then hang back respectfully and squint

at the hired cars, the ceremonial clothes.
My mother, her mother's mother
were brides like these,
country brides teetering up
the gravel-chipped path to the Kirk,
shielding their new shoes from scrapes.
By the sandstone wall, photos were posed,
against a bleak swell of lowland hills;
the photos show puckered faces
and a wind which whips the stiff bouquets.
The dances came and went, and fashions;
my girlfriends and I – in tight skirts
(or tiered), beads which popped
and hooped net petticoats –
crushed into cars and choked
on our own close scent, and smoke, and compliments.
But soon they sobered and they planned –
knitted cardigans all summer, by January
scanned the catalogues for cottons,
drab (for work), dressy (for holidays).
I saw them smooth
and full-blown dreaming of marriage
when I was still pockmarked with envy
and a thousand wants. I became crazy:
'I'll be an artist' I said
and bristled for the skirmish; quite slowly
their eyes scaled and their good sense
bunched against me.
'That's no' for the likes o' us.'
Elizabeth, Elaine, Rhoda of the long legs,
all matrons, mothering, hurrying
their men to work at 7am.
Now hunched round prams,
what landmarks of content do they stake out

as the village circles?
As tractors streak the fields with lime
and all the old women, hushed,
move to the funeral to see the flowers.

1984

Haiku, Moniack Mhor

1

Scottish morning: grey
glue of the porridge-pot
my grandmother left soaking

2

After years of exile
you forget how the hill sheep
run from the train

3

Perthshire summer: in the railway
siding, snowploughs
rust among the lupins

4

Aperitifs on the terrace?
This house
needs a windbreak

1997

Anna Crowe (1945–

The Marriage-Lintels

Along the garden-backs' high sandstone walls,
A carved slab, now and then – linked hearts, initials,
Year in spiky, eighteenth-century numbers –
Straddles a blind doorway. Each one remembers
Small hopeful fires that blazed like candles
Set in a window where love waits and calls.

Those lovers' eyes have closed, candles blown-out,
But where they lived, life goes on taking root.
Hanging from stopped-up doorways, flowers with bells;
And currant's pungent, vanished tom-cat-smells;
And common fumitory, *smoke-of-the-earth*,
Kindling thin yellow flames as on a hearth.

All but one wall, where the coal-tit's note falls
And still falls as last May she watched warm holes
Fill with mortar while, on the ground, all pulled
Apart, the makings of her small fire cooled.

1997

One Moment's Mirror
Translated from Capitale de la Douleur *by Paul Eluard*

It scatters the daylight,
It shows us how thin are the trappings of appearance,
It removes any chance of letting ourselves be distracted.
It is hard like stone,

Like a stone of no particular shape,
The stone of movement and sight,
And its brightness is such that it causes all defences, all
masks, to buckle.
That which the hand took scorns even to take the hand's
shape,
That which once was understood no longer exists,
The bird has melted into the wind,
The sky into its truth,
Ourselves into our own reality.

1997

Joy Pitman (1945–

Ariadne to Theseus

The scarlet cord snakes through my hands
Uncoils the labyrinth
Where groping down the blinded tunnels
Your numb face scents the darkness.

I wait here at the threshold
Remembering the welcome stranger
Who set his key to ingrown locks
And opened for this weary priestess
The unexpected sanctuary above the maze
Where steady candles burn.

Only the monster at the heart
Reveals the dark core of the flame
Enables the rewinding journey,

So I endure your absence
Down the corridors of pain
And spin love's blood thread to its limit.

1993

Sìne M. Cooper/Jean M. Cooper (1946–

Na Cuimhnich, Na Guil

Chaidh sinn gu sunndach
Di-Dòmhnaich àlainn, briagha.
Bha am ministear an sin
ri moladh is ùrnaigh,
mar bha e riamh.
Taing Dhuts' a Dhè
airson siud is seo,
is rud eile.
Dhùisg e cuimhne annainn.
Theich smuaintean aosta
as àiteachan falaich
far an robh sinn air an cur
gu tàmh.
Dh'èirich iad suas
air sgiathan ùrnaigh.
Chuimhnichear am bròn,
chuimhnichear an cràdh,
's cho searbh am blas
nuair chaidh dòchas air chall.
Fhir urramaich,
chan urrainn dut faicinn

slighe na h-inntinn,
no brìgh an smuain a leughadh,
ged a thog thu i
le do bhriathran.
B'e sinne bha gòrach
bhith caoineadh san eaglais
madainn cho àlainn, briagha.
B' fheàrr dhuinn
èisteachd
ris an t-searmon.

1979/80

No Memories, No Tears

We went in good cheer
on a beautiful bright Sunday.
The minister was there
at praise and prayer,
as always.
Thank You, Lord,
for this and that
and the next thing.
He stirred up a memory within us.
Age-old thoughts fled
out of hiding places
where we had laid them
to rest.
Up they rose
on wings of prayer.
A memory of sorrow returned,
a memory of pain,
and the bitter taste

of hope lost.
Reverend,
you cannot see
the path of the mind,
or read the core of the thought,
even though you conjured it up
with your words.
How foolish of us
to mourn in church
on such a beautiful bright morning.
Better
that we listen
to the sermon.

Val Warner (1946–

Pie in the Sky

Ours, in another world of certainties . . .
Their 'script of joy', seeing them through this soil
that yields paper where it's written how
grass withereth, could yet have been our food
for thought, our staff of life to lean on? So
the bible would have still survived, well-thumbed,
intact. A one-time source of daily bread,
it serves here for a book end, propping light
verse, thrillers, 'treasures upon earth, where moth
and rust doth corrupt'. And silver-fish prey
on hosts of wafery words of God . . . changed
into lithe bristle-tails, and silver-scaled
like Victorian mock illumined script.
So thirty silver pieces, many times

over, flash, fade away on hallowed ground.
Transcended, through feeding the multitude
taking and eating as programmed by genes,
the word's made flesh and dwells among us, hosts
of skittering, flittering silver-fish.
Through starchy texts, these insects seize the day,
gutting our promise of pie in the sky.

1986

Letters

This mild night like June, you would linger on
the road, falling away toward the Tay,
wide like a bay and branchy between clouds.
I drop letters in the walled postbox, turn
– one is a paper boat, tossed on the stream.
Beyond the lights' broken necklace cliché,
Errol across the Tay, years fall away
– London, Dover: *je ne regrette rien?*—
from heady springs, North Oxford gardens, nine-
teen's . . . flowering cherry. Almond? 'The breath
of the night-wind' was bitter sweet. This white
spring, only the Post Office on the blink
– subject to Murphy's Law, like life? – held up
a letter. One of the ones that get away,
it drifted round the Borders, picking up
out of line postmarks in its own sweet way.
Like net curtains, the snow was blowing in
the wind . . . to lie like spring's winding sheet. To
'shutt up the storye' of the winter warmth,
I'd long laid by his other letters when
it showed up, weeks on. This mild night might be
July, the potatoes flowering, pale.

1986

Veronica Forrest-Thomson (1947–75)

The Hyphen
For the centenary of Girton College

i hyphen (Gk. together, in one)
a short dash or line used to connect
two words together as a compound
1869-
1969
to connect Chapel Wing and Library.
But also: to divide
for etymological or other purpose.
A gap in stone makes actual
the paradox of a centenary.
'It was a hyphen connecting different races.'
and to the library
'a bridge for migrations'.
In search of an etymology
                         for compound lives,
this architecture,
               an exercise in paleography
(Victorian Gothic)
                  asserts the same intention.
Portraits busts and books
                    the 'context in which we occur'
that teaches us our meaning,
                  ignore the lacunae
of a century
          in their state-
ment of our need to hyphenate.

                                 1990

Sonnet

My love, if I write a song for you
To that extent you are gone
For, as everyone says, and I know it's true:
We are all always alone.

Never so separate trying to be two
And the busy old fool is right.
To try and finger myself from you
Distinguishes day from night.

If I say 'I love you' we can't but laugh
Since irony knows what we'll say.
If I try to free myself by my craft
You vary as night from day.

So, accept the wish for the deed my dear.
Words were made to prevent us near.

1990

I have a little hour-glass

I have a little hour-glass
Nothing will it give
But the trickling sound of
Water through a sieve.

All the bright neuroses
Sparkle as they go
Depression and obsession
Back and forth they flow.

Mingled at the bottom
One and one make two
Waiting the reverse, dear,
Quite like me and you.

1990

I have a little nut-tree

I have a little nut-tree
Nothing will it bear
But a silver anguish
And a golden tear.

Now in return for the kiss
You gave to me
I hand you the fruit of
My little nut-tree.

1990

Liz Lochhead (1947–

What The Pool Said, On Midsummer's Day

I've led you by my garrulous banks, babbling
on and on till – drunk on air
and sure it's only water talking –
you come at last to my silence.
Listen, I'm dark
and still and deep enough.
Even this hottest gonging sun
on this longest day

can't white me out.
What are you waiting for?
I lie here, inviting, winking you in.

The woman was easy.
Like to like, I called her, she came.
In no time I had her
out of herself, slipping on my water-stockings,
leaning into, being cupped and clasped
in my green glass bra.
But it's you I want, and you know it, man.
I watch you, stripped, knee-deep
in my shallows, telling yourself
that what makes you gasp
and balls your gut
is not my coldness but your own fear.

– Your reasonable fear,
what's true in me admits it.
(Though deeper, oh
older than any reason.)
Yes, I could
drown you, you
could foul my depths, it's not
unheard of. What's fish
in me could make flesh of you,
my wet weeds against your thigh, it
could turn nasty.
I could have you
gulping fistfuls fighting yourself
back from me.

I get darker and darker, suck harder.
On-the-brink man, you

wish I'd flash and dazzle again.
You'd make a fetish of zazzing dragonflies?
You want I should zip myself up
with the kingfisher's flightpath, be beautiful?
I say no tricks. I say just trust,
I'll soak through your skin and
slake your thirst.

I watch. You clench,
clench and come into me.

1984

Dreaming Frankenstein

for Lys Hansen, Jacki Parry and June Redfern

She said she
woke up with him in
her head, in her bed.
Her mother-tongue clung to her mouth's roof
in terror, dumbing her, and he came with a name
that was none of her making.

No maidservant ever
in her narrow attic, combing
out her hair in the midnight mirror
on Hallowe'en (having eaten
that egg with its yolk hollowed out
then filled with salt)
– oh never one had such success as this
she had not courted.
The amazed flesh of her

neck and shoulders nettled
at his apparition.

Later, stark staring awake to everything
(the room, the dark parquet, the white high Alps beyond)
all normal in the moonlight
and him gone, save a ton-weight sensation,
the marks fading visibly where
his buttons had bit into her and
the rough serge of his suiting had chafed her sex,
she knew – oh that was not how –
but he'd entered her utterly.

This was the penetration
of seven swallowed apple pips.
Or else he'd slipped like a silver dagger
between her ribs and healed her up secretly
again. Anyway
he was inside her
and getting him out again
would be agony fit to quarter her,
unstitching everything.

Eyes on those high peaks
in the reasonable sun of the morning,
she dressed in damped muslin
and sat down to quill and ink
and icy paper.

1984

Poem For My Sister

My little sister likes to try my shoes,
to strut in them,
admire her spindle-thin twelve-year-old legs
in this season's styles.
She says they fit her perfectly,
but wobbles
on their high heels, they're
hard to balance.

I like to watch my little sister
playing hopscotch, admire the neat hops-and-skips of her,
their quick peck,
never-missing their mark, not
over-stepping the line.
She is competent at peever.

I try to warn my little sister
about unsuitable shoes,
point out my own distorted feet, the calluses,
odd patches of hard skin.
I should not like to see her
in my shoes.
I wish she would stay
sure footed,
              sensibly shod.

1981

Mirror's Song

for Sally Potter

Smash me looking-glass glass
coffin, the one
that keeps your best black self on ice.
Smash me, she'll smash back –
without you she can't lift a finger.
Smash me she'll whirl out like Kali,
trashing the alligator mantrap handbags
with her righteous karate.
The ashcan for the stubbed lipsticks
and the lipsticked butts,
the wet lettuce of fivers.
She'll spill the Kleenex blossoms,
the tissues of lies, the matted
nests of hair from the brushes'
hedgehog spikes, she'll junk
the dead mice and the tampons
the twinking single eyes
of winkled out diamante, the hatpins
the whalebone and lycra,
the appleblossom and the underwires,
the chafing iron that kept them maiden,
the Valium and initialled hankies,
the lovepulps and the Librium,
the permanents and panstick and
Coty and Tangee Indelible,
Thalidomide and junk jewellery.

Smash me for your daughters and dead
mothers, for the widowed
spinsters of the first and every war
let her

rip up the appointment cards for the
terrible clinics,
the Greenham summonses, that date
they've handed us. Let her rip.
She'll crumple all the
tracts and the adverts, shred
all the wedding dresses, snap
all the spike-heel icicles
in the cave she will claw out of –
a woman giving birth to herself.

1984

Almost-Christmas at the Writers' House

Morgan, master of the Instamatic Poem,
has flung open the glass door
– three storeys up –
of this high guest suite, and,
his own camera cocked and ready,
flashgun primed,
is muttering 'Mag-ritte, Mag-grrritte'
with a mock-burr and much glee.
About to freeze-frame the scene before him.

Untouched by even a spring of birdclaw,
perfect behind wrought-iron battlements,
twenty or thirty feet of
snowy rooftop
sports a chair and round terrazzo-table
tipsily iced with an inches-deep drift.
Directly opposite
behind another rooftop door

which mirrors this,
lit up by slicing beams of anglepoise
but quite, quite empty this late at night
is the beautiful Bauhaus calm
of the office of the director of the
Literarisches Colloquium.

Behind Morgan,
Withers, Mulrine, McNaughtan, Lochhead,
well-clad, scarved and booted
stamp and laugh
(impatient for Gulaschsuppe and Berliner Weisse
at the restaurant by Wannsee S. Bahnhof)
then breathe, stilled
as his shutter falls, stopped
by this one moment's
crystalline unbroken vision
of the dreaming order in the
purring electric heart of the house of our hosts.

1991

Sheena Blackhall (1947–

The Dominie

The dominie thocht it an unca thing,
The Mither tongue.
Like Sabbath braws, he glorified gentility
An' hauled ma kail daily throw the rick
Dubbin' the Doric orra, coorse, ill-fared

A peer relation o' the Southern spik
Set by unsung.

The mannie's deid or, if he's nae,
By God! he should be!
Mim-moued, his cantin' quate.
Nae doot, he's since jeloused,
It's deeds that mak the man – nae wards
A thochtie late.

dominie: teacher; *unca*: uncouth;
kail: cabbage; *orra*: worthless; *coorse*:
coarse; *ill-fared*: ugly; *peer*: poor;

spik: speech; *mim-moued*: prim;
quate: quiet; *jeloused*: surmised;
a thochtie late: a bit late

1984

Ophelia

Watter ay jines, leaves nae untidy seam.
A salmon loup's bit a haun's clap,
The neives knit ticht thegither,
Haudin sic thochts! Derk, as Excalibur.

Cast in a random steen,
A muckle, gapin wound, instantly healin.
So saw Ophelia, as she slipped her sorra doon,
Her raivelt wits washed clean awa,
As clear's the meen,
A mirror, saftly sweemin.

jines: joins; *loup*: leap; *bit*: only;
neives: fists; *ticht*: tight; *steen*: stone;

sorra: sorrow; *raivelt*: ravelled;
meen: moon

1986

Persephone

Mother, the life you value's
A skeleton hung with bunting.
A saxophone brash
Blares out *Duty! Duty! Duty!*
Stuck on its one high note.
Mother, your world is trash!

Why can't you let me be?
Dreams are mushrooming
Down in my charcoal chamber,
Under my muffled skies.
Mother, I like my colourful life,
Away from your icicle eyes.
With my Dark Lord
Down in the moist, dank
Alchemy of Earth,
I am becoming whole.
At last I am forming a soul.

Your thoughts are thistles
Rending the tender tissue
Of dream-time's thin cocoon.
They are spawning serpents
Of censure –
I'll stab them, like a stuck Laocoön.

The life you'd fashion for me is
A fetter, a shackle, a sham
A gilded Wiccaman;
Cage of rage, of pain.

I am going to break with tradition, Mother,
I am going to snap your chain.

2000

Christine De Luca (1947–

Wast wi da Valkyries

Dark burn ta voe, a rinkel
bi Nederdale, trist slow slockit
in a sea-baaled ayre. At da beach
o Dale, noosts gaan at Foula, turn
vod een ta her shaalds. Fae Muness
shö's held in an artist's haand:
Valhalla, veiled paradise, built
lik a saga ta swall ta her heichts
wi every seein, every tellin. Winjanes
means whit hit's aye meant:
headland fur pasture. Ponies
startle dere, tak ta da hill.
Der manes lift lik a dizzen Valkyries
fleein da battle. Laand an sea
is still a skirmish. Unawaar,
selkies rowl i da laebrack,
bask safely on Sel Ayre.
An kittiwakes cruise: effortless
rollerbladers o da banks.
Da erne at eence ruled dem
is lang gien fae his stack.
Every sea bicht riven
fae Dale ta Deep Dale

has jaws risped wi yackles.
Time is mizzered here
bi da sea's favours: a tirse
o takkin, grindin,
an endless beachin; but fur wis,
travaillers o da wastern aedge,
hit's a time ta tak, ta pick owre
gaets wir taen, or no taen,
on dis wir langest vaege.

wast: west; *da*: *the*; *Valkyries*: Norse goddesses who conducted the slain from the battlefield to Valhalla; *ta*: to; *rinkel*: tinkling noise; *bi*: past, by; *trist*: thirst; *slockit*: slaked; *baaled*: thrown; *noosts*: beach hollows to shelter boats; *gaan*: gaze; *vod*: empty, unoccupied; *een*: eyes; *shaalds*: shallows (fishing grounds); *shö*: she; *whit*: what; *hit*: it; *dere*: there; *der*: their; *dizzen*: dozen;

selkies, *sels*: seals; *rowl*: roll; *i*: in; *laebrack*: surf; *banks*: sea cliffs; *erne*: sea eagle; *eence*: once; *dem*: them; *gien*: gone; *bicht*: bite; *riven*: torn; *aedged*: edged; *risped*: from noun risp, a rasp or file; *yackles*: molars; *mizzered*: measured; *tirse*: an agitation, temper; *takkin*: taking; *wis*: us; *travaillers*: walkers; *owre*: over; *gaets*: paths; *wir*: we have, our; *taen*: taken; *dis*: this; *vaege*: journey

1995

Catrìona NicGumaraid/
Catriona Montgomery (1947–

Howff

Nan cròileagan aig ceann a' bhàr,
làmh thar làimh a' togail phinnt,
an godail air tighinn gu dralastachd
'O, dùin do bheul, Iain Mhòir –
cuimhnich, tha boireannach sa chuideachd sa.'
Balgam cabhagach de lionn
's thionndaidh an còmhradh gu iasgach chudaigean.

Nan cròileagan an Dùn Dèagh,
tom taobh tuim sa chladh cruinn,
tha na mairbh fo ghiuthaisean ribeagach,
ach fad' air falbh air an taobh a-muigh
tha saighdear bochd air adhlacadh
far nach dèan e air a' chuideachd cron,
oir bhàsaich e le cholera!

1976

Howff

Huddled together at one end of the bar,
hand after hand lifting a pint,
their banter now smutty.
'Och shut it, Big Johnnie –
there's a lady in the company, mind.'
A quick swallow of beer
and the talk moves on to cuddies.

Huddled together in Dundee,
mound by mound, around the cemetery,
the dead lie under ragged conifers
but away over beyond the wall
there's a poor soldier buried
where he can't harm the company,
because he died of cholera!

An Taigh Beag

An seo mar bu dual dhuinn,
taigh beag air na creagan,
ged as e panaichean plastaig bòidheach

tha 'n àite nam pigeachan 's nan sligean;
Monadh Ròdhag air ar cùlaibh,
far an iomadh uair a leighiseadh
greadanadh mo spioraid;
taighean Chornal is ceò ast'
geal, sìos mu mo choinneamh,
ach tha 'm beagan chloinne a th' unnta
gun ach Beurla ac' ga bruidhinn,
is cho fior bheag dhith dha-rìribh
aig aon dhen dubh-sheanair;
'n ann a' greimeachadh ler meòirean
tha sinn air creagan tìm
sa cheart mhionaid?

Ach stad, cò tha seo 's e gluasad
suas chun na creige?
Dòmhnall Peigi le chù ann
's e tighinn air cèilidh
an-diugh oirnn.
Shin thu, sgioblaich an fhàrdaich,
cur fàd air an teine –
san taigh seo co-dhiù
bidh ar còmhradh mar bu mhinig.

1991

Playing at Houses

Here as we always were,
a wee house on the rocks,
although smart plastic pans
have replaced clay jars and shells;
Rodhag Hill rises behind us,
where many a time my broken spirit

found healing;
the houses of Cornal are smoking
white, down below me,
but the few children who live there
speak English only,
they whose great-great-grandfathers
spoke hardly a word of it;
are we clinging by our nails
to the rocks of time
at this very moment?

But wait, who's this now heading
up towards the rock?
It's Peigi's Donald with his dog
paying us a visit
today.
That's it, tidy the hearth,
put a peat on the fire –
in this house at least
we'll talk as we used to.

Cearcall Mun Ghealaich

Bliadhna mhòr na stoirme
   chunnaic mi cearcall mun ghealaich
's dh'fhalbh na h-adagan eòrna
   nan sruth sios chun a' chladaich,
is sheas sinn nar triùir ann
   (mi fhèin, mo phiuthar is m'athair)
a' faicinn obair ar làimhe
   na deann-ruith à sealladh.

Is chunnaic mi uair eile
   cearcall mun ghealaich –

aig deireadh samhraidh sgiamhach
   chaidh gaol às mo shealladh.
Bu riaslach an tìm ud
   gun tàinig leigheas an earraich,
ach thàinig le tìde
   àm grianach gum aire.

Ach a-nis, aig deireadh samhraidh,
   chì mi cearcall mun ghealaich
is tusa a' falbh bhuam
   gu baile an Sasainn,
's mo chridhe cho sgaoilte
   na raon mòr fada farsaing
gun adagan ar gaoil ann
   fon d' fhuair mi fasgadh bha abaich
– 's ma dh'fhalbhas tu
   cha till grian bhrèagha an earraich.

1994

A Circle Round the Moon

In the great year of the storm
I saw a circle round the moon
and the sheaves of barley
went streaming down to the shore,
and all three of us stood there
(myself, my sister, my father)
watching our handiwork
vanish out of view.

And another time I saw
a circle round the moon –

a glorious end of summer
when love went out of view.
Those were turbulent days
till springtime brought healing,
but slowly it came to me
the sunny days were returning.

But now, end of summer,
I see a circle round the moon
as you leave me and head for
a city in England,
and my heart is swept bare
like a vast open field,
without the sheaves of our love
where I took ripened shelter
– and if you leave
the beautiful spring sun will not return.

A' Feitheamh ris a' Phàp: a' Chàisg, 1981

An seo,
    am meadhan an t-saoghail,
    am meadhan na Cruinne,
    an tùis ann am Basilica an Naoimh Peadar,
    mi smaoineachadh air abhainn bhig an Lòin –
    ri taobh gun d' las mi iomadh falaisg.
    'A Rìgh 's a Pheadair 's a Phòil,
    an fhada an Ròimh
    bho Hiort is Ì Chaluim Chille?'*

1994

---

* Tionndadh eile air faclan Mhuireadhaich Albannaich, am bàrd, is e air
tilleadh às an Ròimh. ('Is mi 'm shuidh air cnocan nan deur, / Gun chraicinn
air meur no air bonn; / A Rìgh 's a Pheadair 's a Phòil, / Is fad an Ròimh o
Loch Long!')

Waiting for the Pope: Easter, 1981

Here,
  at the centre of the world,
  at the centre of the universe,
  as incense fills St Peter's Basilica,
  I think of the wee river of Lon –
  where many a time I set fire to the heather.
  'King of Hosts, St Peter, St Paul,
  is Rome so far
  from St Kilda and Columba's Iona?'

Editor's note: The poet Muireadhach Albannach is reputed to have composed a verse on returning from pilgrimage in Rome in the early 1200s, which translates: 'Sitting here on the hillock of tears / I've no skin left on fingers or feet; / King of Hosts and Peter and Paul, / Far is Rome from Loch Long!'

Valerie Gillies (1948–

The Negative

He's come for the pipe-band,
being just big enough
to put on his sporran.
My son is a scrap
of his own tartan:
he is all kilt, save for his brown knees
and the bloodied old scars on them.

It's his everyday kilt, but here, today,
it makes a tourist trample through the crowd:

'Move *there*, little boy.'
She fires the camera, conspires
to steal his virtue into a picture.
He flashes a dour and warring glance
that must be perfect for her.

Now that it's taken, he ought
to spring to life,
flash out a knife,
ask for her money or the negative.
Yet he must know
that will develop into something
different from the youthful Lachlan.

No,
the negative will show
a stony moor,
a twisted tree,
and all around them
the ragged map
of Scotland.

1990

Bass Rock

The rock punctuates the sealine.
Our boat circles the Bass.
Seals swim beneath us,
pop fruit-machine heads up
three at a time, outstare us.

People press towards them,
lean to starboard all at once.
We lurch below the cliffs.
On their dung-yellow rock,
gannets rest a beak-stab apart.

1995

The Night Before Battle

Seeing the wind
before the storm
the king watched Fillan's
miraculous arm
float on its own
through the silver case
till the arm-bone
clakkit into place.

Scotland's pride
at Bannockburn shown,
what mountain hides
his holy bone?
Our saint, our Fillan,
our fate transform,
seeing the wind
before the storm.

1995

Tipu and Archie

Athol of knolls and forests, of whitewater rapids,
India of woods and mountains, of wild waterfalls,
As Athol to Karnataka, as Tummel to Cauvery,
Down the mountain passes and out into the strath
Valleys of the Mysore highlands lead into Karnataka,
Snow-fed or monsoon-fed, their rivers are ready.

Tipu Sultan, the Tiger of Mysore, is India's hero,
Archie Fergusson's brow marked with his sabre-scar,
As Athol to Karnataka, as Tummel to Cauvery,
Between the two highlanders there's a similarity:
Days of fortunes made by men who risked everything,
So Tipu to Archie, well-matched adversaries.

It's all foretold on the cross-slab carved here
Where two beasts are fighting, a tiger and a hound,
As Athol to Karnataka, as Tummel to Cauvery,
Where the swimming elephant incised by the Pict
Is the herd crossing Cauvery, gun-batteries six by six,
Tooth to tooth, claw to claw, Tipu to Archie.

Tipu had a full view of the line as it passed,
Seven miles long, looking down on him from the heights:
Stronghold to stronghold, Seringapatam to Dunfallandy.
Now Archie's house on its own bend of the river
Faces a continuous conveyor-belt of sound and colour,
The endless column moving on the dual carriageway.
As Athol to Karnataka, as Tummel to Cauvery,
No Tipu, no Archie disrupts the march today.

General Archibald Fergusson of Dunfallandy was with the
East India Company from 1776 till he returned to Scotland

in 1814. He received a sabre-wound on the forehead at the storming of Seringapatam in the Anglo–Mysore war of 1799, where his adversary was the great Tipu Sultan.

1995

Margaret Elphinstone (1948–

Potato Cuts

Now girls,
You are taking impressions
And transferring them to paper
Like a mental version of
A half potato dipped in poster colour,
Your neat design gouged out – so –
By a blunt knife.

We encourage you
To make impressions
Only be sure you do it properly –
Tidy potatoes, without smudges
Or fingerprints,
Not using too much paint.
Impressions
Should be contained.
We keep no gold stars
For messy workers.

See that you give a good impression girls –
Look, do as I do,

And don't spill
Anything.

1990

Janet Paisley (1948–

Conjugate

Tensely
premenstrual and
looping the full moon
I am seriously
deranged yet
curiously
in possession of
all my faculties.

Consumed by
feeling for you
biology stands on its head.
What is instead
consummate
in this desire is
I'm seriously
dispossessed.

1996

Mayday

Six other sons, and yet
I know precisely the last pull of pain
when you came out of me,
feet first, each pressured, released,

sucking like drawn plugs
and the wet, warm slither down
the drain of life.

It was the last time we touched.

You sailed beyond me,
bearing only your name.
From your glass shell, a small fist salute,
the final white box your one flag.
All you left, breast full, blood heat, the bluish milk,
fell in the void of your leaving
and destitute, my arms raged.

Such a little life,
twenty-six hours long.
Such a sore tide,
the same in years, still rising.
Time can't heal the hollow that never held you,
your absence is as a fresh wound, widening,
the salt in it your name not said.

1996

Jenny: Weavin the Spell

Ye hae tae feel it.
It's hingin in the air.
Nae wind tae steer things up.
Nuthin movin
The animals ur quate.
The burds peep but dinnae squawk.
The gress an trees an bushes bide at peace.
Watter in the burn gaes by,

slaw slippin ower the stanes wi haurly a wrunkle.
In the seas, the watter lies
like gless that micht shatter.
Even the staurs ur staunin stull.
The wurld haudin its braith.
Waitin while sun an earth
staun at thur furthest pint.
Aw life thit needs the licht is waitin.
Watchin. Kennin thur will hae tae be
a comin back, a new beginnin,
ur the daurk wull never luft
an awthing living wull end this nicht.
Dae ye no feel it?

ur: are	*haurly*: hardly
quate: quiet	*wrunkle*: wrinkle
gress: grass	*pint*: point

2000

Morelle Smith (1949–

Sauchiehall Street

Steps along the street –
The busker playing blues
And the rain canopies –
A leather sandal, slipped over the heel,
Feet damp in the puddles.

The gallery has heavy wooden doors,
Pastel-quiet, out of the
Bargaining and bickering

Of alternating sun and rain.
The quiet of a chandelier,
The imprint of the energy
Inflicting bruises on my eyes.

In the musician's house,
She pours me coffee
In tiny, blue-splashed cups,
Talks of daffodils and dogs
And the inner vision
That completes the eye.
Life burns through her fingers
And the air around her stings
Like too much light –
So much light burns in her eyes
It may just be the shadow of her
That clambers in my throat and fingertips.

She plays piano; all my masks
And insecurities are picked clean.
Like a bone; the dog paws at my hand –
The cow-bells at the door tinsel,
Stream, remind, defy all emptiness,
Each time you close the door.

1998

Catherine Lucy Czerkawska (1950–

The Other Side of the Story

I am no pale princess out of fairy tale.
I would have my skin too thick to feel

The pea through my piled feather beds.
There is no prince charming enough
To dare my Rapunzel tower
Nor bring me a glass slipper
Nor weave me a rose encrusted bower.

But I will be malicious Morgan
Who wished fair Guinevere dead
Or Blodeuedd who was created flowers
And for her lack of faith
Became the hunting owl instead.

And I will be the wicked queen
Who cuts off her suitors' heads
One by gory one,
Who carries fatal apples
And a poisoned spindle
And dances to her death
Beneath the blazing sun.

1973

Old Man

His slippers are mutilated
For the comfort
Of his feet.
His feet are knotted
And broken in sores.
Christ knows
How his blessed feet are.

1976

Mòrag NicGumaraid/
Morag Montgomery (1950–

An-Raoir A-Rithist

An-raoir a-rithist
   leis an aon shàmhachd
's air a ghiùlan thar chuan is bheann
   leis an aon oiteag gaoithe
thàinig an aon ghuth gam ionnsaigh,
   an aon ghuth a chuala mi
nuair a bha mi nam leanabh òg
's mi buain dhearcan air a' Chreig Ghlais.
Dh'innis e dhomh, gu socair ciùin,
am briathran nach do thrèig mi,
cia mheud uair a dheocainn mil às flùran
mus tuiteadh a' ghrian don ùir.

1974

Last Night Again

Last night again
   in the same silence
carried over seas and hills
   by the same breath of wind
the same voice drifted towards me,
   the same voice I heard
as a young child
picking berries on the Grey Rock.
It told me, calmly and gently,

in words which have never left me,
how many times I'd suck the nectar out of flowers
before the sun would sink into the ground.

Muile-mhàgag

Tha muile-mhàgag na cadal air an t-sèise
is srann mòr aice.
Muile-mhàgag 's a craiceann a'
sgagadh le teas na mòine.
Craiceann crocodile.
Buidhe-liath.

I na cadal
agus buille a cridhe a' plapadh
mionaid air mhionaid.
'S iongantach gu bheil a sùilean fosgailte.
Leth fhosgailt'.
Tè dhiubh uaine 's an tèile cho soilleir
ri èibhleag dhearg.
Cho dearg nach aithnichear
dè tha na fhaileas – an èibhleag no 'n t-sùil
a' leigeil a spioraid.

Thàinig fàd mòr boireannaich 's shuidh i air
's cha chualar ach dùd mall ciùin
's chan aithnichear dè rinn am fuaim
– a' chailleach, no a' mhuile-mhàgag
a' leigeil a spioraid.

1974/5

A Toad

There's a toad sleeping on the bench
snoring loud.
A toad with its skin all a-
crackle in the heat of the peat.
Crocodile skin.
Palish yellow.

It sleeps
and its heartbeat throbs
minute by minute.
Bizarre how its eyes are open.
Half open.
One of them green and the other as bright
as a redhot coal.
So red you can't tell
which is the reflection – the coal or the eye
releasing its spirit.

A big clod of a woman came and sat on it
and the only sound was a slow soft toot
and you couldn't tell what made the sound
– the wifie, or the toad
releasing its spirit.

Anne MacLeod (1951–

Standing by Thistles

It's not the beauty of the hill
binds us on this path
by sedge and thistle, such a small path
stony, sharp; a path for
short encounters, yet we stand
and stand
breathless in the summer rain

1997

In the Kibble Palace: Sunday Morning

Old men on benches outstare tired marble
the rippling misery of one distressed
Adonis carved in mid-sigh, tortuous
among chrysanthemums. His head is bowed.
Perhaps he is allergic to chrysanthemums, wishes
to stroll the Systematic Garden
                    the Border Chronological
                                the Arboretum?
Old men know better. Huddled in damp warmth
this early Sunday morning, they have braved the wind
and found it wanting

The glass roof curves in onion splendour
green as unpicked fruit; light struggles
to diffuse through panes as thick
with mould as glass, swims greenly over foliage
preying on deep-sea lack of rays. No fish

fly here; a noisy sparrow shoals
I walk the gravel gravely
Behind me, children shout, escape into the inner swell
of palm and fern and moss, a green confusion
curdling frantic orders from the tired mother
stuck with the push-chair on the dripping stone
unable to pursue the restless feet that prowl
the quiet inner jungle

Statues are strange, the skin as smooth
the arms and legs and hair
as full and free as if each figure breathed
caught in the endless moment of our choosing
and yet the eyes are empty:
                                do not choose the eyes
the fate that tempts those eyes. Pass on to note
the curling hair, the twisting abdomen
the torso thinned implausibly, the bending knees
the veined arms straining still to grip the marble base
                        or choose the toe
pointing towards the stone, the frozen stone
the next step over frozen water: choose that early moment
the child now bent on forward movement
without forward bias, her strength still all behind
the weight, the safety all behind: and yet the child intent
on forward movement
                        Choose that moment, note how heavily
the sheltering rock is built behind the child, not moving yet
set on a course as free as lack of movement
and all her strength so much behind
your child, your own child, pale as marble
weak as water on a split palm leaf; your own child
weaker than the water, set on movement
set on a forward course beyond the palms

and all her strength behind
No due momentum
without clear support, and you intent
on forward movement, lost in outer green
stranded on rain-damp stone

The jungle lives and breathes in glass. Without
the soaring skin, without this constant heat, the leaves
would die, the statues mimic catholic cemeteries
Italian marble, winged, the frozen smile
the sepia photograph
This jungle lives:
children hide and seek within its heart
Old men stare down visitors

1999

Liz Niven (1952–

Stravaigin

Like fitprints
in peat bog,
we've left wir mark.
Even the moon cairries the stamp
o a Borders man.
Strang arms reach roon the globe
sing 'Auld Lang Syne',

The warld wears a kilt,
nane the waur forrit.
A warp an weft o trevellers.

Wha's like us?
Fit prints like?

stravaigin: wandering   *waur*: worse
fitprints: footprints   *fit*: puns on 'foot', 'fit' and 'what'
wir: our

2001

Webs not Roots
For Alastair Reid

The famous writer is leaving:
back to the States.
He's seen his homeland,
small village of childhood,
hasn't changed much.
At root, has he?

Wide-eyed yet, other shores still call,
Curiosity not dulled by sixty years of travel.
'Webs not roots,' he writes,
'Two small bags is all you need.'
Light, easy, he's off.

Left here with our filled house
of books, papers, dishes, chairs,
could we do that?
Dump it all and go?
Lodge (as he does sometimes)
in someone else's clutter?

A groaning bookcase eyes me.
The favourite rug shifts under my foot.
The cat climbs onto my lap
curled like a questionmark.

2001

Devorgilla in the Borderlands

Based in the south,
it's no wonder she was
'active in Anglo-Scots politics'.

Mother of John who ran for the throne
but stripped of insignia, toom tabard he fled.
Grandmother of Edward who was
kicked out of Annan –
'one leg booted the other was bare'.

You can't live near boundaries
without getting involved.
Losing a boot and a badge
are the least of your problems.

Not living at the heart of the matter,
skirting peripheries brings
its own perils;
Like finding your own centre.

2001

Marion Lomax (1953–

Kith

On the other side of the border
they call this *Scozia Irredenta*:
unredeemed.
                    A few coffers of coins
didn't change hands; a battle was lost
instead of won; the in-between land
stays in-between.
                    A line on a map
moved back through the years
                    down to the Tees.
England was never an only child
but has grown to think so. Stone streets dip –
rise. They're burning coal on morning fires
in dark front rooms: smoke gusts over roofs.
Gardens, late coming into flower,
brazen it out with bright aubrietia

I've followed the hills to Carter Bar
past lost peels, and moors where soaking sheep
stagger between tufts of died-back grass.
Standing in the rain, she's there – harassed,
hurt – a foster-mother, telling me
she hasn't much to offer. I'll take
my chance: I don't believe her.
                    The bends
on the border
                    won't make up their minds.
Five times

they twist me round, but I still
head north.

1996

In 1138, David I, King of the Scots, moved the Scottish border down to the Eden and the Tees so that the country was divided into two almost equal parts. At one time Northumbria stretched as far as the Firth of Forth and Cumberland was part of the Celtic kingdom of Strathclyde. For much of the eleventh century Northumbria alternated between Scotland and England and Scottish kings paid homage for Tynedale intermittently for two more centuries. The present border dates from the thirteenth century. [Lomax's note]

Gruoch Considers

Dochter tae a king, faither sin taen,
mairrit, sin weeda. Aa dinna greet.
Ma lad, Lulach, maun gang hes ain gait
an gie's ane bricht chance tae lauch again.
Nae weeda gin wife. Aa'm a steekit yett
sae bleth'rin gabs canna ca' 'Bizzem'.
It's sair ta dae – wha winna fa' whiles?
Aa'm youthfu' an maun hae a man sune
ellis ma saul sall skirl. Aa munna smuir.

MacBeathain cam yestreen. Dander lass,
ye winna swither an baith say ay.

Daith is aye ahint yon spaywife. Juist
tak wha ye wad – MacBeathain, Macbeth.

weeda: widow; *gang hes ain gait*: go
his own way; *steekit yett*: closed
gate; *bleth'rin gabs*: idle mouths;
bizzem: hussy; *skirl*: cry in pain; *aa*

munna smuir: everything can't be
smothered; *yestreen*: last night;
dander: saunter; *swither*: hesitate;
spaywife: fortuneteller

1996

Gruoch was directly descended from Kenneth III of
Scotland (murdered by Malcolm II to secure the throne for
his grandson, Duncan). She married Macbeth *c*.1032, either
when she was pregnant with her son (Lulach) by her first
partner, Gillecomgain, or soon after his birth. Lulach
succeeded to the throne in August 1057 on the death of
Macbeth (who slew Duncan and was, in turn, killed by
Duncan's son, another Malcolm). In 'Gruoch Considers',
having taken stock of her situation, she argues herself into
the second marriage with Macbeth. [Lomax's note]

Marcella Evaristi (1953–

Dogma Change

Ash Wednesday nun shouts.
Little girl thinks:
'Won't cry. Won't cry.'
The will dies, the eyes fill.
The will has turned to chalk dust
watched by the Virgin Mary
and her row of green vases.

'Thy will be done.
Dum diddley-dum.'
Already through the chalk dust
the knowledge there must be

kinder dust than these holy ashes.
Fringe thumb-budged, ash smudged.
She rubbed it off.

O her colour supplement one,
her mug-clutching, play-grouped son.
Thou shalt honour thy Father and thy Mother
by calling them Clare and Simon.
Thou shalt toil diligently
at creative writing and finger painting.
Thou shalt exercise divergent thinking
at all times.

Pill spaced
brown faced
how will you know her?

1974

Magi Gibson (1953–

Planting Crocuses with My Mother

While I dug out the holes
she tipped out the bulbs,
little brown and papery hearts
playing dead beside the granite headstone
on my father's grave.

She popped the nuggets in
her fingers stiffening with cold,
the knuckles swollen-boned and red.
Then we replaced each sod,
patted back the damp October grass
until it looked as if we'd never been.

There should be a fine show in spring,
she said. *Even better the year after*.
We stood and stared as if to visualise
the tiny yellow, white and lilac heads
stretching thin green necks
towards bright April skies.

Then again, she laughed, rubbing her hands
to make them warm. *If I go soon,
you'll have to dig the whole lot up again*.

2000

Helena Nelson (1953–

Cleaner

Mrs Philpott cleans the bathroom
cleaner than any living soul.

She scrubs the bath with a nylon brush,
steams the tiles with her steam machine,
sprays with anti-bacterial spray,
polishes with a spotless cloth

and sometimes as she cleans she sings
in a high clear voice that no-one hears
but the bathroom and its silent walls
and the mirror and the laundered towels
and the patient, gleaming toilet bowl.

If this hadn't been her special gift –
perhaps that day as she stood in the hall
unhooking her coat from the pegs to leave,
he wouldn't have noticed the gentle blush
dusting the inside curve of her arm;
he wouldn't have thought: it is like the rush
of light in the beech hedge when each hard bud,
surprised into softness, unfolds.

2001

Dilys Rose (1954–

No Name Woman

All day she feeds the drunken menfolk
On the terrace: between meals they gamble
Quarrel and groom their fighting cocks.
With one eye on her youngest child
(Grubbing in the dirt for bugs)
She stirs the rice, ladles broth
From spoon to bowl, fans back
The ubiquitous flies. Steaming pots
And hot fat spit their hiss at her.
She wears the same rag constantly
A hand-me-down print wrap, the pattern
Washed away, the hem a tatter –

Eats her dinner standing up
Then clears and lays more tables
Cradling plates to hush their clatter.
When only the rats nag for more
She sweeps the dirt floor clean.

1989

Sister Sirens

Another boat veers for the perch
Where we're tethered.
We preen our feathers,
Croon seductive duets –
The sailor is deaf to all else.
He ignores omens,
Throws sense to the wind
Sets course for the harbour
Of our twin smiles.
The moon conspires with us,
Highlights our allure.
How gorgeously we glimmer.
Our glamour takes his breath away.
If only we'd squawked a warning –
   Beauty is only a trick of the light
   Beneath our flightless wings
   We've talons to tear out your heart –
If only we'd screeched,
   Block up your ears, hide your eyes
   If need be, bind yourself to the mast.

More monster than myth, we'll pick you clean.
Later we'll toss on this rocky bed,

Unable to sleep. We'll bitch, squabble
Over whose good looks charmed him ashore.

But to ourselves curse the gods
Who blessed us with the songbird's voice,
The hawk's claw.

1989

Saint Wilgefortis, Prague

Worse than death: betrothed to an unbeliever.
Despite my father's eagerness for me to wed,
with such a man, how could I live a life
of virtue? On my knees I prayed and begged
deliverance from bondage. In bed, arms
folded across my breast, I lay awake all night.
The cock crowed. Daylight stole into my room.
(Too soon that man would do the same
unless my prayers were answered
and I was spared.) My maid arrived.
Bending to kiss me, she started back
as if I'd slapped her. Words stuck in her throat
like bones. I feared she'd choke. *What do you see?*
Have I broke out in boils, cankers, pustules, pox?
Trembling, she held up the mirror. I confess
I was surprised to see the thick black beard
upon my face but God moves in wondrous ways.
Be not downcast, I said. *It's for the best.*
Now I must dress. The rest is history.
My spouse-to-be could not countenance
the strange-afflicted virgin stood before him.
He saddled, mounted, fled and left me to my fate –

a father's wrath, a father's vengeance wreaked
upon his devout daughter: the cross, the agony
of drawn-out death. I did not wish for martyrdom
but now, above a beaded bodice of blue lace
my painted wooden face, bearded but still beautiful,
takes its place among the saints. What's more:
visitors who marvel at the chapel's baroque glories
have even, on occasion, mistaken me for Our Lord.

2000

Gerrie Fellows (1954–

In His Own Country

Under the flat cap
his head is a round bullcalf head
wax skinned

He walks the wave of the bus
his breath a drunken whistle
at his tongue's edge
A big man in a pale raincoat
sitting heavily down

A bheil Gàidhlig agad?

What's out there
are sodium lights   concrete
expressway   river
unimaginable billboards

A bheil Gàidhlig agad?

he asks again into the crowded bus

where no one speaks his language

1988

A Woman Absent from the Museum
Muses on her Life in South Dunedin

Those of us whom no one thought to photograph
are here as ghosts   to give the lie
to bread without scarceness   freedom by
honest toil   our lungs choked with the motes
of our sewing, its fibres wound around our throats
and lives: a narrative of nights
without coals to keep the grate alight
of eyes sunk into pouches of skin and sleep
of fingers bound by need to the incessant needle

No new world   No paradise
a grime-smeared house where damp clung
to the weather boards   a valley where smoke hung
all year above a clanking factory
and yet we dreamt   of wonderful simplicities:
fresh vegetables in a cottage garden
a geranium on a window sill   and everything clean
We dreamt   for dreaming's free, nothing
could stop us   of what we had been promised
of what bread without scarceness might have meant

2000

Valerie Thornton (1954–

Dark Side Of The Moon

What with the noisy boys
a mile down the loch
shouting and playing Dark Side of the Moon
of all things
on this sunny day,

that, and this black dragonfly
settled on my book,
I could neither concentrate
nor turn the page.

After I'd seen the silver wings,
black-dashed at the outer edge,
the beaded head and black-furred body
and the tear at the base of a wing,

after I'd heard Pink Floyd
and that 'He's no' goat his fucking float wet yet!'

I had to look around,
beyond the cow-churned mud
to pine green hillsides
and birch trees a tree-length away.

A bird rose up
dusty peach as a Barbary dove
but without the clap of wings.
A head, too pointed,
hid among the leaves.

The moment sharpened.

Another, wings tipped white
and barred with blue, flew up.

A third pottered briefly in a tuft
and a fourth confirmed them jays,
looping up the lochside
from bush to tree to shade,
shy and quiet and as rare
as the dark side of the moon.

1998

Kestrel, Conic Hill

Fallen to earth
and mostly spirited away,
all that remains
in the springing heather
are two barred wing tips
shocking and beautiful
linked and separated
by an elegant line
of articulate bone.

Too good to leave
I put boot to carpal
and wrench off
the soiled pinions
trusting there's no blood
no stench.

At lunchtime
with a bird's eye view
over water and green land
I lay them
among bright spirals
of baby bracken.
They rise and try
to reclaim the sky.
I trap them
below my rucksack.

In a city flat
confined to a bucket
they wait for plucking.

Each primary twangs
with a supple crack
shedding debris and raindust
and a small dry smell.

The best, this essence of kestrel,
are stored in a shoebox
in the hall cupboard
beside the cat food.

Some day I'll bind them
to leather jesses
with beads and bells
and let them drift
tethered at the open window
or flutter from my dashboard
as I swoop along
the motorway.

2000

Carol Ann Duffy (1955–

Originally

We came from our own country in a red room
which fell through the fields, our mother singing
our father's name to the turn of the wheels.
My brothers cried, one of them bawling *Home,
Home*, as the miles rushed back to the city,
the street, the house, the vacant rooms
where we didn't live any more. I stared
at the eyes of a blind toy, holding its paw.

All childhood is an emigration. Some are slow,
leaving you standing, resigned, up an avenue
where no one you know stays. Others are sudden.
Your accent wrong. Corners, which seem familiar,
leading to unimagined, pebble-dashed estates, big boys
eating worms and shouting words you don't understand.
My parents' anxiety stirred like a loose tooth
in my head. *I want our own country*, I said.

But then you forget, or don't recall, or change,
and, seeing your brother swallow a slug, feel only
a skelf of shame. I remember my tongue
shedding its skin like a snake, my voice
in the classroom sounding just like the rest. Do I only
think
I lost a river, culture, speech, sense of first space
and the right place? Now, *Where do you come from?*
strangers ask. *Originally?* And I hesitate.

1990

The Way My Mother Speaks

I say her phrases to myself
in my head
or under the shallows of my breath,
restful shapes moving.
The day and ever. The day and ever.

The train this slow evening
goes down England
browsing for the right sky,
too blue swapped for a cool grey.
For miles I have been saying
What like is it
the way I say things when I think.
Nothing is silent. Nothing is not silent.
What like is it.

Only tonight
I am happy and sad
like a child
who stood at the end of summer
and dipped a net
in a green, erotic pond. *The day
and ever. The day and ever.*
I am homesick, free, in love
with the way my mother speaks.

1990

Before You Were Mine

I'm ten years away from the corner you laugh on
with your pals, Maggie McGeeney and Jean Duff.

The three of you bend from the waist, holding
each other, or your knees, and shriek at the pavement.
Your polka-dot dress blows round your legs. Marilyn.

I'm not here yet. The thought of me doesn't occur
in the ballroom with the thousand eyes, the fizzy, movie
    tomorrows
the right walk home could bring. I knew you would dance
like that. Before you were mine, your Ma stands at the
    close
with a hiding for the late one. You reckon it's worth it.

The decade ahead of my loud, possessive yell was the best
    one, eh?
I remember my hands in those high-heeled red shoes,
    relics,
and now your ghost clatters toward me over George
    Square
till I see you, clear as scent, under the tree,
with its lights, and whose small bites on your neck,
    sweetheart?

Cha cha cha! You'd teach me the steps on the way home
    from Mass,
stamping stars from the wrong pavement. Even then
I wanted the bold girl winking in Portobello, somewhere
in Scotland, before I was born. That glamorous love lasts
where you sparkle and waltz and laugh before you were
    mine.

1993

Màiri NicGumaraid/
Mary Montgomery (1955–

Sean Bhalaist

Thiginn thugad le bratach
bho bhlàr Chùil-lodair
's le fèile an tartan an Rìgh;
thiginn thugad le eachdraidh
chaidh a h-abachadh slàn
's a reic mar dhuais do chàch;
ach b'fheàrr leam thighinn thugad
le gunna
bha uair
air rèid anns a' Phàirc.

Bheirinn cunntas air m' àrach
mar sgeul air na mhair dòigh beatha
bha Gaidhealach is Eileanach;
chuirinn blasad bhiodh fìor ann
de smuaintean is bheachdan
bhios daonnan
an inntinn nan Gaidheal.
Ach tha fiachadh le fìrinn
a thig mar cho-dhùnadh air linn;
seòrsa fiachaidh
thug dhuinn
's a thug bhuainn.

Thiginn thugad le amhran
a ghabhadh seòldair
is e fàgail eilean a chridhe;
thiginn thugad le blàths sgeul an taigh-chèilidh

's le càirdeas nas làidir' na th' ann;
ach b'fheàrr leam thighinn thugad
le seòrs' teagaimh
unnta fhèin
a dh'fhàg
a' bhochdainn
na lorg.

1982–3

Old Ballast

I could come with a banner
from the field of Culloden
and with a kilt in the King's tartan;
I could come with a history
that was harvested whole
and sold as a prize to others;
but I would rather come to you
with a gun
once used
in the Park deer raid.

I could relate my upbringing
as the tale of survival of a culture
that was Gaelic and Hebridean;
I could include a smattering, genuine enough,
of thoughts and opinions
invariably found
in the mind of a Gael.
But with truth comes an offer
that brings an age to conclusion;
a kind of offer

which gave to us
and took from us.

I could come with a song
a sailor would sing
as he leaves the isle of his heart;
I could come with a heart-warming ceilidh-house story
and with kinship more wishful than real;
but I'd rather come to you
with the kind of doubt
in themselves
that poverty
left
in its wake.

Nach Goirtichinn A-rithist

Mac mo pheathar
Aig seachd deug
Is e coiseachd ann an solas thràth na maidne
Tro chraobhan
Le duilleagan òga earraich
Leis fhèin
Na chabhaig
Air staran
Air a shlighe dhan a' chaisteal

'S anns a' ghrèin
San t-solas ùr
Reòdh an sealladh
Fo mo shùil
Is m' inntinn

Mar gu fairinn aonarachd
An ionndrainn a rinn e orm
Nuair a dh'fhalbh mi às an dachaigh
San robh mi air àite thoirt dha
'S far nach do dh'fhuirich e fada
As m' aonais

Chan fhac e mi ga fhaicinn
Measg an uaine agus an òir
Tro na deòir

1992–3

Whom I Would Not Hurt Again

My sister's boy
Now seventeen
Walking in the early morning light
Through trees
Of fresh spring leaves
By himself
Hurrying
Along a path
On his way to the castle

And in the sun
In the young light
The picture froze
Before my eye
And in my mind

As if I could feel the desolation
Of his need for me

When I left the home
Where I'd found him a place
And where he didn't stay long
Without me

He didn't see me watching
Amidst the gold and the green
Through the tears

Taigh Ùr na h-Alba

Bidh fuaim as an teant
'S an taigh ga thogail
Cìsean
Is prìsean
Is ailtireachd
Rianachadh
Riarachadh
Deòntachd
Is daingneachd
Is an taigh ga thogail
Air làrach ar n-eòlais eachdraidheil

Air na chaidh fhàgail againn dheth

O bidh fuaim as an teant
'S an taigh ga thogail
Mus fhaigh a h-uile duine steach
'S thig air cuid dhol a sheasamh
No suidhe air being
Gu faigh sinn sèithrichean ceart

Cha bhi cathraichean rìoghail ann

Bidh fuaim as an teant
'S an taigh ga thogail
Gu faigh sinn na rodain a mach
Is feadh Alb' ac' làn thuill
Ach nì sinn arm dhiubh
'S bidh iad grinn a' gabhail dhachaigh

'S lìonaidh sinn na tuill an uair sin

Bidh fuaim as an teant
'S an taigh ga thogail
Beachdan
Reachdan
Is bunaideachd
Teachd-a-steach
Teachd-a-mach
Bonn-shuidheachadh
'S bonn-stèidh
Is an taigh ga thogail
A rèir an nòis neo-eisimeilich

Air nach fhaod sinn maill a chur

Agus nuair a bhios an taigh deiseil
Bidh pàrtaidh againn
'S bidh cèilidh againn cuideachd

1997

Scotland's New House

There'll be noise from the tent
As the house gets built
Taxing

And pricing
And architecturising
Administrations
Administerings
Willingness
And wilfulness
As the house gets built
On the site of our sense of history

On what we have left of it

Oh there'll be noise from the tent
As the house gets built
Before everybody can enter
And some will have to stand
Or sit on a bench
Till proper chairs are found

There will not be thrones

There'll be noise from the tent
As the house gets built
Till we get the rats out
From their holes throughout Scotland
But we'll make an army of them all
And they'll look bonnie heading home

And then we'll fill the holes

There'll be noise from the tent
As the house gets built
Disputes
Statutes
Firm foundations

Income
Outcome
Institution
And constitution
As the house gets built
To an independent design

Which we can delay no longer

And when the house is ready
We'll have a party
And we'll have a ceilidh too.

Baile Ailein

Leam thu
Baile beag mo chiad cheum sgoile
Mo chiad chearcall charaidean
'S mo chiad dhealbh
Mo chiad phàirtidh
'S mo chiad dhannsa
Mo chiad turas oidhche bhom dhachaigh
'S mo chiad chianalas ag iarraidh às

Leam thu
Baile fada clachach cam
Le do thurachan-tharachan sluaigh
'S do chòmhlain threubhan annasach
De dhaoine a bhuineas
Is daoine nach buin
Is daoine nach gabhadh gnothaich
Ri cuid seach cuid

Leam thu
Le do sheann bhòidhchead
'S do sheann luidearachd
Do ghàrraidhean cloiche
'S do thobhtaichean thruagh
'S eadar làraich a sia deug
'S a còig deug thar fhichead
Choinnicheadh mo sheanmhair 's mo sheanair
A phòsadh

Leam thu
Le do chnocan beaga creagach
'S do shaoghal fheansaichean is gheataichean
Is bhodaich bheaga chritheanach
Nach robh mar sin ach chun an-dè
Is tiùrran chloinne ag èigheachd 's a' ruith
Mu chuairt
Far nach robh iadsan a bharrachd
Chun an-dè
Is dè a-rèist an diofar?

'S ged a shaoil mi chun an-dè
Gun taghainn nad aghaidh
Seo sinn fhathast
A' conaltradh.

2001

Balallan

You are mine
Little village of my first step at school
My first circle of friends

My first picture
My first party
and my first dance
My first night-trip away from home
and my first longing to leave

Mine
Long stony ramshackle village
with your topsy-turvy population
and your bizarre tribal groupings
of people who belong
and people who don't
and people who'll have nothing to do
with either

Mine
With your old beauty
And your old bedraggledness
Your stone dykes
And your sad ruins
And between plot sixteen
And thirty-five
My grandfather and my grandmother met
To wed

Mine
With your small rocky hills
And your world of fences and gates
And of small shaky bodachs
Who until yesterday weren't like this
And hordes of children shouting and running about
Where they weren't either
Until yesterday –
And so what does it matter?

And although until yesterday I thought
I would choose against you
Here we are still
Communicating.

Elizabeth Burns (1957–

Valda's Poem/Sleevenotes

Sleevenotes to Hugh MacDiarmid's record *Whaur Extremes Meet*: 'Recorded at Brownbank, the home of Valda and Chris Grieve, near Biggar in the Lanarkshire hills on two sultry days in June 1978. Chris, in his chair by the window, talking with his friend, the poet Norman MacCaig, a wee dram in every glass. Valda in swimsuit, working in the garden, or keeping the soft-coated Wheaten and Border Terrier quiet for the recording.'

June sun presses on my back as I bend
sweat gathers at my neck and under my arms
I am naked as I can be in my bathing costume

I step out onto the flowerbeds
making light footprints with my bare feet
Spray trails from the watering-can
falls in dark circles round the plants

I want to lie out on the parched grass
and let the sun's hands touch me everywhere
let them finger the frail flesh of my breasts
rub gold into the crease and wrinkle of my stomach

Elizabeth Burns (1957–

At the open window edged with ivy
they sit, two old men in their shirt-sleeves
On the table between them a bottle of whisky
the two fat volumes of collected poems
and a tape-recorder lapping up their words

The dog flops in the shade of the back door
I go to her when she stirs, stroke her hot fur
give her water, keep her from barking

I hear their talk and laughter, his and Norman's
I hear the rise and fall of Chris's voice
the rhythms of his favourite poems, over and over

In the afternoon I sit against the apple tree
feeling the dent of bark on my bare shoulders
I close my eyes and the murmur of their voices
blurs with the birdsong that maybe
when we listen to the finished record
will have swum inside the poems

1991

Mother and Child in the Botanic Gardens

Baby carriages are not allowed in the plant houses

The baby floats carriage-less
in her waterlily cradle
that wafts and drifts her round the world

Australasia   Guatemala   Mexico
South Laos   Norfolk Islands   Crete

Wrapped in a coir of coconut
she floats from island to island

A bush with waxy orange flowers
bends between her and the sun
Purple berries fall into her lap
She eats them
and lays her head in the creamy pillow
of a lily flower

She is lost in Tropics of the Old World
Her dreams are scented

The mother comes running through the plant houses
tropical to temperate and back to tropical
frantic between the arms of palm trees
and the tangle of passion flowers
that curl their tendrils into her hair

Fronds of fern tickle and grip
Green surrounds her, a mouth of green is
eating her with jade lips
and a moist and mossy tongue
that licks her with a limey liquid
Cacti crawl at her feet
leer from their gravel and sand
claw their spikes and prickles into her skirts

and the iron skeleton
buckles and caves
Its bony fingers
waver in the lily pond

She looks into
its ochre water
and sees
curled on the deck
of a waterlily leaf
her daughter

her eyes gazing up to the glass roof
and her lips
stained with purple

1991

Deborah Randall (1957–

Danda with a Dead Fish

Here is Danda with a dead fish,
this boy has too many limbs it seems,
more spindles than his running stitch can handle,
in from the green-flax sea-line with bare legs
and his knees clacking, chattering Danda
with a dead fish, what it is and whether fresh
or not they'll pass it over, won't know,
won't eat it she says, though you my dearie
Danda can have it for your supper, how
she teases, his big mother, navvie-built
to be a father; where do all the men go
when they have begot.

Don't look so starving Danda you
little darling, who packs his food away

like a navvie and is growing all slick
and silvery and smells kippery, he's been
hull-picking with fishermen, his father was
one of them, nets going mouldy, Danda
gets moods of the sea, and goose-bumps
can't be scraped off, he'll get them again
on the shore, he lives there looking for
the man in him, they give
tea and talk, slap him on the shoulder,
call him fishy.

Danda's jumper unravelling, coming out
in sympathy, his nose is never cleanly,
dripping brine all the time, scales under
his nails, always flexing, finding, bringing
in, a wind slaps hard on him singing up and
down his ribs, Danda has no colour
except of grey, the colour of
the day he lost his fiery ginger dadda
to the sea, except, his dadda really went away
with a woman not his mother;
never mind our Danda, pass it over
have your supper.

1989

Meg Bateman (1959–

Do Alastair MacIll-Mhìcheil

Chuir na leabhraichean agad tnùth orm
mar nach do chuir càil eile,

oir ghlac mi annta saoghal seunta,
ortha aig an tuath an cois gach gnìomha,
pàirt an urra riutha de rian dìomhair.

Ghabh mi farmad ri Heaney a bharrachd,
is acfhainn an fhearainn mun cuairt air,
na samhla air oidhirp a chuid dhaoine:
fiodh is iarann, leathar is ròp
air an caitheamh ann an dòchas dìolaidh.

A-mach leam à Safeway, na càraichean
stobte le creich às na ceithir àirdean;
a dh'ainneoin nan sanas chan eil ann
na thogas cridhe leis fhèin, is gu leòr
ga phàigheadh leis an aonaranachd.

Bidh mi feuchainn ri mo thàladh fhìn
nach robh cliù do linn-sa, Alastair,
ach cho beannaichte ri do mhac-meanmna,
nach rachadh an tuathanach le Heaney
gum b' e samhla a dh'fheann a bhois.

Ach tha ortha ri lorg fiù 's annamsa,
chan ann gun leig na bà am bainne
bhon a tha lochan againn dheth,
chan ann airson smàladh an teilidh,
no airson teanga an eisgeir,

Ach airson de ghràs agus de mhisneachd
leis an gabh mi ris an linn sa,
oir cha b' fhollaisiche dàn nan daoine ud
am measg salachair is fallais
na mo dhàn-sa am measg ceannachd is reice.

Thug thu dhuinn an ortha bha san àbhaist
a chluinneas mi nist an srann nam wipers,
mi a' feitheamh aig na solais, mo rèis
ga caitheamh am measg pèin agus aigheir –
an dàn a bha aig gach uile urra riamh.

1997

To Alexander Carmichael

Your books made me envious
as nothing else ever did,
for in them I glimpsed an enchanted world,
a people with a prayer for every act,
each with a role to play in an ordered mystery.

I was jealous too of Heaney,
surrounded by tools of the land,
symbols of his people's labour:
wood and iron, rope and leather
worn and frayed in the hope of repayment.

Out I come from Safeway, and the cars are
packed with plunder from every continent;
despite all the ads, there isn't enough here
to uplift the heart, and too much of it
is paid for in loneliness.

I try and lure myself into believing
that your view of the age, Alasdair,
was only as hallowed as your imagination,
and that no farmer would agree with Heaney
that his palms had been skinned raw by a symbol.

But even in me there is a prayer to be found,
not for the cattle to yield their milk
as we have lakes of it,
not for smooring the telly,
or for the sharp tongue of the satirist,

But for the grace and courage
to accept this age I live in,
since the fate of those people was no clearer,
amidst grime and sweat,
than my own fate amidst buying and selling.

You gave us the prayer of ordinary things
which I hear now in the thrum of the wipers,
waiting at the lights, my life
fraying amidst joy and pain –
the fate of every single human before me.

Editor's note: Alexander Carmichael (1832–1912), collector and original
editor of the folklore material published as *Carmina Gadelica – Hymns and*
Incantations.

Leigeil Bhruadaran Dhìom

Tha am feasgar ciùin,
an t-adhar san uinneig
gun smal . . .
Ist, m' eudail,
na bruidhinn an-dràst,
tha taibhsean a' dol siar.

Chan e fear àraidh a chaoininn

ach beatha de mhiann,
gach roghainn neo-thaghte gam thrèigsinn
air do shàillibh, fhir bhàin.

Dèan caithris leam
gus an tèid iad à sealladh.
Cha tig iad nar dàil, oir
is euchdaiche na iadsan
do shìol nam bhroinn, is dèine
bhios gul ar ciad-ghin
nuair a thogas tu e os àird.

1997

Letting Go of Dreams

The evening is calm,
in the sky through the window
not a blot . . .
Hush, my darling,
don't speak just yet,
there are ghosts passing by.

It is no one man I would mourn
but a lifetime of hunger,
every untaken choice that now slips away
because of you, fair man.

Keep vigil with me
till they vanish from sight.
They will not come near us, for
mightier than they

is your seed in my womb, and fiercer
will be the cry of our first-born
when you hold him aloft.

Ugh Briste
do Cholm, aig trì bliadhna a dh'aois

Sheas thu air ugh na Càisge
a bh' agam bho aois m' òige
's tu dannsadh mun teine casrùisgte.

Smaoinich mi mar a chomharraicheadh na Sìnich
le duilleig de dh'òr
an sgoltadh ann an soitheach briste,
is iad a' dèanamh toileachas às a bhreòiteachd,
às a chàradh eadar bith is neo-bhith . . .
ach 's ann a bha an t-ugh na mhìle pìos.

Is ged nach robh càil de bhreòiteachd
anns an ràn a thàinig asad
's tu bàthadh a' chiùil
ris an robh thu a' dannsadh,
no anns na deòir theth
bha a' taomadh far do ghruaidhean,
chuirinn-sa òr air do phianadh aig an àm ud
's tu ag aithneachadh nach buan a' bhòidhchead.

2000

A Broken Egg
for Colm, at three years of age

You stood on the Easter egg
I'd had since childhood
as you danced barefoot round the fire.

I remembered that the Chinese would mark
with gold leaf
the crack in a broken vessel,
to celebrate its fragility,
its repair into being and non-being . . .
but the egg, it turned out, was in a thousand pieces.

And though there wasn't a shred of fragility
in the howl you let out,
drowning out the music
you'd been dancing to,
or in the hot tears
teeming down your cheeks,
what I would gild was your pain at that moment
as you realised that beauty does not last.

Walzer

Fhuair mi luach m' fharaidh air a' Walzer
is an duine gu borb a' cur car sa charbad
gach uair a thigeadh e gu tàmh,
's mi nam laighe lem shliasaidean sgèapte,
sùilean dùinte, 's mi a' sgreuchail,
car mar a laigh mi fichead bliadhna air ais
fo smachd fir eile dham b' ionann
fiamh na dòrainn is an aigheir,

fear a bha titheach
gum faighinn luach m' òigheachd
's e a' cur aon char eile nam chorp-sa,
ag ràdh, 'Bheir thu taing dhomh fhathast;
tha thu nas fheàrr dheth às aonais.'

'S ann a thug mi taing do dh'fhear a' Walzer
's mi tighinn gu cugallach bharr an inneil,
dìreach mar a thug mi taing dhan a' chiad fhear
's e sìneadh mo bhagaichean thugam aig an stèisean,
's shiubhail mi gu tuath fad an latha nam thuaineal
seach nach robh nighean m' athar a' tilleadh mar a bha i.

2000

Walzer

I got my full money's worth on the Walzer,
with that man giving the car a violent spin
every time it came to a rest,
and me lying back, thighs wide,
eyes shut, screaming,
rather as I lay back twenty years ago
pinned down by another man who couldn't distinguish
the face of pain from the face of pleasure,
a man determined
I should get my full virginity's worth
as he gave my body one more spin,
saying 'You'll thank me yet;
you're better off without it.'

I actually thanked the man on the Walzer
as I stumbled off the machine,

just as I thanked that first man
as he handed me my bags at the station,
and I travelled north all day in a daze
knowing my father's daughter was not returning unchanged.

Maud Sulter (1960–

Flight

To the frozen north I flee. Another country.

Well a hid tae get awae couldn'y staun the pressure
n a couldn'y face the reality o bein sae loved   So
here in the room o ma adolescence a'm awake again
before daylight filters perculated through bamboo
blinds   Fearful

Paint dapples the morning
I paint
to make this space a sanctuary
for us
so that somewhere we have security
knowing
that as soon as we do our own place
should follow.

n the poor n the needy n the spiritually
lost are still here n the city gets greyer
again   edges sharpened voices mair piercin in
desperation we try tae survive another winter here
in *thatchur's britain* wains wi runnin noses auld wimmin
wi nae enough money fur heatin n the cauld   the cauld

seems
wirse than last year   aye the cauld seems wirse than last
    year
the seventies promise of a better future tastes bitter on ma
tongue nae mair   a wunder wit happened tae the
    semblance
o tolerance now replaced wi mair bigotry in the wake o
the anglo-irish agreement   graffiti reminds us that
the bitterness remains n tho it isn'y ma main
concern it's a shame fur the wains is it no
aye a shame fur the wains is it no?

1989

Jackie Kay (1961–

My Grandmother's Houses

1
She is on the second floor of a tenement
From her front room window you see the cemetery

Her bedroom is my favourite: newspapers
dating back to the War covering every present
she's ever got since the War. What's the point
in buying her anything my mother moans.
Does she use it. Does she even look at it.
I spend hours unwrapping and wrapping endless
tablecloths, napkins, perfume, bath salts,
stories of things I can't understand, words
like conscientious objector. At night I climb

over all the newspaper parcels to get to bed,
harder than the school's obstacle course. High up
in her bed all the print merges together.

When she gets the letter she is hopping mad.
What does she want with anything modern,
a shiny new pin? Here is home.
The sideboard solid as a coffin.
The newsagents next door which sells
Hazelnut toffees and her *Daily Record*.
Chewing for ages over the front page,
her toffees sticking to her false teeth.

2
The new house is called a high rise.
I play in the lift all the way up to 24.
Once I get stuck for a whole hour.
From her window you see noisy kids
playing hopscotch or home.
She makes endless pots of vegetable soup,
a big bit of hoch floating inside like a fish

Till finally she gets to like the hot
running water in her own bathroom
the wall-to-wall foam-backed carpet
the parcels locked in her air-raid shelter.

But she still doesn't settle down;
even at 70 she cleans people's houses
for ten bob and goes to church on Sundays,
dragging me along to the strange place where the air
is trapped and ghosts sit at the altar.
My parents do not believe. It is down to her.
A couple of prayers. A hymn or two.

Jackie Kay (1961–

Threepenny bit in the collection hat.
A flock of women in coats and fussy hats
flapping over me like missionaries, and that is that,
until the next time God grabs me in Glasgow with Gran.

3
By the time I am seven we are almost the same height.
She still walks faster, rushing me down the High Street
till we get to her cleaning house. The hall is huge.
Rooms lead off like an octopus's arms.
I sit in a room with a grand piano, top open –
a one-winged creature, whilst my gran polishes
for hours. Finally bored I start to pick some notes
oh can you wash a sailor's shirt oh can you wash and clean
till my gran comes running, duster in hand.
I told you don't touch anything. The woman comes too;
the posh one all smiles that make goosepimples
run up my arms. Would you like to sing me a song?
Someone's crying my Lord Kumbaya. Lovely, she says,
beautiful child, skin the colour of café au lait.
'Café oh what? Hope she's not being any bother.'
Not at all. Not at all. You just get back to your work.
On the way back to her high rise I see her
like the hunchback of Notre Dame. Everytime I crouch
over a comic she slaps me. Sit up straight.

She is on the ground floor of a high rise.
From her living-room you see ambulances,
screaming their way to the Royal Infirmary.

1991

The Red Graveyard

There are some stones that open in the night like flowers
Down in the red graveyard where Bessie haunts her lovers.
There are stones that shake and weep in the heart of night
Down in the red graveyard where Bessie haunts her lovers.

Why do I remember the blues?
I am five or six or seven in the back garden;
the window is wide open;
her voice is slow motion through the heavy summer air.
Jelly roll. Kitchen man. Sausage roll. Frying pan.

Inside the house where I used to be myself,
her voice claims the rooms. In the best room even,
something has changed the shape of my silence.
Why do I remember her voice and not my own mother's?
Why do I remember the blues?

My mother's voice. What was it like?
A flat stone for skitting. An old rock.
Long long grass. Asphalt. Wind. Hail.
Cotton. Linen. Salt. Treacle.
I think it was a peach.
I heard it down to the ribbed stone.

I am coming down the stairs in my father's house.
I am five or six or seven. There is fat thick wallpaper
I always caress, bumping flower into flower.
She is singing. (Did they play anyone else ever?)
My father's feet tap a shiny beat on the floor.

Christ, my father says, that's some voice she's got.

I pick up the record cover. And now. This is slow motion.
My hand swoops, glides, swoops again.
I pick up the cover and my fingers are all over her face.
Her black face. Her magnificent black face.
That's some voice. His shoes dancing on the floor.

There are some stones that open in the night like flowers
Down in the red graveyard where Bessie haunts her lovers.
There are stones that shake and weep in the heart of night
Down in the red graveyard where Bessie haunts her lovers.

1993

The Shoes of Dead Comrades

On my father's feet are the shoes of dead comrades.
Gifts from the comrades' sad red widows.
My father would never see good shoes go to waste.
Good brown leather, black leather, leather soles.
Doesn't matter if they are a size too big, small.

On my father's feet are the shoes of dead comrades.
The marches they marched against Polaris. UCS.
Everything they ever believed tied up with laces.
A cobbler has replaced the sole, the heel.
Brand new, my father says, look, feel.

On my father's feet are the shoes of dead comrades.
These are in good nick. These were pricey.
Italian leather. See that. Lovely.
He always was a classy dresser was Arthur.
Ever see Wullie dance? Wullie was a wonderful waltzer.

On my father's feet are the shoes of dead comrades.
It scares me half to death to consider
that one day it won't be Wullie or Jimmy or Arthur,
that one day someone will wear the shoes of my father,
the brown and black leather of all the dead comrades.

1993

Lucozade

My mum is on a high bed next to sad chrysanthemums.
'Don't bring flowers, they only wilt and die.'
I am scared my mum is going to die
on the bed next to the sad chrysanthemums.

She nods off and her eyes go back in her head.
Next to her bed is a bottle of Lucozade.
'Orange nostalgia, that's what that is,' she says.
'Don't bring Lucozade either,' then fades.

'The whole day was a blur, a swarm of eyes.
Those doctors with their white lies.
Did you think you could cheer me up with a
    Woman's Own?
Don't bring magazines, too much about size.'

My mum wakes up, groggy and low.
'What I want to know,' she says, 'is this:
where's the big brandy, the generous gin, the
  Bloody Mary,
the biscuit tin, the chocolate gingers, the dirty big
    meringue?'

I am sixteen; I've never tasted a Bloody Mary.
'Tell your father to bring a luxury,' says she.
'Grapes have no imagination, they're just green.
Tell him: stop the neighbours coming.'

I clear her cupboard in Ward 10B, Stobhill Hospital.
I leave, bags full, Lucozade, grapes, oranges,
sad chrysanthemums under my arms,
weighted down. I turn round, wave with her flowers.

My mother, on her high hospital bed, waves back.
Her face is light and radiant, dandelion hours.
Her sheets billow and whirl. She is beautiful.
Next to her the empty table is divine.

I carry the orange nostalgia home singing an old song.

1998

Kathleen Jamie (1962–

Clearances

The wind sucks clouds. In the indrawn breath
grass bends and nods, like Mandarins.
The sun hunches, and begins to set no sooner
than it's risen. This
depopulated place! Where moorland birds
repeat a sound, like copper, beaten.
The very moon imagines things –
a desert dusk, with itself as scimitar . . .

As the wind keeps up, closer than
I've heard my name in . . . how long?
and the dark coheres; an old idea
returns again, the prodigal friend:
of leaving: for Szechwan, or Persia.

1987

For Paola

A boomin echo doon the corridor,
her door's the only ane open

lik a shell, an a wumman sweepin:
saft soun, wings.

A licht-bulb, hingit fi the ceilin
by a short cord.

A slever o gless in the oose
an a black hair. she telt me

they've killed 5000 people in Beijing.
Nou this wumman's haunin her gear

brushes an pens, her worn claes
for me tae cairry. But she'd a bin waitin

when they cam, chewin her gum
blawn them a bubble size o China.

This is a place your friens disappear:
trust naebody. Luve a.

The smearit wa's o a concrete room,

slever: sliver   *oose*: fluff
gless: glass

a wumman sweepin.

1993

Mother-May-I

Mother-May-I
go down the bottom of the lane,
to the yellow-headed piss-the-beds,
and hunker at the may-hedge, skirts
fanned out
       in the dirt and see the dump
where we're not allowed –
twisty trees, the burn, and say:
all hushed sweetie-breath:
  they are the woods
where men
      lift up your skirt
and take down your pants
even although you're crying.
Mother may I
     leave these lasses' games
      and play at Man-hunt, just
in the scheme Mother
may I
  tell small lies: *we were sot*
in the lane, sat on garage ramps,
picking harling
with bitten nails, as myths

rose thick as swamp mist
from the woods behind the dump
                              where hitch-hikers rot
in the curling roots of trees,
and men
leave tight rolled-up
dirty magazines.
Mother may we
                    pull our soft backsides
through the jagged may's
white blossom, run across the stinky dump
and muck about
at the woods and burn
                              dead pleased
to see the white dye

we were sot: we were so (to rhyme with 'not')

of our gym-rubbers seep downstream?

                                        1994

Fountain

What are we doing when we toss a coin,
just a 5p-piece into the shallow dish
of the fountain in the city-centre
shopping arcade? We look down
the hand-rail of the escalator
through two–three inches of water
at a scatter of coins: round, flat, worthless,
reflections of perspex foliage
and a neon sign – FOUNTAIN.

So we glide from mezzanine to ground,
laden with prams, and bags printed
Athena, Argos, Olympus; thinking: now
in Arcadia est I'll besport myself
at the water's edge with kids,
coffee in a polystyrene cup.
We know it's all false: no artesian well
really leaps through strata
fathoms under *Man at C&A*, but
who these days can thrust her wrists
into a giggling hillside spring
above some ancient city?
So we flick in coins, show the children how:
make a wish! What for, in the shopping mall?
A wee stroke of luck? A something else, a nod
toward a goddess we almost sense
in the verdant plastic? Who says
we can't respond; don't still feel,
as it were, the dowser's twitch
up through the twin handles of the buggy.

1994

Ultrasound

For Duncan

i. Ultrasound

Oh whistle and I'll come to ye,
my lad, my wee shilpit ghost
summonsed from tomorrow.

Second sight,
a seer's mothy flicker,

an inner sprite:

this is what I see
with eyes closed;
a keek-aboot among secrets.

If Pandora
could have scanned
her dark box,

and kept it locked –
this ghoul's skull, punched eyes
is tiny Hope's,

hauled silver-quick
in a net of sound,
then, for pity's sake, lowered.

1999

Bolus

So little of the world is bequeathed
through us, our gifts
instead, are passed among the living
– like words, or the bolus
of chewed bread
a woman presses with her tongue
into the gorgeous open mouth of her infant.

1999

Meadowsweet

Tradition suggests that certain of the Gaelic women poets
were buried face down.

So they buried her, and turned home,
a drab psalm
hanging about them like haar,

not knowing the liquid
trickling from her lips
would seek its way down,

and that caught in her slowly
unravelling plait of grey hair
were summer seeds:

meadowsweet, bastard balm,
tokens of honesty, already
beginning their crawl

toward light, so showing her,
when the time came,
how to dig herself out –

to surface and greet them,
mouth young, and full again
of dirt, and spit, and poetry.

1999

Angela McSeveney (1964–

Clichés

Once upon a time I uttered words
as meaningless as myself.

They could only be approximations
and always of someone else's feelings

but Autumn leaves do look like carpet on the ground
and hearts can at least come close to breaking.

1992

My Breasts . . .

My breasts
walk ahead of me.

They collect crumbs and bruises.
Dripping coffee makes them wince.

Pallid as flour sacks
they sag from their lace-trimmed harness
and take up my lap like twin babes.

Roll over in the night
and they spill into my arms
I can curl myself around them
alone in the dark.

Their imagination moves them.

The nipples stir in search
of a sucking mouth.

Or tense with expectation
they lean against my ribcage
and wait.

1992

Crockery

My mother stood her potplants on old saucers,
all of them survivors from separate sets.

Each item had been packed into a tea-chest at least

once

then laid out on another shelf.

I remember playing among the balled-up newspaper
on a different kitchen floor.

My mother tended to her red geraniums
and wondered at the crockery
we must have gone through.

1992

Angela McSeveney (1964–

Windowbox

I sowed nightscented stocks with the halfgrown hope
that this was more like gardening
than impatiens in pots.

They grew anaemic and spindly
coated by dust from the street.
From the ground they looked like weeds.

Nothing flashy or flowery
like a trumpetting hippaestrum
or a petal drenched Black-eyed Susan

and even I who planted them
rarely thought to look out
except maybe in the evenings

when the cool damp of Summer rain
sweated in the air
like an extra sense

and the night scent swam in
clear as spearmint
and soothed away the city noise.

Then there grew a garden:
rosebeds and herbs,
tangles of scarlet runners.

1992

Kate Clanchy (1965–

For a Wedding
(Camilla and Kieran 9/8/94)

Cousin, I think the shape of a marriage
is like the shelves my parents have carried
through Scotland to London, three houses;

is not distinguished, fine, French-polished,
but plywood and tatty, made
in the first place for children to batter,

still carrying markings in green felt tip,
but always, where there are books
and a landing, managing to fit;

that marriage has lumps like
their button-backed sofa, constantly,
shortly, about to be stuffed;

and that love grows fat
as their squinting cat, swelling
round as a loaf from her basket.

I wish you years that shape, that form,
and a pond in a Sunday, urban garden;
where you'll see your joined reflection tremble,

stand and watch the waterboatmen
skate with ease across the surface tension.

1995

The Bridge Over the Border

Here, I should surely think of home –
my country and the neat steep town
where I grew up: its banks of cloud,
the winds and changing, stagey light,
its bouts of surly, freezing rain, or failing that,

the time the train stuck here half an hour.
It was hot, for once. The engine seemed
to grunt and breathe with us,
and in the hush, the busker at the back
plucked out *Scotland the Brave*. There was

a filmic, golden light and the man opposite
was struck, he said, with love.
He saw a country in my eyes.
But he was from Los Angeles,
and I was thinking of another bridge.

It was October. I was running to meet a man
with whom things were not quite settled,
were not, in fact, to ever settle, and I stopped
halfway to gaze at birds – swallows
in their distant thousands, drawn

to Africa, or heat, or home, not knowing
which, but certain how. Shifting on the paper sky,
they were crosses on stock-market graphs,
they were sand in a hoop shaken sideways,
and I stared, as if panning for gold.

1999

Alison Kermack (1965–

The Shadow Minister

by meenzy a contrapshun
like a perryscoap
wi a tellyscoap
attachd tay it
while cashully stroalin
aloang downin street
ah chansd tay look
in thi uppur windy
i nummer ten

ah seen thi pee em
sittin inna big arrum chare
in frunty a big coal fyur
hoaldin a mappy scoatlin
oan thi endy a toast foark

funny thing wiz
thoah kidny see it say cleerly
kizzit happind tay faw
oan thi oappisit waw
thi shaddy i thi pee em
wiz dane igzackly
thi same thing

1991

Time and Again

thi cloak
oan thi waw
sezitz timety

get thi bairnz reddy
get thi hoose tidy
get thi messijis in
get thi tee oan

get inty bed
an gee um hiz conjuggles

thur wizza time when
I

naw thur wizny

1993

Gillian K. Ferguson (1967–

Dear Norman
(for the late Norman MacCaig)

I blew in from my own young night
and demented Edinburgh November,
magnetised leaves tangled in Ophelia hair.

Whisky soon lay like a cat
on my stomach – its water, like you,
ran briskly forty years ago;

each year we celebrated with a Silk Cut –
mist peered at our lung-blown rival,
a dovetail of poems fanned in your hand.

How your chameleon mind, frail giant,
whose words skewer fragments of the world –
butterflies in boxes of books –

alchemised the blades of wit
to feathers. Your wife dead;
our pain surpassing all soberness.

Your hieroglyphs translated my pages,
laughter poulticed dry tears;
words summed like scars on stone.

Your tongue still speaks like light
in black holes of belief –
I remember my homeward, hovercraft feet.

1997

Scan

In me a moonscape of organs,
bloodless, maybe a monster;

my blood thuds. Until a black
bubble. Silent, slow as a flower,

opening from limb buds,
an anemone pulse of fingers.

Under my thick skin veil,
not me, plugged; blind,

bulb-headed, spinning invisible
tissue on bones fine as fish.

Mouse-big, sparrow-hearted,
it becoming *you*, new from

nothing; the miraculous alien,
eel-supple in blank dreams.

And like men loving the blue
planet, the world is changed.

2001

Everything is More

Why is it with you, everything is more?
From recent crushed and bruised, cut blades,
grass blood smell is a keen green hand around
my throat, the rhododendron displays deep red
velvet whorls like cheap sex, unfurls glistening
for the sun. I must resist a public urge to hug trees –
trunks are waists drunk, welcoming. Dying daffodils
that lit your face with spring whisper to wind about
the existence of bulbs. How unbearable the sky-
rejecting willow's hang, trailing skinny fingers
in the earth like a hopeless person in a boat –
sadness twists thin wires in my juicy heart.

Paradise-breasted pigeons explode, then slide air
down again, swarming bread; a panic of ducks water-

skis back. I am in their wings light as the feather gleam,
my toes dabbling mud with lily roots. Water smooths
over drowned trees calm as a nurse. A drug you are
in my veins, my brain – an intoxication, living supply.
You are my second chance at the world, my new blood.

2001

Anna Frater (1967–

Màiri Iain Mhurch' Chaluim

Mo sheanmhair, a chaill a h-athair air an Iolaire, *oidhche na bliadhn' ùir, 1919.*

Tha mi nam shuidhe ag èisteachd ribh
agus tha mo chridh' a' tuigsinn
barrachd na mo chlaisneachd;
's mo shùilean a' toirt a-steach
barrachd na mo chluasan.

Ur guth sèimh, ur cainnt
ag èirigh 's a' tuiteam mar thonn
air aghaidh fhuar a' chuain
's an-dràst' 's a-rithist a' briseadh
air creag bhiorach cuimhne;
's an sàl a' tighinn gu bàrr
ann an glas-chuan ur sùilean.

'Bha e air an ròp
an uair a bhris e . . .'

Agus bhris ur cridhe cuideachd
le call an ròpa chalma
air an robh grèim gràidheil agaibh
fhad 's a bha sibh a' sreap suas
nur leanabh.

Agus, aig aois deich bliadhna
cha robh agaibh ach cuimhne air a' chreig
a bhiodh gur cumail còmhnard;
's gach dòchas a bha nur sùilean
air a bhàthadh troimhn oidhch' ud,
's troimh gach bliadhn' ùr a lean.

Chàirich iad a' chreag
agus dh'fhàg sin toll.
Chruadhaich an sàl ur beatha
agus chùm e am pian ùr;
agus dh' fhuirich e nur sùilean
cho goirt 's a bha e riamh;
agus tha pian na caillich
cho geur ri pian an nighinn,
agus tha ur cridhe
a' briseadh às ùr
a' cuimhneachadh ur h-athar.

'. . . oir bha athair agam . . .'

1995

Anna Frater (1967–

Màiri Iain Mhurch' Chaluim

My grandmother, who lost her father on the Iolaire, *New Year's Night, 1919*
(Translated by Anne Frater)

I sit listening to you
and my heart understands
more than my hearing;
and my eyes absorb
more than my ears.

Your soft voice, your speech
rising and falling like waves
on the cold surface of the sea,
and now and again breaking
on the sharp rock of memory;
and the brine rises up
in the grey seas of your eyes.

'He was on the rope
when it broke . . .'

And your heart also broke
with the loss of the sturdy rope
which you had clung to lovingly
while you were growing up
as a child.

And, at ten years of age,
you had only a memory of the rock
that used to keep you straight;
and every hope that was in your eyes
was drowned on that night
and through each New Year that followed.

They buried the rock
and that left a hole.
The salt hardened your life
and kept the pain fresh;
and it stayed in your eyes
as stinging as it ever was;
and the old woman's pain
is as keen as the girl's,
and your heart
breaks anew
remembering your father.

'. . . *because I had a father* . . .'

Connadh

Rùisg sinn na poill,
bhuain sinn a' mhòine,
rùdh sinn na fàdan
agus rinn sinn ath-rùdhadh.
Chruinnich sinn na caorain
agus chuir sinn ann am pocannan iad
agus, nuair a bha sinn deas,
lìon sinn an làraidh leotha.

Nuair a thill sinn dhachaigh,
gàirdeanan lag le tilgeil,
pian crùbach anns gach druim,
cha robh cruach a' feitheamh rinn.
chaidh an làraidh seachad oirnn –
fuar falamh –
agus e air ar mòine a reic
air sràidean a' bhaile.

Nis tha sinn air ar fàgail
gun nì ach smùr
a chuireas sinn air an teine,
agus muinntir a' bhaile ag ràdh
gum bu chòir dhuinn a bhith taingeil
gu bheil sinn a' faighinn
barrachd smùr gach duine
na tha iadsan;
agus cuiridh iad fàd eile
air an teine.

Dè nì sinn le na leacan falamh?
Critheadh le fuachd
no lasadh le fuath?

1995

Fuel

We stripped the banks,
we cut the peat,
we stacked the slices to dry
then turned them over.
We gathered the broken peats
and stuffed them into sacks
and, when we were finished,
we filled up the lorry.

When we got home,
arms weak from throwing,
every back stiff from bending
there was no peatstack awaiting us,
and the lorry drove past –

bare and empty –
having just sold our peat
on the streets of the town.

Now we are left
with nothing but dust
to throw on the fire,
while the townies tell us
we ought to be grateful
since we get more dust per head
than they;
as they throw another peat
onto the fire.

What shall we do now the hearthstones are bare?
Shiver with cold
or flare up with hate?

Oidhche Reòite

Nuair a bha an t-adhar buidhe
's nach robh dorchadas ann
's nach robh fuaim na mara nam chluaisean
neo fàileadh ceò na mòine nam chuinnlean
cha do smaoinich mi oirbh
's fios a'm nach biodh ann
ach ionndrainn gun fheum.

Ach dh'fhuirich sibh far an robh sibh
a' feitheamh rium.

Agus air oidhche reòite
's mi air teiche bho sholais a' bhaile mhòir

chì mi sibh a' deàlradh
mar a bha sibh riamh
's sibh a' cur fàilt' air an nighean stròdhail
a thill.

2001

Frosty Night

When the sky was golden
and there was no darkness
no sound of the sea in my ears
no reek of peat-smoke in my nostrils,
I never gave you a thought,
knowing it would bring only
pointless longing.

But you stayed where you were
waiting for me.

And on a frosty night
having fled the city lights
I see you shine
as you have always shone,
welcoming the prodigal daughter's
return.

Tracey Herd (1968–

Paris in the Spring

Mother is in Paris for the spring collections.
She flies there and back within the hour.
In the kitchen, Father impatiently shakes out
his paper, scanning the business pages.
Outside the clouds air their linens
briskly; mother's laundry billows
into flower; the roses sway
in April's warm pastels.

Faces ring the catwalk. She is their centre.
Flashbulbs almost break her concentration
but she focuses ahead on a point the size of a coin
and spins triumphantly on one spike-heel.
Her mind winds the spool back thirty years
to a beach in Spain where a girl poses stiffly
in a swimsuit of dark green, her arms
stapled to her sides. She struggles
to free them, jumping back as she slops tea
over the mug's rim. Father tuts
and lays aside his paper.
Her head is in the clouds again.

1996

Ophelia's Confession

Every day God pats my head and calls me
angel, his little broken woman
and gives me flowers as if I hadn't had enough of these

and I choke back my rage and he mistakes this
for distress as I stand there shaking
in my little sackcloth dress.

Had I ever had the choice
I'd have worn a very different dress,
slit from breast to navel and far too tight
and I'd have smoked and sworn and been
out of my head on drugs, not grief, and the flowers
would have been a tattoo around my ankle,
not an anchor to drag me down, and as for
being a virgin, I'd have slept with both men and women.

I would never recommend a shallow stream
and what was no more than a daisy chain
as being the ideal way to die.
It was far too pretty but I had to improvise
and I was a poet, far more so than him,
who threw out every word he ever thought
as if that might have kept his sorry life afloat.

I didn't drown by accident. I was a suicide.
At least let me call my mind my own
even when my heart was gone beyond recall.

Today, a car crash might have been my final scene,
a black Mercedes in a tunnel by the Seine,
with no last words, no poetry,
with flashbulbs tearing at my broken body
because broken was the way I felt inside,
the cameras lighting up the wreckage of a life.
That would, at least, have been an honest way to die.

2001

Eleanor Brown (1969–

The Lads

The lads, the lads, away the lads;
we are the Boys, who make this Noise: hoo, ha; hoo-*ha*;
a-*way*, awayawayaway, a-way, away;
ere we go, ere we go, ere we go;
we are the Boys, who make this Noise:
hoo *ha*.

Away the lads. I love your poetry.
It strips the artform down to nakedness,
distilling it to spirituous drops
of utter purity.
I like the way you shout it all so loud,
revelling in the shamelessness
of its repetitiousness; the way it never stops
delighting
you. You've every right to be proud
of your few, brief, oral formulae –
any of which will do, for *Match of the Day*,
or Friday night, Lads' Night Out,
lagered up and fighting –
you are the lads. You've every right to shout.

Your poetry belligerently asserts
what nobody would trouble to deny:
that you are the lads; that there you go;
that yours will never be to reason why.
My unsingable songs cannot do more for me
than rid me of my epicene disgust,
after I've served you all ten pints and watched
you flushing up with random rage and lust.

You'll smack each other's heads tonight
and shag each other's birds;
you are the Boys, who make this Noise.
What need have you for words?

We will not argue, therefore, you and I.
Your poetry serves your purpose; mine serves mine.
You only tell me what I don't deny,
and I don't tell you anything. That's fine.

Away, the lads. Your deathless chants will be
heard in these bars and streets long after we
are dead (for lads are mortal too); your sons
will never feel the need for different ones.

1996

Leda, no Swan

Where I'm not given a complaisant smirk,
my mouth might be a slightly startled 'O' –
a half a 'no', that needn't count as No.
You will deduce he didn't have to work
so very hard, to part my pretty legs.
His curving neck, my curving arm, his beak
in almost a caress against my cheek –
no, this is not a scene, you'll say, that begs
use of the hard word Rape. Where is the rape?
Look how the gentle victim's dreamy eyes
register nothing more than 'vague' surprise;
those limbs suggest no effort at escape.

Ever been frightened by an animal?
Ever get knocked sprawling flat on your back
in the senseless impact of brute attack?
Ever been winded, *and* hysterical?

Wings that could break your arm thrashing your chest,
a black bill hissing in your eyes, obscene,
inhuman, spitting noises that can mean
nothing but let-me-get-it-in; you, pressed
with the weight of a foreign body on
your guts, clammy webbed feet scrabbling to get
a purchase; two or three rough jerks; a jet
of alien slime.
        Don't get raped by a swan.

That's my advice. They said he was divine,
when they found me retching myself inside
out, afterwards, throwing up as if I'd
never stop. They said, treat it as a sign
of enviable favour. You're a myth,
now, they said; try to behave like one. Though
what I always wished, if you want to know,
was that I'd had something to hurt him with.

1996

Biographical and

Bibliographical Notes

The practice in this section is to give a selection of the bio-graphical and bibliographical information available on the writers. The bibliographies aim to be complete on published poetry collections but, for reasons of space, normally only to give a selection of other work.

Adam, Helen (1909–92)

Helen Adam was born on 2 December 1909 in Glasgow; she died in New York City on 19 September 1993. She was a writer of Scottish ballads and later participated in the Beat poetry movement. After attending Edinburgh University for two years, she worked as a journalist in London. In 1939 she moved to the United States, to New York and San Francisco. In San Francisco she worked with such influen-tial poets as Allen Ginsberg and Robert Duncan. Her early publications, *The Elfin Pedlar and Tales Told by the Pixy Pool* (1923) and *Charms and Dreams from the Elfin Pedlar's Pack* (1924), include poems written in early childhood. She followed these with a number of collections of poems and a collection of short stories, *Ghosts and Grinning Shadows* (1977). She collaborated with her sister and with Auste Adam on a play entitled *The City is Burning*, published in 1963. She also acted in two films: *Death* and *Our Corpses Speak*, both of which were filmed in Germany. Her life was the subject of a documentary film directed by experimental film maker Rosa von Praunheim.

The Elfin Pedlar and Tales Told by the Pixy Pool (London: Hodder & Stoughton, 1923); *Charms and Dreams from the Elfin Pedlar's Pack* (London: Hodder & Stoughton, 1924); *Shadow of the Moon* (London: Hodder & Stoughton, 1929); *The Queen o' Crow Castle* (San Francisco: White Rabbit Press, 1958); *Ballads* (New York: Acadia Press, 1964); *Counting Out Rhyme* (New York: Interim Books, 1972); *Selected Poems and Ballads* (New York: Helikon Press, 1974); *Gone Sailing* (West Branch, IA: Toothpaste Press, 1980); *The Bells of Dis* (West Branch, IA: Coffee House Press, 1985); and others.

Adamson, Margot Robert (1898–?)

As well as poetry, Margot Robert Adamson wrote novels, travel literature 'for those who stay at home' and an anthology of middle-English verse, rendered into modern English by herself.

A Year of War, and Other Poems (London: David Nutt, 1917); *The Desert and the Sown; and Other Poems* (London: Selwyn & Blount, 1921); *Up the Hill of Fairlight* (London: Selwyn & Blount, 1925); *A Northern Holiday* (London: Cobden-Sanderson, Thavies Inn, 1928); *A Treasury of Middle-English Verse* (London: Dent, 1930); and others.

Angus, Marion (1866–1946)

Marion Angus was born in Aberdeen. Her father, the Rev. Henry Angus, was a minister of the United Presbyterian Church; her mother came from the Scottish Borders. Much of her childhood was spent in Arbroath but on the death of her father she moved with her mother and sisters to

Aberdeen, where she lived most of her adult life. She spent some time in Greenock but died in Arbroath. She contributed poetry and stories to journals for a number of years and was published in MacDiarmid's *Northern Numbers* (1921–22). Her first collection of poems was *The Lilt; and Other Poems* published in 1922, when she was 56. Her *Selected Poems*, edited by Maurice Lindsay, contains a moving personal tribute by Helen Cruickshank (q.v.). Her poems are mostly written in the Angus Scots of her native north-east and show marked influence from ballads and folk song. She was an early member of Scottish PEN.

The Lilt; and Other Poems (Aberdeen: Wylie, 1922); *The Tinker's Road; and Other Verses* (London & Glasgow: Gowans and Gray, 1924); *Sun and Candelight* (Edinburgh: Porpoise Press, 1927); *The Singin' Lass*, (Edinburgh: Porpoise Press, 1929); *The Turn of the Day* (Edinburgh: Porpoise Press, 1931); *Lost Country; and Other Verses* (Glasgow: Gowans and Gray, 1937).

Armour, Margaret (18?–1943)

Margaret Armour was born at Philipston House on the Hopetoun estate, where her father was factor. She was educated locally and at George Watson's Ladies' College, where she was dux and gold medallist. She studied German, taught English in Munich and translated *The Fall of the Nibelungs* and *The Gudrun*, as well as making verse translations of Heine's poems (1917). Although she studied singing, she was prevented from pursuing a singing career by ill health. She was associated with the group that gathered round Patrick Geddes (Outlook Tower), contributed to the *Evergreen* and attended the 'Ryme and Reason' Club. She taught English at Lansdowne until 1895, when she married W. B. Macdougall, who illustrated most of her books. Having lived in or near London until the death of her husband in

1936, she returned to Edinburgh and died in 1943. Two novels, *Agnes of Edinburgh* (Melrose) and *The Impostor and the Poodle* were also published (1940). Her poems, revised by her before her death, were posthumously published.

The Home and Early Haunts of Robert Louis Stevenson (1895); *The Eerie Book* edited by Margaret Armour; XV full page illustrations by W. B. Macdougall (London: J. Shiells & Co., 1898); *The Fall of the Nibelungs*, translated by Margaret Armour, 1908; *Gudrun* (1928); *The Imposter and the Poodle* (London: Hodder & Stoughton, 1940); *Singing Down the Years: Selected Poems* (Edinburgh: The Albyn Press, 1954).

Bateman, Meg (1959–

Meg Bateman was born in Edinburgh in 1959. She became attracted to Gaelic culture in her late teens, studied Gaelic at Aberdeen University, then completed a PhD in classical Gaelic religious poetry. Her experience of family and community life in South Uist was a determining one. After tutoring and lecturing in Edinburgh then at Aberdeen University, she moved to Skye in 1998 with her son to take up a post at Sabhal Mòr Ostaig. Her first collection, *Òrain Ghaoil*, was published in Dublin with translations in Irish, and a recapitulative collection with English translations, *Aotromachd agus Dàin Eile*/'Lightness, and Other Poems' (1997) won her a Scottish Arts Council book award. Thirteen more recent poems appeared in *Etruscan Reader IX* (2000). She has also published widely in magazines and has co-edited several poetry and other anthologies.

Òrain Ghaoil (Baile Átha Cliath: Coiscéim, 1990); *An Anthology of Scottish Women Poets*, ed. Catherine Kerrigan, with Gaelic translations by Meg Bateman (Edinburgh: Edinburgh University Press, 1991); *Aotromachd agus Dàin*

Eile (Edinburgh: Polygon, 1997); *Etruscan Reader IX* (Buckfastleigh: Etruscan Books, 2000)

Blackhall, Sheena Booth (1947–

Sheena Blackhall is an illustrator, singer, poet and short-story writer who has published fifteen volumes of poems and seven short-story collections. Born Sheena Middleton, in Aberdeen, she studied for a year at Gray's School of Art, then qualified as a primary teacher, subsequently working in Easterhouse, Fraserburgh and County Durham. She then married and moved to Skene in Aberdeenshire; after the failure of her marriage, she was left with four children to bring up. She is an Open University graduate in Psychology, has worked as a receptionist with an oil company and has been Creative Writing Fellow of the Elphinstone Institute, Aberdeen. She writes in Scots and English, and sings in Gaelic and Scots.

The Cyard's Kist, and Other Poems (Dyce, Aberdeen: Rainbow Books, 1984); *The Spik o' the Lan'* (Dyce, Aberdeen: Rainbow Books, 1986); *Back o Bennachie: Poems in Scots and English* (Aberdeen: Hammerfield Publishing, 1993); *Braeheid, A Fairm and its Fowk an' Ither Tales in Doric* (Aberdeen: Hammerfield Publishing, 1993); *Druids, Drachts, Drochles: Poems and Short Stories* (Aberdeen: Hammerfield Publishing, 1994); *A Kenspeckle Creel: Tales* (Aberdeen: Hammerfield Publishing, 1995); *Selected Poems* (Stagwyse, Charles Murray Trust, 1995); *Wittgenstein's Web: Scottish Short Stories* (Aberdeen: GKB Enterprises, 1996); *Lament fur the Raj: an' Ither Poems* (Aberdeen: GKB Enterprises, 1996); *The Life-Bluid o Cromar* (Aberdeen: Hammerfield Publishing, 1997); *The Bonsai Grower: Short Stories* (Aberdeen: GKB Enterprises, 1998); *Millennium Blues: Poems in Scots and English* (Aberdeen: Hammerfield Publishing, 1998); *The Singing Bird: Poems* (Aberdeen: GKB Books, 2000); and others.

Bone, Kate Y.A. (1897–1986)

Kate Bone was born Kate Dryburgh. She was educated at Kirkcaldy High School and graduated from Edinburgh University in 1917. After a teacher training course at St George's College, Edinburgh, she taught in an infant school in Kirkcaldy. She married a CA and after his death went back to part-time teaching, also working in Brunton's second-hand bookshop. She wrote a life of St Kentigern for younger children and published limited editions of her contributions to the private circulation magazine, *The Thistle*. Her poems are in English and Scots and have an introduction by Robert Garioch.

Thistle By-blaws, 2 vols (West Linton: Castlelaw Press, 1956); *Thistle By-blaws*, new ed. (1971).

Boyle, Mary Elizabeth (1881–1974)

Mary Boyle published poetry and verse for children before becoming the secretary of the great archaeologist, Henry Breuil. She also wrote on archaeology on her own and in collaboration with Breuil. The sonnet sequence, *Aftermath*, from which the poem in this anthology is taken, was written for her brother, killed at Le Cateau, 26 August 1914.

Pilate in Exile at Vienne: a Poem (Cambridge: W. Heffer & Sons, 1915); *Aftermath* (Cambridge: Heffer & Sons, 1916); *Drum-Na-Keil* (Stirling: Eneas Mackay, 1921); *Daisies and Apple Trees, or Secrets Children Share* (Stirling: Eneas Mackay, 1922); *Herodias Inconsolable* (London: Chelsea Publishing Co., 1923); and others.

Brown, Eleanor (1969–

Eleanor Brown was born in 1969 and grew up as an English child in Scotland. She claims that she 'learned early about racial feeling, being personally blamed for the beheading of Mary Queen of Scots, and being ostracised during a primary-school trip to the site of the battle of Bannockburn'. She studied English at York University and has had a number of jobs since. She has lived in Hertfordshire but now lives in Scotland and has been Writing Fellow of the universities of Glasgow and Strathclyde. In 1993 she received a Gregory Award from the Society of Authors.

Maiden Speech (Newcastle-upon-Tyne: Bloodaxe, 1996); *Franziska* [Frank Wedekind], adapted by Eleanor Brown from a translation by Philip Ward (London: Oberon, 1998).

Brown, Margaret Gillies (1929–

Margaret Gillies Brown was born near Edinburgh and trained as a nurse when young. She is a farmer and mother of seven. She has been writing poetry for 25 years and has also written a biographical story, *Far from the Rowan Tree*, about when she and her first husband, Ronald Gillies, and their young family emigrated to a Prairie farm in the hinterland of Canada in the 1950s. *Around the Rowan Tree* continues the story of her travels, this time with her second husband, Henry Brown, in their camper van. As well as six collections, she has had many poems published in magazines and anthologies and has gained Scottish Arts Council awards for her books.

Give Me the Hill-Run Boys (1978); *The Voices on the Marches* (1979); *Hares on the Horizon* (1981) (all Walton-on-Thames: Outpost Publications); *No Promises* (Nottingham/Edinburgh: Akros, 1984); *Looking Towards Light* (Dundee: Blind Serpent Press, 1988); *Footsteps of the Goddess* (Nottingham/Edinburgh: Akros, 1994); and others.

Bulter, Rhoda (1930–94)

Much of Rhoda Bulter's poetry in Shetland dialect is popular verse but it handles the complexities of relationships with some subtlety.

Doobled-up: All the Shetland Poems from 'Shaela' and 'A Nev Foo A Coarn' (Sandwick, Shetland: Thuleprint Ltd, 1978); *Link-stanes: Shetland Poems* (Lerwick: The Shetland Times, 1980); *Snyivveries* (Lerwick: Shetland Times, 1986).

Burns, Elizabeth (1957–

Elizabeth Burns has worked in bookselling and publishing in Edinburgh. She now lives in Lancaster where she teaches creative writing.

Ophelia and Other Poems (Edinburgh: Polygon, 1991); *The Gift of Light* (Edinburgh: Diehard, 1999).

Caird, Janet (1913–92)

Janet Caird was born Janet Kirkwood in 1913 in Livingstonia, Malawi (then Nyasaland), where her father was an educational missionary. She was educated at Dollar Academy, Edinburgh University, Grenoble University and the Sorbonne. She married James B. Caird in 1938 and they had two daughters. She was a professional teacher who lived for some time in Inverness. Her career as a writer did not begin until her middle years and she is perhaps better known for her crime fiction than her poetry. She also wrote for children.

Murder Reflected (London: Bles, 1966); *Murder Remote* (New York: Doubleday, 1973); *Some Walk a Narrow Path* (Edinburgh: Ramsay Head, 1977); *A Distant Urn* (Edinburgh: Ramsay Head, 1983); *John Donne You Were Wrong* (Edinburgh: Ramsay Head, 1988); and others.

Carswell, Catherine (1879–1946)

Catherine Roxburgh Macfarlane was born in Glasgow on 27 March 1879. She was educated at Park School for Girls, then spent two years studying music at the Frankfurt Conservatory before in 1901 enrolling at Glasgow University to study English. Her first marriage to Herbert Jackson was annulled on the ground of Jackson's mental illness, and her daughter by that marriage died tragically when only eight. Her second, happy marriage to Donald Carswell gave her a son and a literary partnership. She is best known for her two novels, *Open the Door!* (1920) and *The Camomile* (1922), and her biographies of Burns (1930) and D.H. Lawrence (1932). She also wrote a life of Boccaccio (1937). Her autobiographical work was edited by her son, John, and published posthumously as *Lying Awake* (1950), from which the poems in this volume are taken.

Open the Door! (London: Melrose, 1920); *The Camomile* (London: Chatto & Windus, 1922); *The Life of Robert Burns* (London: Chatto & Windus, 1930); *The Savage Pilgrimage: A Narrative of D.H. Lawrence* (London: Chatto & Windus, 1932); *Lying Awake* (London: Secker & Warburg, 1950); and others.

Chisholm, Lillias Scott (Lillias Forbes) (*fl.* 1966–

Born Lillias Scott, daughter of Francis George Scott, the composer best known for his settings of MacDiarmid, she was the second wife of the composer Erik Chisholm and her first poems were published under the name Lillias Scott Chisholm. Her second collection is published under her new married name, Lillias Forbes. She lives in St Andrews and is an active member of PEN. MacDiarmid paid tribute to her verse as she to his.

Poems of Love (Edinburgh: M. MacDonald, 1966); *Turning a Fresh Eye* (Kirkcaldy: Akros, 1998).

Clanchy, Kate (1965–

Kate Clanchy was born in Glasgow and educated in Edinburgh and Oxford. She won an Eric Gregory Award in 1994. For her first collection, *Slattern*, she won in 1996 the Forward Prize for Best First Collection, the Saltire Prize for the Scottish First Book of the Year, a Scottish Autumn Book Award and a New London Writers Award. In 1997 she was awarded a Somerset Maugham Award and was shortlisted for the John Llewllyn Rhys Prize. She has worked as a teacher in the East End of London and now lives with her husband, Matthew Reynolds, in Oxford, where she also teaches.

Slattern (London: Chatto & Windus, 1995); *Samarkand* (London: Picador, 1999); *Newborn: Poems on Motherhood* (London: Picador, 2004).

Cooper, Sìne M./Jean M. Cooper (1946–

From Aberdeen Jean Cooper learned Gaelic as an adult. Three of her poems won the Bardic Crown at the national Mod in 1976, and she contributed a further nine poems to *Gairm* between 1977 and 1984. Further poems appeared in *New Writing Scotland 13*.

Crowe, Anna (1945–

Anna Crowe was born in Devonport, Plymouth, and grew up in France, Belgium, Sussex and St Andrews. She is married with a grown-up daughter and sons and has now lived in Fife for 25 years. A poet, translator, reviewer and creative writing tutor, she has herself been translated into Catalan. She won the Peterloo Poets Open Competition in 1993 and 1997. Her work has appeared in anthologies such as *Images for Africa* (Water Aid, 1988), *The Golden Goose Hour* (Edinburgh: Scottish Book Trust, 1994) and *New Writing Scotland*. She has also worked with visual artists.

Skating out of the House (Calstock: Peterloo Poets, 1997).

Cruickshank, Helen B(urness) (1886–1975)

Helen Cruickshank was born in Hillside, Angus, on 15 May 1886. When she left school she joined the Civil Service, working in London for the Post Office from 1903 to 1912; she moved to National Health Insurance in Edinburgh, remaining there for the rest of her working life. She was an active Suffragette and a committed Scottish Nationalist. She began contributing poems to magazines and in time she became a close friend of Hugh MacDiarmid, with whom she founded Scottish PEN, serving as secretary from 1927 to 1934. Throughout her life she moved in literary circles, always encouraging young writers and in many cases looking after old. Many of her own poems are in Scots, including her most anthologised, 'Shy Geordie'. Cruickshank, always cheerfully self-sacrificing, cared for her mother for many years. She retired from the Civil Service in 1946 and was awarded an honorary MA by Edinburgh University in 1971. Two years later, poor health forced her to leave her house in Corstorphine and move to Queensberry Lodge in the Canongate, where she died on 2 March 1975. Her autobiography, *Octobiography*, another work which reveals her generosity by its very reticence, was published posthumously.

Up the Noran Water and Other Scots Poems (London: Methuen, 1934); *Sea Buckthorn* (Dunfermline: Macpherson, 1954); *The Ponnage Pool* (Edinburgh: Macdonald, 1971); *Collected Poems* (Edinburgh: Reprographia, 1971); *Octobiography* (Montrose: Standard Press, 1976); *More Collected Poems* (Edinburgh: Gordon Wright, 1978).

Czerkawska, Catherine Lucy (1950–

Catherine Czerkawska was born in Leeds and received her early education there and in Ayr and Kilwinning. She attended Edinburgh and Leeds universities. She is well known as a playwright and writer of fiction as well as a poet winning the Tom-Gallon Short Story Award for 1973–4. Her play, *The Hare and the Fox*, was broadcast on Radio 4 in March 1973. She now lives in Ayrshire with her family.

White Boats [with Andrew Greig] (Edinburgh: Garret Arts, 1973); *A Book of Men, and Other Poems* (Preston: Akros, 1976); *Shadow of the Stone* (Glasgow: Drew, 1989); *The Golden Apple* (London: Century, 1990); *Wormwood* (Edinburgh: Traverse Theatre, 1997); *Quartz* (Edinburgh: Traverse Theatre, 2000); and others.

Daiches, Jenni (1941–

Jenni Daiches was born in Chicago, the daughter of scholar and critic, David Daiches. She was educated in America and England, and took degrees from Cambridge and London, after which she began a career in teaching and writing. She has taught in the University of Nairobi, travelled and lectured in America, China and Europe, and lived since 1971 in Scotland. She has two daughters and a son from her marriage to the writer Angus Calder. As Jenni Calder, she has published widely on aspects of English and American literature and history. She is an expert on a number of Scottish writers, including Robert Louis Stevenson and Margaret Oliphant, and has recently published a biography of Naomi Mitchison (q.v.). She says that her poetry 'arises mainly out of everyday experience of life and work, and is much influenced by place and landscape'.

Robert Louis Stevenson: A Life Study (London: Hamish

Hamilton, 1980); *Margaret Oliphant* (Edinburgh: Scottish Academic Press, 1992); *Mediterranean* (Aberdeen: Scottish Cultural Press, 1995); and many others.

De Luca, Christine (1947–

Christine De Luca was born in Bressay, Shetland, and brought up in Waas, where her father was Headmaster of the local Junior Secondary School. She now lives in Edinburgh and works in assessment research at the Scottish Qualifications Authority. She taught geography for ten years at Broughton High School, Edinburgh. She writes poetry in both Shetland dialect and English. Her first collection, *Voes & Sounds*, won the Shetland Literary Prize in 1996. Christine De Luca is possibly the first Viking for 1,000 years to read Shetland dialect/Norse poetry in Milan. She is currently Secretary of Shore Poets, Edinburgh, and a member of the School of Poets.

Voes & Sounds: Poems in English and Shetland Dialect (Lerwick: Shetland Library, 1995); *Wast wi da Valkyries* (Lerwick: Shetland Library, 1995).

Dhòmhnallach, Oighrig (nì 'Illeasabaig)/Euphemia Macdonald (1842–1936)

She came from Caolas in Tiree where her mother, Catherine MacFadyen, and her brother Donald were also respected poets. All three, as well as Oighrig's son and her nephew, are featured in the Tiree anthology *Na Bàird Thirisdeach* ('The Tiree Bards') edited by Hector Cameron (1932). Catherine MacFadyen's short reflection on the introduction of the old age pension (1908/09) is in Black's *An Tuil* (1999).

Na Bàird Thirisdeach (Tiree: Tiree Association, 1932).

Duffy, Carol Ann (1955–

Carol Ann Duffy was born in Glasgow, 23 December 1955. Her family left Glasgow when she was a child and she grew up in Stafford; she was educated at St Joseph's Convent, Stafford, and Stafford Girls' High School. She attended the University of Liverpool, where she took a degree in Philosophy in 1977. Awards for her poetry include the Forward Prize and the Whitbread Prize for *Mean Time* (1993). She has also written poems for children, edited anthologies of poetry and edited the magazine, *Ambit*. She currently lives in Manchester with her partner, Jackie Kay (q.v.), and lectures at the Writing School of Manchester Metropolitan University. She received a CBE in the 2002 New Year's Honours.

Standing Female Nude, (1985); *Selling Manhattan* (1987); *The Other Country* (1990); *Mean Time* (1993); *The Pamphlet* (1998) (all London: Anvil); *The World's Wife* (London: Picador, 1999); *Feminine Gospels* (London: Picador, 2002); and others.

Dunbar, Dorothy (1915–

'Born beneath Ru'glen's wee roon rid lums, educated Rutherglen Academy. Has been social worker, still church worker, no houseworker! Very fond of cats, friends, the living theatre and poetry which scans': Dorothy Dunbar's self-description from an Octopus Poetry Group collection some time in the 1970s. Until recently she lived in Rowan Cottage, Dalrymple Junction, near Ayr.

Dunbar's work appears in an Octopus Poetry Group collection and some anthologies.

Elphinstone, Margaret (1948–

Margaret Elphinstone is best known as a novelist but she has also published short stories, poems, critical articles and gardening books. She teaches at Strathclyde University, where she has been Convener of the M.Litt. in Creative Writing jointly taught by the universities of Glasgow and Strathclyde. She has two grown-up daughters.

The Incomer (London: Women's Press, 1987); *A Sparrow's Flight* (Edinburgh: Polygon, 1989); *Outside Eden: Poems* (Stroud: Sundial Press, 1990); *An Apple From a Tree* (London: Women's Press, 1991); *Islanders* (Edinburgh: Polygon, 1994); *The Sea Road* (Edinburgh: Canongate, 2000); and others.

Evans, Sally (1942–

Sally Evans lived in England, Wales and Italy before moving in 1979 to Edinburgh, where she runs a bookshop with her publisher husband. Her first book, *Millennial* (1995), was a long poem and she is a member of the Long Poem group. Her collection of short poems, *Looking for Scotland*, was published in 1996. She is the editor of *Poetry Scotland*.

Millennial (Edinburgh: Diehard Press, 1995); *Looking for Scotland* (Salzburg: University of Salzburg, 1996).

Evaristi, Marcella (1953–

Marcella Evaristi was born in Glasgow and educated at Glasgow and Edinburgh universities. She is best known as a playwright and journalist and has written for theatre, television and radio. Her play, *Dorothy, the Bitch*, was produced in Edinburgh in 1976 and her 1982 play, *Commedia*, was produced by both the Sheffield Crucible and the Lyric Hammersmith Studio in London. Her first television play, *Eve Set the Balls of Corruption Rolling*, won her the 1982 Pye Award for Best Writer New to Television. She was playwright-in-residence at the University of St Andrews in Fife, 1979–80. The same year she was a creative writing fellow at the University of Sheffield in Yorkshire. Between 1984 and 1985, she was writer-in-residence at the universities of Glasgow and Strathclyde. She now lives in London with her two children. She is also an actress.

Commedia (Edinburgh: Salamander Press, 1983).

Fell, Alison (1944–

Born 4 June 1944 in Dumfries and brought up in villages in the Highlands and the Borders, Alison moved to London in 1970 to work in the Women's Street Theatre and later on *Spare Rib*. She married in 1964 and divorced the following year: she has one son. Her first volume of poetry, *Kisses for Mayakovsky*, won the Alice Hunt Bartlett Award of the National Poetry Society in 1984. Her stories, poems and essays have been widely anthologised and she has edited and appeared in a number of feminist anthologies of poetry and prose. She is also the author of five novels and her work was featured on the BBC Scotland TV film, *Whispers in the Dark*, winter 1995–6.

The Grey Dancer: Children's Stories in English (London: Collins, 1981); *Kisses for Mayakovsky* (London: Virago, 1984); *Every Move You Make* (London: Virago, 1988); *The Bad Box* (London: Virago, 1987); *The Crystal Owl* (London: Methuen, 1988); *Mer de Glace* (London: Methuen, 1991); *The Pillow Book of the Lady Onogoro*, ed. Alison Fell, trans. Arye Blower, with an introduction by Sir Geoffrey Montague-Pollock (London: Serpent's Tail, 1994); *Dreams Like Heretics* (London: Serpent's Tail, 1997); *The Mistress of Lilliput; or, The Pursuit* (London: Doubleday, 1999); and others.

Fellows, Gerrie (1954–
Gerrie Fellows was born in Roxburgh, Otago, New Zealand, of Scottish descent. Her family moved to England in 1963. She now lives in Glasgow.

Technologies, and Other Poems (Edinburgh: Polygon, 1990); *The Powerlines* (Edinburgh: Polygon, 2000).

Ferguson, Gillian K. (1967–
Ferguson's *Air for Sleeping Fish* was shortlisted for the Saltire First Book of the Year and she won the top award in the SAC's Writer's Bursary for *Baby*, her collection of poems on pregnancy, birth and babies. She is a columnist at the *Scotsman* newspaper. Her work also appears in *Making for Planet Alice*, in *New Blood*, and *The Faber Book of Twentieth-Century Scottish Poems* (1992). In 2002 she won the Creative Scotland Award for Literature. She is currently working on a book of poems about the Human Genome.

Air for Sleeping Fish (Newcastle-upon-Tyne: Bloodaxe Books, 1997); *Making for Planet Alice: New Women Poets* (Bloodaxe Books, 1997); *New Blood* (Bloodaxe Books, 1999); *Baby* (Edinburgh: Canongate Books, 2001).

Forbes, Lillias see **Chisholm, Lillias Scott**

Forrest-Thomson, Veronica (1947–75)
Veronica Forrest-Thomson was born in 1947 and grew up in Glasgow. She studied at Liverpool and Cambridge universities; she subsequently taught at Leicester and Birmingham. She was a poet, a theorist and a critic. Her critical study, *Poetic Artifice* (Manchester: Manchester UP, 1978), is scathing about customary methods of critical analysis of poetry. She married the writer Jonathan Culler in 1971 but died, tragically early, in 1975.

Poetic Artifice: A Theory of Twentieth-Century Poetry (Manchester: Manchester University Press, 1978); *Collected Poems and Translations* (Edinburgh: Allardyce, Barnett, 1990).

Fraser, Olive (1909–77)

Olive Fraser's is a tragic story: she was the unwanted child of a secret marriage, deserted by her father before her birth and by her mother shortly after. She was educated at Aberdeen University, where she won accolades and awards as scholar and poet. She then went as a graduate student to Cambridge, where she showed the first signs of the manic-depressive illness that affected her for nearly the whole of her life. She was an officer in the WRNS during the Second World War: this exacerbated her psychological suffering and from this point most of her life was spent in and out of mental institutions. She never, however, completely ceased to write poetry. In 1969 she was diagnosed as suffering from hyperthyroidism and treatment effected a cure that allowed her to write freely in her last years. Her work was publicised through the generous advocacy of Helen Mennie Shire, who had met her at university in Aberdeen and remained her friend throughout her life.

The Pure Account (Aberdeen: Aberdeen University Press, 1981); *The Wrong Music: The Poems of Olive Fraser* (Edinburgh: Canongate, 1989).

Frater, Anna (1967–

From the Point peninsula of Lewis, Anna Frater comes from the same village as Ciorstai NicLeòid (q.v.), Carstìona Anna Stiùbhart (q.v.) and poet and scholar Derick Thomson. She developed her poetry in Gaelic while studying Gaelic and French at Glasgow University. A substantial selection of her work was featured in *An Aghaidh na Sìorraidheachd* (1991), and her own collection, *Fon t-Slige*/'Under the Shell', was published in 1995. After completing a PhD thesis on Scottish Gaelic women's poetry up to 1750, she worked in Gaelic television in Glasgow and now tutors at Lews Castle College, Stornoway. See also Black's *An Tuil* (1999).

Fon t-Slige (Glasgow: Gairm, 1995).

Garry, Flora (1900–2000)
Flora Garry was born at New Deer in Aberdeenshire and educated at New Deer village school, Peterhead Academy and Aberdeen University. She taught English in schools in Dumfries (Dumfries Academy), Strichen and Glasgow; her husband, Robert Campbell Garry, was Regius Professor of Physiology at Glasgow University. She started writing poetry in the 1940s by submitting a poem for a competition in which it won first prize. Her collection, *Bennygoak*, was an instant success.

Bennygoak, and Other Poems (Preston: Akros, 1974); *Collected Poems* (Edinburgh: Gordon Wright, 1995).

Gibson, Magi (1953–
Magi Gibson was educated at Kilsyth Academy and Glasgow University. She taught Modern Languages in Cumbernauld High School and English as a foreign language in Paris. She has also worked as creative writing tutor with the Workers' Educational Association. She has been Scottish Arts Council Writing Fellow and won the *Scotland on Sunday*/Women 2000 Poetry Prize in 1990. *Kicking Back* was nominated for a Saltire Award for best first book. She was Writing Fellow with Renfrew District Libraries 1992–94 and has been tutor to the Stirling Writers' Group. She has also written a play, *Elleva Day*, with

inmates of Cornton Vale Prison and has completed a novel for 10–12 year olds. She teaches special needs.

Kicking Back (Edinburgh: Taranis, 1994); *Strange Fish*, with Helen Lamb (Glasgow: Duende, 1997); *Premier Results*, with Brian Whittingham (Glasgow: Neruda, 1997).

Gillies, Valerie (Simmons) (1948–

Born in Edmonton, Canada, she was brought up in Edinburgh and at her grandparents' house on the Lanarkshire moors, which inspired her to begin writing at 14. She was educated at Edinburgh University, where she was taught by Norman MacCaig, who was Writing Fellow there. She was awarded a Commonwealth Scholarship to study contemporary Indian writers at the University of Mysore, an experience that has also fed her poetry. She has worked as a poet and scriptwriter for radio and television and has taught creative writing in schools and colleges: as well as being Writer in Residence at Duncan of Jordanstone College of Art, Dundee, from 1988 to 1990, she has held a fellowship in the Lothians. She lives in Edinburgh with her husband and children. A lot of her work has involved collaboration with visual artists and musicians.

Bed of Stone (Edinburgh: Canongate, 1984); *Each Bright Eye: Selected Poems, 1971–1976* (Edinburgh: Canongate, 1977); *Tweed Journey* (Edinburgh: Canongate, 1989); *The Chanter's Tune* (Edinburgh: Canongate, 1990); *The Ringing Rock* (Edinburgh: Scottish Cultural Press, 1995); *Men and Beasts: Wild Men and Tame Animals of Scotland*, photographs by Rebecca Marr (Edinburgh: Luath, 2000); *The Lightning Tree* (Edinburgh: Polygon, 2002) and others.

Herd, Tracey (1968–

Tracey Herd was born in East Kilbride and then moved to

Fife. She graduated in English and American Studies from the University of Dundee in 1991 and subsequently worked in a Dundee bookshop. Her first collection, *No Hiding Place* (1996), was short-listed for the Forward Prize. She won an Eric Gregory Award in 1993 and was awarded a Scottish Arts Council Bursary in 1995. She became Writer in Residence at the University of Dundee in 1998.

No Hiding Place (Newcastle-upon-Tyne: Bloodaxe, 1996); *Dead Redhead* (Newcastle-upon-Tyne: Bloodaxe, 2001).

Hutchison, Isobel Wylie (1889–1982)

Isobel Hutchison was born 1889 at Carlowrie, Kirkliston, and educated at Rothesay House School and Studley Horticultural College for Women. She was a traveller and botanist, a collector of plants in Arctic Regions for the Royal Horticultural Society. She was also an accomplished water-colourist who enjoyed physical exercise. Member of PEN. Gwyneth Hoyle, *Flowers in the Snow: The Life of Isobel Wylie Hutchison* (Lincoln & London: University of Nebraska Press, 2001).

Lyrics from West Lothian (Edinburgh: printed by H. & J. Pillans & Wilson, [1916]); *How Joy was Found: a Fantasy in Verse in five acts* (London: Blackie & Son, 1917); *The Calling of Bride* (Stirling: Eneas Mackay, [1926]); *The Northern Gate* (Alexander Moring: London, 1927); *Lyrics from Greenland*, with 4 plates from water-colour sketches by the author (London & Glasgow: Blackie & Son, 1935).

Jacob, Violet (1863–1946)

Violet Jacob was born Violet Kennedy-Erskine at the House of Dun near Montrose. In 1894 she married Arthur Jacob, an Irishman serving in the British Army. She accompanied him when he was stationed in Central India and Egypt, after which the Jacobs lived in various parts of England, particularly Shropshire and Herefordshire. She published fiction, novels and short stories, and poetry in Scots and English. Her Indian diaries were published in 1990. The heaviest blow in Violet Jacob's life was the loss of her only son, Harry, at the Battle of the Somme in 1916. After her husband's death in 1937, Jacob returned to Angus where she died in 1946, having received an honorary degree from Edinburgh University in the previous year. Jacob was writing in the Scots vernacular long before the Scottish Renaissance of the 1920s when Hugh MacDiarmid and others came to the fore. Violet knew MacDiarmid, who was a reporter on the *Montrose Review* during the 1920s. She met him on her visits to Angus on holiday, usually during the autumn, and he included some of her poetry in the first edition of his anthology, *Northern Numbers*.

The Sheep Stealers (London: Heinemann, 1902); *The Infant Moralist* with Lady Helena Carnegie (Edinburgh: Grant & Son, 1903); *The Golden Heart and Other Fairy Stories* (1904); *The Interloper* (1904); *Verses* (1905); *Songs of Angus* (1915); *More Songs of Angus* (1918); *Bonnie Joann* (1921); *Northern Lights* (1927); *The Scottish Poems of Violet Jacob* (Edinburgh: Oliver & Boyd, 1944) and others.

Jamie, Kathleen (1962–

Kathleen Jamie was born in Renfrewshire, grew up in Midlothian and studied Philosophy at Edinburgh University. At 19 she won a Gregory Award and a Scottish Arts Council Book Award for *Black Spiders* (1982). She has since published four collections of poems. With Andrew Greig, she published *A Flame in Your Heart* (1986) and, with the photographer Sean Mayne Smith, *The Autonymous Region* (1993). She has also published *The Golden Peak* (1992), an account of her travels in northern Pakistan. She currently teaches creative writing at St Andrews University and lives with her family in Fife.

Black Spiders (Edinburgh: Salamander Press, 1982); *The Way We Live* (Newcastle-upon-Tyne: Bloodaxe, 1987); *The Golden Peak* (London: Virago, 1992); *The Autonymous Region* (Bloodaxe, 1993); *The Queen of Sheba* (Bloodaxe, 1994); *Jizzen* (London: Picador, 1999); *Mr and Mrs Scotland are Dead: Poems 1980–1994* (Bloodaxe, 2002); *The Tree House* (London: Picador, 2004); *The Tree House* (London: Picador, 2003).

Kay, Jackie (1961–

Born in Edinburgh and brought up by adoptive parents in Glasgow, Jackie Kay was educated at Stirling University, and has written drama, poetry and fiction, for children as well as adults. Her first poetry collection, *The Adoption Papers* (1991), received a Scottish Arts Council book award, a Saltire First Book of the Year Award and a Forward Prize. *Two's Company*, her poems for children, won the Signal Poetry Award in 1993. *Off Colour* (1998) won a Somerset Maugham Award. Her novel, *Trumpet* (1998), won the Guardian Fiction Award. Her latest collection of short stories has been widely well-reviewed.

'Twice Over', in *Gay Sweatshop: Four Plays and a Company* (London: Methuen, 1989); *The Adoption Papers* (Newcastle-upon-Tyne: Bloodaxe, 1991); *That Distance Apart* (London: Turret Books, 1991); *Two's Company* (London: Blackie Children's Books, 1992); *Other Lovers* (Newcastle-upon-Tyne: Bloodaxe, 1993); *Three Has Gone* (London: Blackie Children's Books, 1994); *Bessie Smith* (Bath: Absolute, 1997); *The Frog Who Dreamed She Was an Opera Singer* (London: Bloomsbury Children's, 1998); *Off Colour* (Newcastle-upon-

Tyne: Bloodaxe, 1998); *Trumpet* (London: Picador, 1998); *Why Don't You Stop Talking?* (London: Picador: 2002).

Kermack, Alison (1965–

Alison Kermack was born in Edinburgh. She now lives in Orkney and works for Stromness Books and Prints. She writes poetry and short stories, has published two pamphlets of poetry and has appeared in various magazines and anthologies.

Restricted Vocabulary (Stromness: Clocktower Press, 1991); *Writing like a Bastard* (Edinburgh: Rebel Inc. Publications, 1993)

Lochhead, Liz (1947–

Liz Lochhead was born in Motherwell on 26 December 1947. Educated at Dalziel High School, Motherwell, she studied painting at the Glasgow School of Art (1965–70) and during the early seventies took part in a writing group co-ordinated by Philip Hobsbaum that was also attended by Alasdair Gray and James Kelman. Lochhead worked as an art teacher until she became a full-time writer in 1979. She has held writing residencies in Britain and Canada, and lives in Glasgow. In addition to her poetry collections, her published stage works (with dates of first production) include *Blood and Ice* (1982; revised 1984), *Dracula* (1985), a Scots version of *Tartuffe* (1985) and *Mary Queen of Scots Got Her Head Chopped Off* (1987). Her other plays include *The Big Picture* (1988), *Them Through The Wall* (with Agnes Owens, 1989), *Patter Merchants* (1989), *Jock Tamson's Bairns* (1990) and *Quelques Fleurs* (1991). Her most recent play, *Perfect Days*, was one of the hits of the 1998 Edinburgh Festival.

Blood and Ice (Edinburgh: Salamander Press, 1982); *Silver Service* (1984); *Dreaming Frankenstein and Collected Poems* [includes *Memo for Spring, Islands, The Grimm Sisters*] (Edinburgh: Polygon, 1984); *True Confessions and New Clichés* (Edinburgh; Polygon, 1985); *Tartuffe, a translation into Scots* (Edinburgh: Polygon; Glasgow: Third Eye Centre, 1985); *Mary Queen of Scots Got Her Head Chopped Off* and *Dracula* (Harmondsworth: Penguin, 1989); *Bagpipe Muzak* (Harmondsworth: Penguin, 1991); *Medea* (London: Nick Hern in association with Theatre Babel, 2000); *Colour of Black and White* (Edinburgh: Polygon, 2003) and others.

Lochhead, Marion (Cleland) (1902–85)

Marion Lochhead was born in Wishaw on 19 April 1902. She was educated at Glasgow University (English and Latin) but later lived mostly in Edinburgh. She was at first a teacher and then turned to journalism and other writing. She wrote fiction, novels and stories for adults and children, biography and cultural and social history. Along with Helen Cruickshank (q.v.), she was one of the founder members of Scottish PEN in 1927. She was made a fellow of the Royal Society of Literature in 1955. Music was always important to her.

Poems (Glasgow: Gowans & Gray, 1928); *Painted Things* (Glasgow: Gowans & Gray, 1929); *Anne Dalrymple* (Edinburgh: Moray Press, 1934); *Cloaked in Scarlet* (1935); *Adrian was a Priest* (1936); *Island Destiny* (1936); *Feast of Candlemas and Other Devotional Poems* (1937), *The Dancing Flower* (1938) [all Edinburgh & London: Moray Press]; *Fiddler's Bidding* (Edinburgh: Oliver & Boyd, 1939); *Highland Scene* (Glasgow: Smith's, 1939); *The Scots Household in the Eighteenth Century* (Edinburgh: Moray Press, 1948); *The Victorian Household* (London: John Murray, 1964); *The Battle of the Birds and Other Celtic Tales* (London: Hamilton, 1981); and others.

Lomax, Marion (1953–

Marion Lomax is the pseudonym of Robyn Bolam, Professor of English Language and Literature, St Mary's College, University of Surrey. Robyn Bolam was born in Newcastle and grew up in Northumberland; she is Chair of the National Association of Writers in Education. She has reviewed Renaissance literature and contemporary poetry in several journals, including *The Times Literary Supplement*, *Modern Language Review*, *Literature and History*, *Poetry Wales* and *Writing in Education*. She contributed to the ABES bibliography on CD ROM (Caroline Drama) and wrote the seventeenth-century drama sections for *The Year's Work in English Studies* vols. 95–8, 1998–2001. In April 2000 she was co-chair of the British Council's Fifteenth Annual Conference on the Teaching of Literature at Corpus Christi College, Oxford, and, in October 2000, was a keynote speaker at the British Council's international 'anti-conference' at the University of Constanta, Romania. In April 2001 she was a member of a panel invited to speak about creative writing in UK universities at the Associated Writing Programs' conference at Palm Springs.

The Peepshow Girl (Newcastle-upon-Tyne: Bloodaxe, 1989); *Beyond Men and Dreams: A Chamber Opera* [composer: Bennett Hogg], commissioned by the Royal Opera House (Garden Venture) and performed at the Riverside Studios, 1–8 June 1991; *Raiding the Borders* (Newcastle-upon-Tyne: Bloodaxe, 1996); and critical and editorial works as Marion Lomax and as Robyn Bolam.

MacArthur, Bessie J.B. (Jane Bird) (1889–1983)

She was born in Duns, Berwickshire and spent her childhood in Edinburgh, living in the Bank of Scotland on the Mound, where her father worked. Educated at the Charlotte Square Institute and St George's School, Edinburgh, she married a sheep farmer in Upper Clydeside with whom she had three sons and a daughter. She lost two of her sons in the Second World War and after an immediate period of silence wrote moving poetry about this loss. Their deaths are also commemorated in a stained glass window in Elvanfoot Parish Church. She also wrote plays and local history and was an accomplished pianist.

Clan of Lochlann, and Silis: Two Celtic Plays (Edinburgh: W.M. Urquart & Son, 1928); *The Starry Venture, and Other Poems* (London: Elkin Mathews & Marrot, 1930); *Scots Poems* (Edinburgh: Oliver & Boyd, 1938); *Last Leave* (Edinburgh: Oliver & Boyd, 1943); *From Daer Water: Poems in Scots and English* (Dunfermline: H.T. Macpherson, 1962); *And Time Moves On* (West Linton: The Castlelaw Press, 1972); *Song o' the Lairock* (Biggar: Biggar Museum Trust, 1976) and others.

MacDonald, Catherine see NicDhòmhnaill, Catrìona

McDonald, Ellie (1937–

A native of Dundee, Ellie has been an office worker, a shop assistant and a freelance calligrapher. Below her photograph in *The Gangan' Fuit* is the following: 'Biographical note: The long-established tradition of autobiographical notes may satisfy the curious but answers no relevant questions.
The poet is merely a go-between,
It is the message which matters.
To the lover of words I offer my poems.'

The Gangan' Fuit, with an Introduction by Anne Stevenson (q.v.) (Edinburgh: Chapman, 1991); *Pathfinder* (Kingskettle: Kettillonia, 2000).

Macdonald, Euphemia see Dhòmhnallach, Oighrig

MacDonald, Mairi see **NicDhòmhnaill, Màiri**

Mackay, Christina A. see **NicAoidh, Cairstìona Anna**

Mackay, Christina see **NicDh'àidh Curstaidh**

McKay, Elise (1920–
Unravelling Knots (Walton-on-Thames: Outposts, 1984); *Floating Lanterns* (Envoi Poets, 1988).

Maclean, Mary M. see **NicIlleathain, Màiri M.**

MacLeod, Anne (1951–
Born of Anglo-Irish parents, the second of five children, she has lived most of her life in or near Inverness. She studied medicine at Aberdeen University, after which she returned to Inverness. She now works as a dermatologist, serving communities throughout the Highlands. She is married with four children, and, is currently working on an adult novel.

Just the Caravaggio (Salzburg; Oxford: Poetry Salzburg at the University of Salzburg, 1999); *Standing by Thistles* (Edinburgh: Scottish Cultural Press, 1997); *The Dark Ship*, (Glasgow: 11/9, 2001).

MacLeod, Christina see **NicLeòid, Ciorstai**

McSeveney, Angela (1964–
Angela McSeveney was born and brought up in Ross-shire, Livingston and the Scottish Borders. She is a graduate of Edinburgh University. Her poetry has appeared in various collections and she has held a Scottish Arts Council Bursary. She now lives in Edinburgh.

Coming Out With It (Edinburgh: Polygon, 1992); *ibid* (issue 5) (Edinburgh: Department of English, University of Edinburgh, 1997).

Mirrlees, Hope (1887–1978)

Raymond Mortimer, in his 'Preface' to her poems, calls her 'a Celt descended from ancient Picts'. She was educated at home and at St Leonard's School, St Andrews. She wrote novels, poems and translations but is perhaps most remembered for her circle of literary friends, which included T.S. Eliot, Virginia Woolf and Lady Ottoline Morrell. She published two novels, *Lud-in-the-Mist* and *Counterplot*, and a book of poetry, *Moods and Tensions: Poems*. She began, but never completed, a biography of seventeenth-century British antiquarian Sir Robert Bruce Cotton; part of this was published as *A Fly in Amber* in 1962. With Jane Harrison, she produced two translations of Russian literature, *The Life of the Archpriest Avvakum by Himself* and *The Book of the Bear*. Her unpublished papers consist solely of correspondence; significant correspondents include T.S. Eliot, Ottoline Morrell, Virginia Woolf and Leonard Woolf. She lived for many years in South Africa but her poetry was published while she was living in Oxford and is dedicated to Mary Lascelles.

Moods and Tensions: Poems (Oxford and Tehran: The Amate Press, 1976); and others.

Mitchell, Elma (1919–2000)

Elma Mitchell was born in Airdrie. She worked as a professional librarian and in publishing, journalism and broadcasting in London. In Somerset, she worked as a freelance writer and translator. Several collections of her poetry have been published and in 1977 she was one of the five first-prize winners in the Cheltenham Festival Poetry Competition.

The Poor Man in the Flesh (Calstock, Cornwall: Peterloo Poets, 1976); *The Human Cage* (Peterloo Poets, 1979); *Furnished Rooms* (Peterloo Poets, 1983); *People Etcetera: Poems New and Selected* (Peterloo Poets, 1987)

Mitchison, Naomi (1897–1999)
Naomi Mitchison was born Naomi Haldane on 1 November 1897 in Edinburgh and was educated at the Dragon School and St Anne's College, Oxford. Her father was a noted physiologist and her brother the genetic scientist and essayist, J.B.S. Haldane. She married the barrister and Labour politician Dick, later Baron, Mitchison in 1916 and during their time in London she took an active part in social and political affairs. She had published several novels before she returned to Scotland in 1937 to live in Carradale in Kintyre. Widely travelled and politically active, she was adopted as adviser and Mmarona (mother) of the Bakgatla tribe in Botswana in the 1960s. Her many books include historical novels, science fiction and fantasy, children's novels, memoirs, poetry and stories. She died on 11 January 1999.

The Corn King and the Spring Queen (1931; Edinburgh: Canongate, 1990); *The Blood of the Martyrs* (1939; Edinburgh: Canongate, 1988); *The Bull Calves* (1947; Glasgow: Drew, 1985); *All Change Here: Girlhood and Marriage* (London: Bodley Head, 1975); *The Cleansing of the Knife* (Edinburgh: Canongate, 1978); *Among You Taking Notes: The Wartime Diary of Naomi Mitchison, 1939–1945* (London: Gollancz, 1985); *A Girl Must Live: Stories and Poems* (Glasgow: Drew, 1990); and many others.

Montgomery, Catriona see **NicGumaraid, Catrìona**

Montgomery, Mary see **NicGumaraid, Màiri**

Montgomery, Morag see **NicGumaraid, Mòrag**

Muir, Willa (1890–1970)
Willa Anderson was born and brought up in Shetland. She took a first in Classics at St Andrews University; after graduation in 1910 she studied educational psychology and moved to London, becoming first a lecturer and then vice-principal of Gipsy Hill Training College for teachers. She married the poet, Edwin Muir, in 1919. The Muirs worked as writers and journalists in London and then for the British Council in Edinburgh, Prague and Rome. Willa translated Kafka, Feuchtwanger and Broch, among other writers, with her husband and wrote several novels and polemic pieces. She is not best known for her poetry but her poetic translations are, nevertheless, worth attention.

Women: An Inquiry (London: Hogarth Press, 1925); *Imagined Corners* (London: Martin Secker, 1931); *5 songs from the Auvergnat; done into Modern Scots by Willa Muir* [Warlingham: Samson Press, 1931]; *Mrs Ritchie* (London: Martin Secker, 1933); Mrs Grundy in Scotland (London: Routledge, 1936); 'Women in Scotland', *Left Review*, 1936; [all published as *Imagined Selves*, ed. Kirsty Allen (Edinburgh: Canongate, 1996)] *Living with Ballads* (London: Hogarth Press, 1965); *Belonging: A Memoir* (London: Hogarth Press 1968).

Murray, Janetta I.W. (*fl.* 1922–52)
Janetta Murray was born and brought up in Glasgow.

The Ship-Makers, and Other Verses (Glasgow: Gowans & Gray, 1922); *A Legendary of St Mungo* [poems] (Glasgow: Gowans & Gray, 1923).

Nelson, Helena (1953–

Helena Nelson was born in Knutsford, Cheshire. She read English at the University of York and then an took an MA in eighteenth-century literature at the University of Manchester. Her work was first published in *Spectrum* magazine in 1992 and subsequently in *The Dark Horse*. She has published in a number of other literary magazines and her poetry regularly features in the webzine *Snakeskin*; she reviews for *The Dark Horse*, *Thumbscrew* and *Second Light*. In 2000, she was winner of the Keats Shelley Memorial Association Millennium Competition for an essay on Keats. For the last 12 years she has worked at Glenrothes College in Fife, teaching core-skill communication and creative writing.

Mr and Mrs Philpott on Holiday at Auchterawe, and Other Poems (Kingskettle: Kettillonia, 2001)

NicAoidh, Cairstìona Anna/Christina Anna MacKay (1928–

From Achmore, Lewis, she was a primary teacher till retirement in 1991. She has written many poems for children (all unpublished) but has since 1988 published some of her verse in *Gairm* under her married name, NicÌomhair. See also *An Tuil*, p.796.

NicDh'àidh, Curstaidh/Christina Mackay (1914–2001)

Née MacPhee, from Iochdar, South Uist, she taught in the Highlands and in Uist (mainly at Garrynamonie Primary School) until she retired. Her songs were sung at local cèilidhs and are still heard on radio.

NicDhòmhnaill, Catrìona/MacDonald, Catherine (1925–

From Staffin, Skye, she has been writing religious verse since 1972. She has published two collections: *Sgeul na Rèite*/"The

Story of the Atonement' (1981) and *Na Bannan Gràidh*/'The Bonds of Love' (1987). See also Black's *An Tuil* (1999).

Sgeul na Rèite: Laoidhean (Stornoway: Stornoway Religious Bookshop, 1981) and *Na Bannan Gràidh* (Stornoway: Stornoway Religious Bookshop, 1987).

NicDhòmhnaill, Màiri/Mary MacDonald

From Grimsay, North Uist, she has been a primary teacher in Skye and Glen Etive and has worked as Gaelic tutor at Sabhal Mòr Ostaig. She was married to the late Norman Malcolm MacDonald, novelist and playwright. In 1985 she brought out her one poetry collection, *Mo Lorgan Fhìn*/'My Own Footprints', and five years later a book of short stories, *Grima* (1990). She also writes stories for radio. See Black's *An Tuil* (1999).

Mo Lorgan Fhìn ([Skye]: Crois-Eilein Pubs; John Eccles, Inverness, printers, 1985); *Grima* (Steòrnabhagh/Stornoway: Acair, 1990). *Sràid na h-Eala* [children's stories] (Steòrnabhagh/ Stornoway: Acair, 1994).

NicGhill-eathain, Màiri M./Mary M. Maclean (1921–

Born in Carinish, North Uist, and attended the local primary school there, after which she educated herself through correspondence courses. She worked on the mainland through the 1940s before returning to Uist, where she settled in Grimsay. She won the Bardic Crown in 1951. Her published work includes a booklet of poetry in English and Gaelic, *Sunbeams and Starlight* (1947), a short story collection *Lus-Chrùn à Griomsaidh* (1970), and a novella *Gainmheach an Fhàsaich* (1971). In Timothy Neat's *The Voice of the Bard* (Edinburgh: Canongate, 1999) she speaks of her life and poetry, recounting how she broke her engagement to a fellow Uist poet and joined the Free Church: 'Marriage, in those days, was an absolute giving of one's life and I, in all honesty, felt unable to give my life to a single man. I wanted to write great poetry . . . I felt I had a vision of the world which I had a duty to express through my poetry' (p.43). See also *An Tuil*.

Sunbeams and Starlight (1947); *Lus-Chrùn à Griomsaidh* (Inbhirnis, 100 Church Street Inverness: Club Leabhar Ltd/Highland Book Club, 1970); *Gainmheach an Fhàsaich* (Inbhirnis: Club Leabhar Ltd/Highland Book Club, 1971).

NicGumaraid, Catrìona/Catriona Montgomery (1947–
Born Dunvegan, Skye, Catrìona has spent most of her adult life in Dundee and Glasgow. A graduate in Celtic and Scottish history of Glasgow University, she has worked as a teacher, acted for theatre and television, and is also a scriptwriter. She collaborated with her sister Mòrag (q.v.) in the collection *A' Choille Chiar*/'The Dusky Forest' (1974). A collection of old and new material, *Rè na h-Oidhche*/'The Length of the Night', appeared in 1994. See also Black's *An Tuil* (1999).

A' Choille Chiar, with Mòrag NicGumaraid (Glaschu/ Glasgow: Clo-Beag, 1974); *Rè na h-Oidhche*, introduction by Sorley MacLean (Edinburgh: Canongate, 1994).

NicGumaraid, Màiri/Mary Montgomery (1955–
From Arivruaich in Lewis, she began writing poetry seriously while studying Gaelic and English at Aberdeen University. She worked as a BBC radio producer and scriptwriter in the 1980s, returning to Lewis in the '90s to lecture at Lews Castle College, Stornoway. She is now studying Law. Her poems were published for over ten years in *Gairm* and other periodicals before her first collection, *Eadar Mi 's a' Bhreug*/'Between Me and the Lie', appeared in 1988 under

the Irish imprint Coiscéim. A second collection, *Ruithmean's Neo-Rannan*/'Rhymes and Non-verse', which included early poems, followed in 1997. Both collections are bilingual Gaelic–Irish. She has also written a children's story *Am Baile Beag Annasach*/'The Bizarre Little Village' (1990), a novel *Clann Iseabail*/'Ishbel's Children' (1993) and a variety of short stories and stories for radio. See also Black's *An Tuil*, p.795.

Eadar Mi 's a' Bhreug, poems in Scottish Gaelic with Irish translations, (Baile Atha Cliath: Coiscéim, 1988); *Ruithmean 's Neo-Rannan*, poems in Scottish Gaelic with Irish translations (Baile Atha Cliath: Coiscéim, 1997).

NicGumaraid, Mòrag/Morag Montgomery (1950–

From Dunvegan, Skye, she studied briefly at Glasgow School of Art before returning to Skye to assume croft and family responsibilities. In 1974 she published a joint collection, *A' Choille Chiar*/'The Gloomy Forest', with her sister Catrìona (q.v.). She is now a trained puppeteer and a television scriptwriter. See also Black's *An Tuil*.

A' Choille Chiar, with Catrìona NicGumaraid (Glaschu/ Glasgow: Clo-beag, 1974)

NicLeòid, Ciorstai/ Christina MacLeod (1880–1954)

She was born in Bayble on the Point peninsula of Lewis (also the native village of poets Christina Ann Stewart (q.v.), Derick Thomson, Iain Crichton Smith and Anne Frater). She spent most of her adult life in Fortrose, where her husband was rector of the local Academy: they had six children. Throughout her life she was a teacher, choirleader, poet and writer of drama and songs for children. She published a booklet of original songs, *Ceòlradh Cridhe*, in 1943 and her 1952 collection, *An Sireadh* ('The Quest'), was the first book

of Gaelic non-devotional poetry by a woman in forty years.
A study of her work by Catherine M. Dunn can be found in
Transactions of the Gaelic Society of Inverness 49 (1974–76),
97–134. Two of her longer war poems are featured in Ronald
Black's anthology *An Tuil*, 1999.

An Sireadh (Struibhle/Stirling: Aonghas MacAoidh, 1952).

Niven, Liz (1952–

Born in Glasgow, she has worked as a teacher and Scots
Language Development Officer. She moved to Galloway with
her family in 1982 and was Writer in Residence for Dumfries
and Galloway Arts Association from 1998 to 2001. Awarded
Scottish Arts Council Writers' Bursaries in 1986 and 2003.
She has published a wide range of resources for the increased
use of Scots language in Education, including 'The Scots
Language: its Place in Education' and 'It's a Braw Brew'. She
was one of the commissioned writers for Scottish Cultural
Enterprise's Year of the Artist, 2000–01.

A Drunk Wumman Sittin oan a Thistle (Kircudbright:
Marketing Publications, 1997); *A Play Aboot Ninian*
(Dumfries: Watergaw, 1997); *Past Presents* (Kirkcaldy:
Akros, 1997); *Cree Lines* (Dumfries: Watergaw, 2000);
Stravaigin (Edinburgh: Canongate, 2001).

Orr, Christine Grant Millar (1899–1963)

Christine Orr was born in 1899, daughter of Sheriff Robert
Low Orr. She was educated at St George's High School,
Edinburgh, and Somerville College. She was a prolific
writer, although not of poetry. She wrote novels, romances,
comedies and farces. *The Player King* is a story of Scotland
at the time of Flodden. She worked with the BBC as an
organiser of *Children's Hour*.

The Glorious Thing (1919); *Kate Curlew: A Romance of the Pentland Country* (1922); *The House of Joy* (1926); *Hogmanay* (1928) [all London: Hodder & Stoughton]; *The Loud-Speaker, and Other Poems* (Edinburgh: The Porpoise Press, 1928); *Artificial Silk: A Novel* (London: Hodder & Stoughton, [1929]); *Flying Scotswoman* (London: Rich & Cowan, 1936); and until 1951 many other romances, comedies and farces.

Paisley, Janet (1948–

Born in Ilford, Essex, Janet Paisley grew up in Avonbridge in central Scotland. She has won many awards for her fiction, poetry and plays, including: Creative Scotland Award 2000, Scots Language MacDiarmid trophy, Poetry Society Prize and the Peggy Ramsay Memorial Award for her play *Refuge*. She has also received two SAC writing fellowships and a play-wright's bursary. She also writes for radio and television and her most recent screenplay was shortlisted for a BAFTA award. Her work has been widely translated.

Pegasus in Flight (Edinburgh: Rookbook, 1989); *Biting through Skins: Poems & Illustrations* (Edinburgh: Rookbook, 1992); *Wild Fire* (Edinburgh: Taranis, 1993); *Alien Crop* (Edinburgh: Chapman, 1996); *Reading the Bones* (Edinburgh: Canongate, 1999); *Ye Cannae Win* (Edinburgh: Chapman, 2000); and others.

Paulin, Dorothy Margaret (1904–?)

Dorothy Margaret McBirnie was born in Dumfries and educated at Dumfries Academy, St Margaret's, Polmont and Edinburgh University (MA, BCom). She married Neil Godfrey Paulin, WS, 1931; they had one daughter. Her husband was editor of the *Gallovidian Annual* and she took over from him, 1926–36; she also edited the poetry section of *Poetry Review*, 1943–44. She worked as Liaison Officer,

Dept of Agriculture for Scotland, 1942–47, and farmed for a period. The Paulins had houses in Edinburgh and Seton Court, Gullane. She gives hunting as her recreation.

Country Gold, and other poems (Edinburgh & London: Moray Press, 1936); *The Wan Water, and other poems* (Oxford: Shakespeare Head Press, sold by Basil Blackwell, 1939); *Solway Tide* (Glasgow: William Hodge & Co, 1955); *Springtime by Loch Ken, and other poems* (Castle Douglas & Dumfries: J.H. Maxwell, 1962).

Pitman, Joy (1945–

Joy Pitman was born in Bristol; she started writing poetry at boarding school at thirteen. Her first degree was in English and Philosophy; her second in Drama and Theatre Arts. She has taught English in England and has worked as an archivist in the USA. She moved to Scotland in 1973 and has lived in Edinburgh since 1976. A founder-member of Stramullion, the Scottish feminist publishing co-operative, she has also worked as a psychotherapist and has published articles on figures in the history of medicine.

Telling Gestures (Edinburgh: Chapman Publications, 1993).

Prince, Alison (1931–

Born in London of a Scottish mother and a Yorkshire father, Alison Prince won a scholarship to the Slade School of Art and began writing when marriage and three children inter-rupted her career as an art teacher. She has written for chil-dren's television and is author and illustrator of more than twenty children's books. She has also written a series of essays on formative thinking, *The Necessary Goat* (1992), and *An Innocent in the Wild Woods*, a biography of Kenneth Grahame, author of *The Wind in the Willows* (1994). After running a farm in Suffolk for eight years, she returned, after her children grew up, to Scotland, where she now lives on the Isle of Arran.

The Necessary Goat (Edinburgh: Taranis Books, 1992); *An Innocent in the Wild Wood* (London: Allison & Busby, 1994); *Having Been in the City* (Edinburgh: Taranis Books, 1994); and many others.

Raine, Kathleen (1908–2003)

Kathleen Raine was brought up in Ilford, where her father was a teacher; she found the place ugly. Her mother was Scottish and was steeped in the poetry of Scotland, from the ballads to Burns, but Kathleen Raine says she loved all poetry and could almost recite *Paradise Lost*. She has published eleven volumes of poetry since 1943. She was a graduate of Cambridge University and a celebrated scholar and critic of William Blake and W.B. Yeats. Her autobiography has been published in several volumes. She was the founder of the Temenos Academy, London, and Editor of the *Temenos Review*. She won many literary awards, including the Harriet Monroe Prize and the Edna St Vincent Millay Prize from the American Poetry Society. She lived in London.

Shore and Flower: Poems 1935–43 (London: Nicholson & Watson, 1945); *The Pythoness, and Other Poems* (1949); *The Collected Poems* (1956); *The Hollow Hill, and Other Poems* (1965) [all London: Hamish Hamilton]; *Defending Ancient Springs* (London: Oxford University Press, 1967); *Farewell Happy Fields* (1973); *The Land Unknown* (1975); *The Lion's Mouth* (1977) [all London: Hamish Hamilton]; *Collected Poems, 1935–1980* (London: Allen & Unwin, 1981); *Autobiographies* (London: Skoob Books, 1991); and many others.

Randall, Deborah (1957–

Deborah Randall was born in Gosport, Hampshire. She had various jobs, including working in a plastics factory, hotels and a children's home before studying English at Sheffield University. She moved to Kirkwall in Orkney and subsequently to Ullapool. In 1987 she won first prize in the Bloodaxe and Bridport poetry competitions.

The Sin Eater (Newcastle-upon-Tyne: Bloodaxe, 1989); *White Eyes, Dark Ages* (Bloodaxe, 1993).

Ransford, Tessa (1938–

Tessa Ransford was born in India, educated at boarding school in St Andrews and at Edinburgh University; she has lived most of her adult life in Scotland apart from eight years working in Pakistan in the 1960s. She has published eleven books of poems since the mid-1970s, the most recent being *When It Works It Feels like Play*. Tessa was founder/director of the Scottish Poetry Library when it opened in 1984 until after its establishment in new premises in 1999 (she was awarded the OBE in 2000 for her services to poetry); founder/organiser of the School of Poets poetry workshop (1981–99) and editor of *Lines Review* poetry magazine from 1988 until its final issue, number 144 in 1998. She is now working as a freelance poetry adviser and practitioner. Tessa Ransford has recently been awarded a writing fellowship with the Royal Literary Fund (working currently at the Centre for Human Ecology in Edinburgh) and has set up the Callum Macdonald Memorial Award to encourage the publishing of poetry in pamphlets.

Poetry of Persons (London: Quarto Press, 1976); *While It Is Yet Day* (London: Quarto Press, 1977); *Light of the Mind* (Edinburgh: Ramsay Head Press, 1980); *Fools and Angels*

(Edinburgh: Ramsay Head Press, 1984); *Shadows from the Greater Hill* (Edinburgh: Ramsay Head Press, 1987); *A Dancing Innocence* (Edinburgh: Macdonald Publishers, 1988); *Seven Valleys* (Edinburgh: Ramsay Head Press, 1991); *Medusa Dozen and Other Poems* (Edinburgh: Ramsay Head Press, 1994); *Scottish Selection* (Kirkcaldy: Akros Publications, 1998 (reissued 2001); *When It Works It Feels like Play* (Edinburgh: Ramsay Head Press, 1998); *Indian Selection* (Kirkcaldy: Akros Publications, 2000); *Natural Selection* (Kirkcaldy: Akros Publications, 2001); and others.

Richardson, Maimie (Alexandrina) (*fl.* 1926–1937)

Maimie Richardson (Mrs) published several collections of poetry, including *Stirling Castle*, a collection illustrated by D.Y. Cameron. She lived at Blairforkie, Bridge of Allan, and celebrated the area in her poetry. *Moods and Dreams*, foreword by John Campbell, Middleton, Northumberland, March 1926. There is a photograph in *Song of Gold*. Her 1931 poems have a Foreword by Hugh de Selincourt.

Moods and Dreams (London: Selwyn & Blount, 1926); *Song of Gold* (London: Hodder & Stoughton, 1929); *Poems* (London: Selwyn & Blount, 1931); *Stirling Castle, and Other Poems* (Glasgow: Maclehose, 1934); *The Dark Flower, and Other Poems* (London: Selwyn & Blount, 1937).

Robertson, Edith Anne (1883–1973)

Born in Glasgow, eldest daughter of Robert Stewart of Clarewood, Limpsfield, Edith Anne was educated at Glasgow High School, and in London and Germany. In 1919 she married the Rev. Prof. James Alexander Robertson: they had three daughters. She published biography and drama as well as poetry in English and Scots. She was a keen walker and gardener.

He is Become My Song: Carmen Jesu Nazareni (London: J. Clarke & Co., 1930); *Francis Xavier, Knight Errant of the Cross, 1506–1552* (London: Student Christian Movement, 1930); *Voices frae the City of Trees and Ither Voices frae Nearbye* (Edinburgh: M. Macdonald, 1955); *Poems frae the Suddron o' Walter de la Mare, Made ower intil Scots, wi' Foreword by Walter de la Mare* (Edinburgh: M. Macdonald, 1955); *Collected Ballads and Poems in the Scots Tongue* (Aberdeen: Aberdeen University Press, 1967); *Translations into the Scots Tongue of Poems by Gerard Manley Hopkins* (Aberdeen University Press: Aberdeen, 1968); *Forest Voices, and Other Poems in English* (Aberdeen: Aberdeen University Press, 1969).

Robertson, Jenny (1942–

Jenny Robertson grew up in Glasgow but now lives in Edinburgh. In addition to her poetry, she has written a number of children's books; she has also been involved in radio programmes and has written plays. Her study of Polish included a year spent in Warsaw, which influenced her poetry. Later she spent time in St Petersburg before writing *Loss and Language* (1994).

Beyond the Border (Edinburgh: Chapman, 1989); *Ghetto: Poems of the Warsaw Ghetto, 1939–43* (Oxford: Lion, 1989); Loss and Language (Edinburgh: Chapman, 1994); *Don't Go to Uncle's Wedding: Voices from the Warsaw Ghetto* (London: Azure, 2000); and others.

Rose, Dilys (1954–

Dilys Rose was born in Glasgow. She read English and Philosophy at Edinburgh University before travelling widely and working in various capacities at home and abroad. From 1991 to 1993 she held a Creative Writing Fellowship in Castlemilk and from 1995 to 1998 in Mid/East Lothian. Her stories and poems have often been broadcast on BBC Radio and on STV. Her work has also been included in several anthologies such as the *Faber Book of 20ᵗʰ-century Poetry* and the *Oxford Book of Scottish Short Stories*. She has won the MacAllan/*Scotland on Sunday* Short Story Competition, several Scottish Arts Council Awards and the McVitie (now Stakis) Scottish Writer of the Year Award. She has published three volumes of poetry, one of them for children, several short-story collections and a novel. She has also written drama. She lives in Edinburgh with her family.

Beauty is a Dangerous Thing; Madame Doubtfire's Dilemma (Edinburgh: Chapman, 1989); *Our Lady of the Pickpockets* (London: Secker & Warburg, 1989; London: Minerva, 1990); *Red Tides* (London: Secker & Warburg, 1994); *When I Wear My Leopard Hat: Poems for Young Children* (Edinburgh: Scottish Children's Press, 1997); *War Dolls* (London: Headline, 1998); *The Pest Maiden* (London: Headline, 1999); *Lure* (Edinburgh: Chapman, 2003); and others.

Sackville, Lady Margaret (1881–1963)

Margaret Sackville was born in 1881, third daughter of the 7th Earl de la Warr; her mother was Scottish. She published many collections of poetry as well as dramatic works. Edinburgh was the scene of much of her working and social life. She was a steady pacifist during the First World War and met Sassoon and probably Owen in Edinburgh in 1917. Sassoon unfortunately thought her verse 'fairly rotten' (quoted in Dominic Hibberd and John Onions, eds, *Poetry of the Great War*, 1986). While she lived in Edinburgh she acted as hostess in the famous salon of André Raffalovich (supposedly the original of Dorian Gray) and the poet, John Gray, until their deaths in 1934, when she contributed to a volume of reminiscences of them. She was first President of Scottish

PEN and an encourager of young poets; she was, of course, acquainted with MacDiarmid. She died 18 April 1963.

Poems (London: John Lane, 1901); *A Hymn to Dionysus, and Other Poems* (London: Elkin Mathews, 1905); *Hildris the Queen: A Play in Four Acts* (Manchester: Sherratt & Hughes, 1908); *A Book of Verse by Living Women*; with an introduction by Lady Margaret Sackville (London: Herbert & Daniel, [1910]); *Bertrud, and Other Dramatic Poems* (Edinburgh: William Brown, 1911); *Lyrics* (London: Herbert & Daniel, 1912); *Jane Austen* (London: Herbert & Daniel, [1912]); *Songs of Aphrodite, and Other Poems* (London: Elkin Mathews, 1913); *The Career Briefly Set Forth of Mr Percy Prendergast Who Told the Truth* [in verse], Illustrations by Cecil Ingram (London: Arthur H. Stockwell, [1914]; *The Pageant of War, and Other Poems* (London: Simpkin, Marshall & Co., 1916); *Twelve Little Poems* (London: E. Lahr, 1931); *Selected Poems* (London: Constable & Co., 1919), preface Wilfred Scawen Blunt; *Epitaphs* (Edinburgh: William Brown, 1921); *Poems* (London: Allen & Unwin, 1923); *A Rhymed Sequence* (Edinburgh: Porpoise Press, 1924); *Collected Dramas: 'Hildrid, Bertrud'* (London: G. Allen & Unwin, 1926); *Romantic Ballads* (Edinburgh: Porpoise Press, 1926); *100 Little Poems* (Edinburgh: Porpoise Press, 1928); *Ariadne by the Sea* (London: Red Lion Press, 1932); *The Double House; and Other Poems* (London: Williams & Norgate, 1935); *Collected Poems of Lady Margaret Sackville* (London: Martin Secker, 1939); *Tom Noodle's Kingdom, etc.* (London & Edinburgh: W. & R. Chambers, 1941); *Return to Song, and Other Poems* (London: Williams & Norgate, 1943); *Paintings & Poems*, with paintings by H. Davis Richter (Leigh-on-Sea: F. Lewis, 1944); *Country Scenes and Country Verse* (Leigh-on-Sea: F. Lewis, 1945); *The Lyrical Woodlands* [poems], with drawings by Lonsdale Ragg (Leigh-on-Sea: F. Lewis, 1945); *Miniatures* [poems] (Bradford:

Beamsley Press, 1947); *Harp Aeolian: Commentaries on the work of Lady Margaret Sackville*, edited by Georgina Somerville (Cheltenham: Burrow's Press, 1953); *Miniatures*, second series (Crayke: Guild Press, 1956); *Quatrains, and Other Poems* (Llandeilo: St Albert's Press, 1960); and others.

Shepherd, Nan (Anna) (1893–1981)

Nan Shepherd was born in Cults, Aberdeenshire, 11 February 1893. Her father John Shepherd was an engineer. Brought up in West Cults, Aberdeenshire she was educated at Aberdeen High School for Girls and Aberdeen University, graduating in 1915. She lectured in English at Aberdeen College of Education from 1915 until her retirement in 1956. In addition to her own work, she encouraged the writing of Jessie Kesson. She wrote three novels, a non-fiction celebration of the Cairngorms and a volume of poetry. Awarded an Honorary Degree by Aberdeen University in 1964, she also corresponded with Neil Gunn, who shared her love of the Scottish landscape.

The Quarry Wood (1928); *The Weatherhouse* (1930); *A Pass in the Grampians* (1933); *The Living Mountain: A Celebration of the Cairngorm Mountains of Scotland* (1977) [all published as *The Grampian Quartet* (Edinburgh: Canongate, 1996)]; *In the Cairngorms: Poems* (Edinburgh & London: Moray Press, 1934).

Simpson, Margaret Winefride (1888–1971)

Born in Buckie and educated in Flanders, Belgium.

Carols of the Wayfarer (London: Burns, Oates & Co., 1923); *Day's End, poems in Scots and English* (Paisley: Alexander Gardner, [1929]); *The Amber Lute, poems from the French, etc.* (Edinburgh: Grant & Murray, 1932); *The Wind's Heart. Poems from the Gaelic, French, Spanish, Portuguese, Italian and German* (Edinburgh & London: Moray Press, 1934); *Keys of Morning: Poems in English and Scots* (Edinburgh & London: Moray Press, 1935); *Aisles of Song; Poems in English and Scots and Translations, etc.* (Edinburgh & London: Moray Press, 1937); *Heart's Country, Songs of Home and the North* ([Elgin]: Moray & Nairn Newspaper Company [1945]).

Smith, Jean Guthrie (*fl.* 1922)

Jean Guthrie Smith published her collection *Adventure Square* in 1922. The volume contains poems that have already appeared in various journals, including *The Nation*, *The Atheneum*, *The Glasgow Herald*, *The New Age*. In these poems she refers to herself in a way that suggests that she is still in her twenties. The volume is divided into three sections: Glasgow, London, 'Malabar'. There is, however, a Jean Guthrie Smith who, along with Lucy and Nannie, were authors of a privately printed family poem, 'The Gathering of the Clan, or, The Carbeth Meeting of 1882: A Mugdock Lay' (NLS). If this is the author then she would have been older and also the sister of Herbert Guthrie Smith (1861–1940), who emigrated to New Zealand and wrote about wildlife and farming there.

Adventure Square (London: Hodder & Stoughton, 1922).

Smith, Morelle (1949–

Morelle Smith was born in Edinburgh and graduated from Edinburgh University with a degree in English and French. She writes poetry, short stories and novels. Her latest poetry collection is *Deepwater Terminal* (1998), published by Diehard, Edinburgh. Poems and short stories have been published in magazines and anthologies. She was a recipient of a Scottish Arts Council Writers' Bursary in 1994. Her first novel is soon to be published on the Internet. Current projects include a book on travel experiences and another novel.

Deepwater Terminal (Edinburgh: Diehard, 1998).

Stevenson, Anne (1933–

Anne Stevenson was born in Cambridge but grew up in the US and was educated at the University of Michigan, Ann Arbor. Although a citizen of the US, she returned to Britain and has lived since then in England, Scotland and Wales. She has published over a dozen volumes of poetry and has also written several volumes of criticism and a biography, the controversial *Bitter Fame: A Life of Sylvia Plath*. She was writer-in-residence at the University of Dundee, 1973–75, fellow of Lady Margaret Hall, Oxford, 1975–77, and writer-in-residence at the University of Edinburgh, 1987–89; she was Northern Arts Literary Fellow at Newcastle and Durham, 1981–82 and 1984–85.

Living in America (Ann Arbor: Generation, *c.* 1965); *Reversals* (Middleton, CT: Wellesley UP, 1969); *Correspondences: A Family History in Letters* (London: OUP, 1974); *Travelling Behind Glass: Selected Poems, 1963–1973* (London: OUP, 1974); *Enough of Green* (Oxford: OUP, 1977); *Sonnets for Five Seasons* (Hereford: Five Seasons Press, 1979); *New Poems* (Leamington Spa: Other Branch Readings, 1982); *Minute by Glass Minute* (Oxford: OUP, 1982); *Green Mountain, Black Mountain* (Boston, MA: Rowan Tree, 1982); *Making Poetry* [a poem] (Oxford: Pisces Press, 1983); *A Legacy* (Durham: Taxus, 1983); *Black Grate: Poems* (London: Inky Parrot, 1984); *The Fiction-makers* (Oxford: OUP, 1985); *Winter Time* (Mid Northumberland Arts Group, 1986); *Selected Poems by Frances Bellerby*, selected and edited by Anne Stevenson, with a biographical introduction by Robert Gittings (London:

Enitharmon, 1986); *Selected Poems, 1956–1986* (Oxford: OUP, 1987); *Bitter Fame: A Life of Sylvia Plath* (London: Viking, 1989); *The Other House* (Oxford: OUP, 1990); *Four and a Half Dancing Men*, (Oxford: OUP, 1993); *The Collected Poems* (Oxford: OUP, 1996); *Five Looks at Elizabeth Bishop* (London: Bellew, 1998); *Between the Iceberg and the Ship: Selected Essays* (Ann Arbor: University of Michigan P, *c.* 1998); *Granny Scarecrow* (Newcastle-upon-Tyne: Bloodaxe, 2000); and others.

Stiùbhart, Carstìona Anna/Christina Ann Stewart (1914–83)

Born in Bayble, Lewis, where she attended the local school until she was sixteen; she was awarded the new MacAulay Cup for Gaelic. She worked as a herring girl and in various employment in the Lowlands before returning after the war to Bayble, where she married. According to Ronald Black, 'She did not begin composing until late in life when her children had left home' (*An Tuil*, p.773). Ten of her poems were published in *Gairm* magazine between 1979 and 1982 under her married name NicLeòid. Black offers a more extensive biography (*An Tuil*, pp.772–773).

Stewart, Christina Ann see Stiùbhart, Carstìona Anna

Stuart, Alice V(andockum) (1899–1983)

Alice Stuart was born in Rangoon to Scottish parents (her father was managing proprietor of the *Rangoon Gazette*) and was educated at St Hilda's School, Edinburgh, and at Somerville College, Oxford. She settled in Edinburgh and worked as a tutor to foreign students and a freelance writer. She was a founder member of the Scottish Association for the Speaking of Verse. Her recreations were mountain-climbing and amateur acting.

The Far Calling (London: Poetry Lovers' Fellowship, Williams & Norgate, 1944); *The Dark Tarn* (London: OUP, 1953); *David Gray: the Poet of 'The Luggie'* (Kirkintilloch: Burgh of Kirkintilloch, 1961); *The Door Between* (Dunfermline: H.J. Macpherson, 1963); *The Unquiet Tide* (Edinburgh: Ramsay Head Press, 1971) and others.

Sulter, Maud (1960–

Maud Sulter was born in Glasgow and received her primary and secondary education there. She was MoMart Artist in Residence at the Tate Gallery, Liverpool, 1990–91. She published a novel, *Necropolis*, in 1991, as well as poetry. Her long poem, 'As a Black Woman', was written in London in 1984.

'For the Love of Atalanta' [in *The Crazy Jig: Gay and Lesbian Writing from Scotland* (Edinburgh: Polygon, 1992)]; *As a Black Woman* (Hebden Bridge: Urban Fox, 1985); *Zabat: Poetics of a Family Tree* (Hebden Bridge: Urban Fox, 1989).

Symon, Mary (1863–1938)

Mary Symon was educated at Aberdeen University. The Deveron is the river valley and district on the eastern edge of Speyside.

Deveron Days (Aberdeen: D. Wylie, 1933 & 1938).

Taylor, Rachel Annand (1876–1960)

Rachel Annand Taylor was born Rachel Annand in Aberdeen and educated at Aberdeen University, where she studied under Herbert Grierson. She married Alexander Cameron Taylor and lived in Aberdeen, Dundee and London, until she died on 15 August 1960. Her work included history and literary criticism. In 1943 she was awarded an honorary LLD by Aberdeen University.

Poems (London: J. Lane, 1904); *Rose and Vine* (London: E. Mathews, 1908); *The Hours of Fiammetta* (London: E. Mathews, 1909); *Aspects of the Italian Renaissance* (London: G. Richards, 1923); *The End of Fiammetta* (London: G. Richards, 1923); *Leonardo the Florentine* (London: G. Richards, 1927); *Dunbar: The Poet and his Period* (London: Faber, 1931); and others.

Thornton, Valerie (1954–

Valerie Thornton was born and educated in Glasgow. She is both a poet and a short-story writer. She edited *Working Words*, which was joint winner of the TESS/Saltire Society Educational Book of the Year 1996, and received a Scottish Arts Council Writer's Bursary in 1989. Her poems and short stories are included in many collections. She has done a great deal of work with writers' groups and is currently Royal Literary Fellow at Glasgow University.

Catacoustics (Glasgow: Mariscat, 2000).

Turner, Anne (1925–

Her poems have appeared in a number of collections and anthologies.

Sudden Shards (Leeds: The Grackle Press, 1968).

Walker, Kathrine Sorley (*fl.* 1945–

As well as poetry, Kathrine Sorley Walker has written a number of books on ballet and on Raymond Chandler, and a biography of Saladin. She reviews dance for a number of newspapers and journals.

Beauty is Built Anew: A Selection of Poems (Glasgow: William Maclellan, 1949); *The Heart's Variety* (London: Mitre Press, 1959); *Emotion and Atmosphere* (Enfield [44 Wellington Road, Enfield, Middx]: Beacon Press, 1975); *Late Century Poems* (Shrewsbury: Feather Books, 1999); and others.

Walton, Dorothy Seward (*fl.* 1934–52)

Born in Cambridge, daughter of Sir Archibald Seward, and educated at Prior's School, Godalming, Surrey, she married John Walton and had a son and a daughter. Her husband was Regius Professor of Botany at Glasgow University.

When Evening Comes to the City, and Other Poems (Cambridge: Heffer & Sons, 1934); *The Hidden Stream: The Story of St Mungo* [in verse] (Edinburgh: The Moray Press, [1948]); and others.

Warner, Val (1946–

Val Warner read Modern History at Oxford and has worked as a teacher, freelance copy-editor and freelance writer. She was Creative Writing Fellow at the University College of Swansea and Writer in Residence at the University of Dundee. She has received a Gregory Award. Her Carcanet publications include the pamphlet *These Yellow Photos* (1971) and the full collections *Under the Penthouse* (1973) and *Before Lunch* (1986); *The Centenary Corbière* (translations of Tristan Corbière, 1975); and an edition of *The Collected Poems and Prose of Charlotte Mew* (1981).

These Yellow Photos (Oxford: Carcanet, 1971); *Under the Penthouse* (Cheadle: Carcanet, 1983); *Before Lunch* (Manchester: Carcanet, 1986); *Tooting Idyll* (Manchester: Carcanet, 1997); and others.

Wells, Nannie Katharin (1875–?)

Born in Morayshire and educated in Berlin, Paris, Aberdeen and Fochabers, Nannie Wells married in 1901 and had three sons. She served in the Foreign Office during the First World War, was Secretary of the Edinburgh Women's Citizens' Association and, from 1929, Secretary Depute to the SNP. She described her recreation as 'managing rheumaticky minds with modern electric shock treatment'. Nannie Wells wrote poetry, a novel and literary criticism. Of her verse she said in 1958, 'I have not . . . attempted to be "modern", in the austere restrained, almost genteel and ladylike manner now fashionable in England. For a Scot that would be to "droon The Miller".'

Diverse Roads: A Novel (Edinburgh: Grant & Murray, 1932); *Byronic Comments on the Twentieth Century* (Collieston: Michael Slains, 1962); *George Gordon, Lord Byron: A Scottish Genius*, with a foreword by Hugh MacDiarmid (Michael Slains, 1962); *Twentieth Century Mother and Other Poems* (Fantasy Press, 1952); *The Golden Eagle* (Edinburgh: Castle Wynd Printers, 1958)

Wood, Wendy (1892–1981)

A well-known Scottish Nationalist activist. She was a broadcaster and artist ('Auntie Gwen' of the BBC's *Children's Hour*).

I Like Life (Edinburgh: Moray Press, 1938); *Tales of the Western Isles* (Oliver & Boyd, 1952); *The Silver Chanter: Traditional Scottish Tales and Legends*, illustrated by Colin McNaughton (London: Chatto & Windus, 1980); *Astronauts and Tinklers: Poems and Pictures by Wendy Wood*, ed. Joy Hendry (Edinburgh: Edinburgh Heritage Society of Scotland, 1985); and others.

PERMISSIONS ACKNOWLEDGEMENTS

Various publishers, poets and Estates have generously given permission to reproduce the following copyrighted works:

'The Wild Geese' from *Songs of Angus* (1915), 'The End o't', 'The Jaud' from *Bonnie Joann* (1921), 'Donald Maclane' from *Northern Lights* (1927) by Violet Jacob reproduced with permission of John Murray (Publishers) Ltd. 'Mary's Song' from *The Tinker's Road* (1924), 'At Candlemas', 'The Fiddler', 'Think Lang', 'The Wild Lass' from *Sun and Candlelight* (1927), 'The Can'el', 'The Blue Jacket' from *The Turn of the Day* (1931), by Marion Angus reproduced with permission of Faber and Faber Ltd. 'V', 'VI' from *Lying Awake* (1997) by Catherine Carswell reproduced with permission of Canongate Books. Dr Deirdre (MacLeod) Loughlin, on behalf of her family, is honoured to give permission to reproduce the following poems: 'Litir Chun a' Bhàird', 'Dia', 'As-creideamh' by Ciorstaidh NicLeòid/Christina MacLeod. 'Original Sin' by Wendy Wood reproduced with permission of Chapman Publishing. 'The House of the Hare', 'Living in a Village', 'Buachaille Etive Mor and Buachaille Etive Beag' and 'XIII. Work and Love' from *The Cleansing of the Knife* (1978) by Naomi Mitchison, reproduced with permission of Canongate Books and David Higham Associates. 'Skeletons of Honesty' from *Thistle By-blaws* (1971) by Kate Y. A. Bone reproduced by permission of Reinold Gayre. 'The Professor's Wife' from *Bennygoak and Other Poems* (1974) by Flora Garry (Campbell), reproduced with kind permission of the poet's granddaughter, Elizabeth Bell and Savage Press. 'Coinneamh nan Cearc mun Ghràn' reproduced with kind permission of the poet's son, Fr Donald Mackay. 'Thoughts after Ruskin', and 'This Poem . . .' from *People Etcetera* (1987) by Elma Mitchell, reproduced with permission of Peterloo Poets. Copyright for 'Thoughts after Ruskin', Harry Chamber. 'Cum Sinn Dlùth', 'Trusgan na Fèin-Fhìreantachd' by Catrìona NicDhòmhnaill, reproduced with kind permission of the poet. Permission to reproduce translation of 'Cum Sinn Dlùth' granted by Ronald Black. 'An Druidheachd' by Cairstìona Anna NicAoidh, reproduced with kind permission of the poet. 'An Teine Beò', 'Crom-Lus Arrais' by Màiri NicDhòmhnaill, reproduced with kind permission of the poet. 'Scottish Woman' from *Looking Towards Light* (1988), by Margaret Gillies Brown, reproduced with kind permission of the poet. 'With my Sons at Boarhills' from *The Collected Poems 1955–1995* (2000) by Anne Stevenson, reproduced with permission from Bloodaxe Books. 'Scotland' from *Poems of Love* (1966) and 'La Grande Jatte' from *Turning a Fresh Eye* (1998) by Lillias Scott Chisholm (Lillias Forbes) used by permission. 'Flying Lessons' from *The Gangan Fruit* (1991), 'On Not Writing Poetry' from *Pathfinder* (2000), by Ellie McDonald, reproduced with kind permission of the poet. 'The Poet's Daughters' and 'In the Royal Botanic Garden' from *A Dancing Innocence* (1988), 'Blake's Wife' from *When It Works it Feels Like Play* (1988) by Tessa Ransford, reproduced with kind permission of the poet and Ramsay Head Press. 'Reading by a Window' and 'Carradale' from *Meditterzanean* (1995), by Jenni Daiches, reproduced with the kind permission of the poet. 'Black

Houses, Ardnamurchen' and 'Old Communist' from *Beyond the Border* (1989) and *Loss and Language* (1994) respectively by Jenny Robertson. Reproduced with permission of Chapman Publishing. 'Looking for Scotland' from *Looking for Scotland* (1996) by Sally Evans, reproduced with permission of Poetry Salzburg. 'Border Raids' from *Kisses for Mayakovsky* (1984), 'Women in the Cold War' and 'Haiku, Moniack Mhor' from *Dreams Like Heretics* (1997) by Alison Fell, reproduced with permission of Serpent's Tail Ltd. 'The Marriage-Lintels' and 'One Moment's Mirror' from *Skating Out of the House* (1997) by Anna Crowe, reproduced with permission of Peterloo Poets. 'Pie in the Sky' and 'Letters' from *Before Lunch* (1986) by Val Warner, reproduced with permission of Carcanet Press Ltd. 'The Hyphen', 'Sonnet', 'I have a little hour-glass', 'I have a little nut-tree' from *Collected Poems and Translations* (1990) by Veronica Forrest-Thomson, reproduced with kind permission of Jonathan Culler. 'What the Pool Said, On Midsummer's Day', 'Dreaming Frankenstein', 'Poem For My Sister', 'Mirror's Song', from *Dreaming Frankenstein and Collected Poems* (2000), by Liz Lochhead, reproduced with permission from Polygon Books, an imprint of Birlinn Ltd. 'Almost Christmas at the Writers' House' from *Bagpipe Muzak* (1992) by Liz Lochhead, published by Penguin Books. Reproduced with permission of The Rod Hall Agency. 'The Dominie' from *The Cyard's Kist* (1984), 'Ophelia' from *The Spik o' the Lan'*, 'Persephone' from *The Singing Bird* (2000) by Sheena Booth Blackhall, reproduced with kind permission of the author. 'Wast wi da Valkyries' from *Wast wi da Valkyries* (1997), by Christine De Luca, reproduced with kind permission from the poet. 'Howff', 'An Taigh Beag', 'Cearcall mun Ghealaich', 'A' Feitheamh ris a' Phàp: a' Chaisg, 1981' from *Na h-Oidhche* (1994), by Catrìona NicGumaraid reproduced with kind permission of the poet. 'Na Cuimhnich, Na Guil' by Sìne M. Cooper, reproduced with kind permission of the poet. 'The Negative' from *Each Bright Eye* (1977), 'Bass Rock', 'The Night Before Battle' 'Tipu and Archie' from *The Ringing Rock* (1995) by Valerie Gillies, reproduced with kind permission of the poet. 'Potato Cuts' from *Inside Eden* (1990) by Margaret Elphinstone, reproduced with kind permission of the poet. 'Conjugate' from *Alien Crop* (1996), 'Mayday' from *Reading the Bones* (1999), 'Jenny: Weavin the Spell' from *Ye Cannae Win* (2000) by Janet Paisley, reproduced with kind permission of the poet. 'Sauchiehall Street' from *Deepwater Terminal* (1998), by Morelle Smith, reproduced with kind permission of the poet. 'The Other Side of the Story' from *White Boats* (1973), 'Old Man' from *Book of Men* (1976) by Catherine Lucy Czerkawska, reproduced with kind permission of the poet. 'Standing by Thistles' from *Standing by Thistles* (1997) by Anne MacLeod, reproduced with kind permission of the poet. 'In the Kibble Palace: Sunday Morning' from *Just the Caravaggio* (1999) by Anne MacLeod, reproduced with permission of Poetry Salzburg. 'Stravaigin', 'Webs not Roots' and 'Devorgilla in the Borderlands' from *Stravaigin* (2001) by Liz Niven, reproduced with permission of Canongate Books. 'Kith' and 'Gruoch Considers' from *Raiding the Borders* (1996) by Marion Lomax (Robyn Bolam), reproduced with permission of Bloodaxe Books. 'Dogma Change' from *Scottish Poetry* 7 (1974) by Marcella Evaristi, reproduced with kind permission of the poet. 'Planting Crocuses with My Mother' from *Wild Women* (2000) by Magi Gibson, reproduced with permission of Chapman Publishing. 'No Name Woman', 'Sister Sirens' and 'Saint Wilgefortis, Prague' from *Madame Doubtfire's Dilemma* (1989) by Dilys Rose, reproduced with kind permission of the poet. 'In His Own Country' from *Technologies* (1990) and 'A Woman Absent from the Museum Muses on her Life in South Dunedin' from *Powerlines* (2000) by Gerrie Fellows, reproduced with permission of Polygon Books, an imprint of Birlinn Ltd. 'Dark Side of the Moon' from *After the Watergaw*, Scottish Cultural Press (1998); 'Kestrel, Conic Hill' from *Catacoustics* (2000) by Valerie Thornton, Mariscat Press. Reproduced with kind permission of the poet. 'Originally' from *The Other Country* (1990), 'The Way My Mother Speaks' and 'Before You Were Mine' from *Mean Time* (1993) by Carol Ann Duffy, reproduced with permission of Anvil Press Poetry. 'Sean Bhalaist', 'Nach Goirtichinn A-rithist', 'Taigh Ùr na h-Alba', and 'Baile Ailein', by Màiri NicGumaraid, reproduced with kind permission of the poet. 'Valda's Poem/Sleevenotes' and 'Mother and Child in the Botanic Gardens' from *Ophelia and Other Poems* (1991) by Elizabeth Burns, reproduced with permission of Polygon Books, an imprint of Birlinn Ltd. 'Danda with a Dead Fish' from *The Sin Eater* (1989) by Deborah Randall, reproduced with permission of Bloodaxe Books. 'Do Alastair MacIlleMhìcheil', 'Leigeil Bhruadaran Dhìom', 'Ugh Briste' and 'Walzer' reproduced with kind permission of Meg Bateman. 'My Grandmother's Houses', from *The Adoption Papers* (1991), 'The Red Graveyard' from *Other Lovers* (1993), 'The Shoes of Dead Comrades' and 'Lucozade'from *Off Colour* (1998) by Jackie Kay, reproduced with permission of Bloodaxe Books. 'For Paola' from *The Autonomous Region* (1993), 'Clearances', 'Mother-May-I', 'Fountain', from *Mr & Mrs Scotland are Dead: Poems 1980–1994* (2002), by Kathleen Jamie, reproduced with permission of Bloodaxe Books. 'Ultrasound', 'Bolus', 'Meadowsweet', from *Jizzen* (1999) by Kathleen Jamie. Reproduced with permission of MacMillan Publishers Ltd. 'Cliches', 'My Breasts', 'Crockery', and 'Windowbox', from *Coming Out With It* (1992), by Angela McSeveney, reproduced with permission of Polygon Books Ltd, an imprint of Birlinn. 'For a Wedding' from *Slattern* (1995) by Kate Clanchy, 'The Bridge Over the Border' from *Samarkand* (1999) by Kate Clanchy, reproduced with permission of Macmillan Publishers Ltd. 'Scan', 'Everything is More' from *Baby* by Gillian K. Ferguson, reproduced with permission of Canongate Books. 'Dear Norman' from *Air for Sleeping Fish* (1997) published by Bloodaxe Books. Reproduced with kind permission of the poet. 'Oidche Reòite', 'Connadh', 'Màiri Iain Mhurch' Chaluim' (and translation) by Anna Frater, reproduced with kind permission of the poet. 'Paris in the Spring' from *No Hiding Place* (1996), 'Ophelia's Confession' from *Dead Redhead* (2001), by Tracey Herd, reproduced with permission of Bloodaxe Books. 'The Lads' and 'Leda, No Swan' from *Maiden Speech* (1996) by Eleanor Brown, reproduced with permission of Bloodaxe Books.

Every attempt has been made to contact copyright holders, but if any material has been included for which permission has not been granted, apologies are tendered in advance to proprietors and publishers concerned.